Why Do Linguistics?

ALSO AVAILABLE FROM BLOOMSBURY

Developing Materials for Language Teaching, 2nd edition, edited by Brian Tomlinson

Forensic Linguistics, 3rd edition, John Olsson and June Luchjenbroers

Introduction to Interaction, Angela Cora Garcia

Language in Education, Rita Elaine Silver and Soe Marlar Lwin

Linguistics: An Introduction, William McGregor

Why Do Linguistics?

Reflective linguistics and the study of language

FIONA ENGLISH

AND

TIM MARR

BLOOMSBURY

NEW DELHI • LONDON • OXFORD • NEW YORK • SYDNEY

BLOOMSBURY INDIA
Bloomsbury Publishing India Pvt. Ltd
Second Floor, LSC Building No. 4, DDA Complex, Pocket C–6&7,
Vasant Kunj, New Delhi 110070

BLOOMSBURY, BLOOMSBURY ACADEMIC INDIA and the Diana logo are
trademarks of Bloomsbury Publishing Plc

First published in India 2022
First published 2015
Reprinted 2020

This edition published with permission from Bloomsbury Publishing Plc,
50 Bedford Square, London, WC1B3DP, UK

British Library Cataloguing-in-Publication Data
A catalogue record for this book is available from the British Library.

Library of Congress Cataloging-in-Publication Data
A catalog record for this book is available from the Library of Congress

ISBN: 978-93-89391-20-6

For sale in the Indian subcontinent only

Typeset by Deanta Global Publishing Services, Chennai, India
Digitally printed and bound in India by Replika Press Pvt. Ltd.

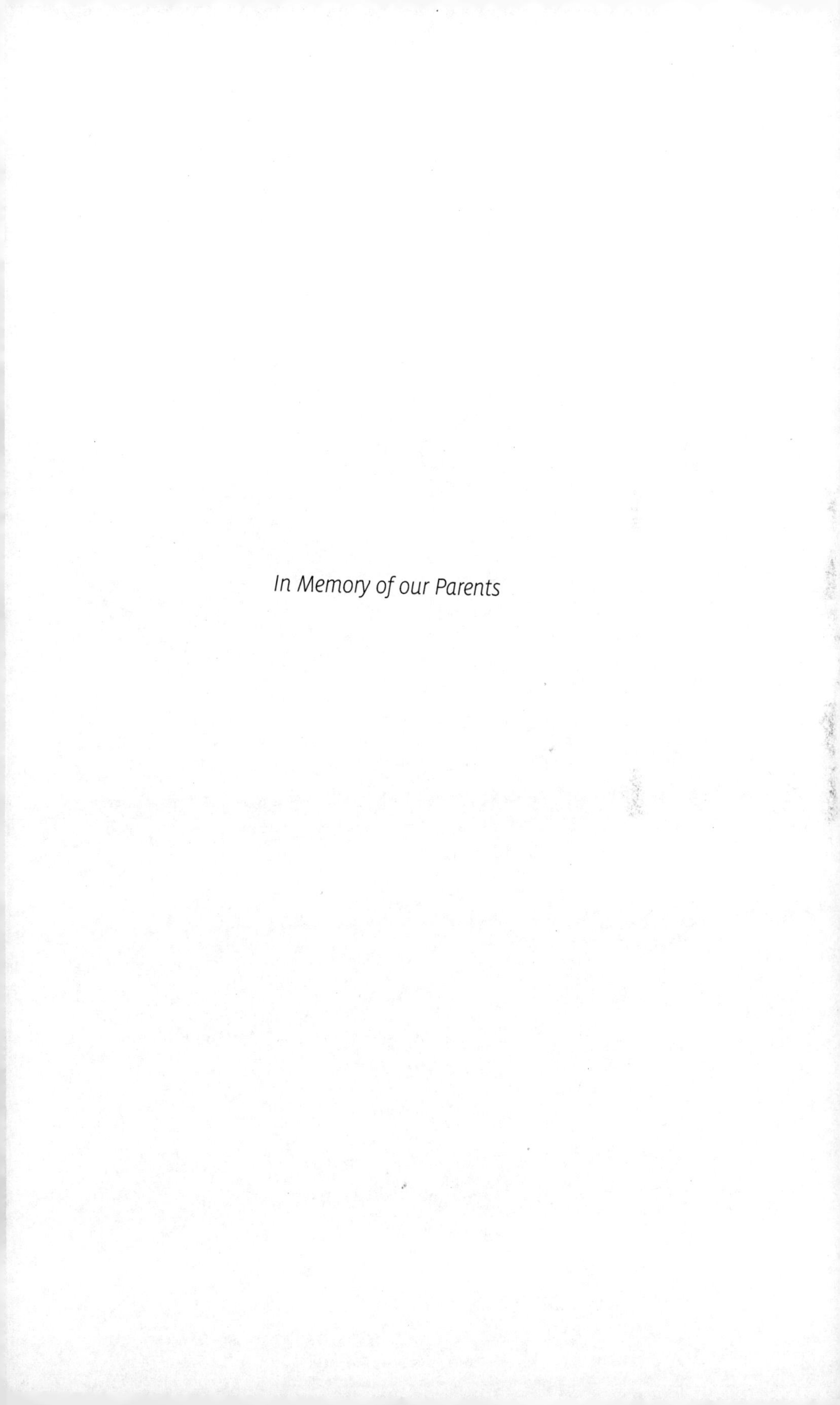

In Memory of our Parents

Contents

Authors' acknowledgements

It is common practice for teachers to thank their students and declare that they have learned a huge amount from them. In our case this is nothing less than the truth. We have had the great good fortune to have worked, separately and together, with hundreds of students from all over the world, who have opened our eyes to all sorts of aspects of language, culture and communication. Their enthusiasm and curiosity were what impelled us to first think of writing a book like this. Thanks are due in particular to Katia Sarno-Pedreira, Sheraz Ahmad and Michael Howard for allowing us to use extracts from their research and Di Mai, Arif Chowdhury and Lubna Zia, all of whom have helped us greatly in different ways.

We were lucky also to have been part of a singularly supportive and dedicated team of teacher-researchers, whose insights and inspiration were always invaluable: thanks, then, to Janet Enever, Karen Malan, Parvaneh Tavakoli and Inge Weber-Newth. We are grateful too to the other people who gave freely of their time to help us better understand the issues surrounding language in their different contexts: Samantha Parsons, Chris Shaw, Steve Collins, Iskandar Yakubov. Thanks also go to Gurdeep Mattu and Andrew Wardell at Bloomsbury for their support, advice and for chivvying us along.

Finally, our heartfelt love and thanks go to Ana, Mark and Stanley for their patience, forbearance and above all, encouragement. We could not have done it without them.

Publisher's acknowledgements

While every effort has been made to contact all copyright holders, this has not always been successful. However, we would like to thank Specsavers (La Villiaze St Andrews Guernsey Channel Islands GY6 8YP) for allowing us to use one of their advertisements and Swpix (Simon Wilkinson Photography, T/A Photography Hum Ltd) for the photograph of the ball boy in that advertisement.

General introduction

A married couple, the man a linguist and the woman a development economist, are on holiday in east Africa. As their bus trundles along a dusty highway, it passes an old woman selling vegetables from a blanket spread at the side of the road. A few prospective customers are gathered around her, and some bargaining is evidently going on. The couple both find this scene interesting, and it immediately raises questions in their minds. 'Hmm', thinks the development economist to herself: 'I wonder if that woman needed credit to buy the seeds and the equipment she needed to grow those vegetables . . .? And if so, where did the credit come from? A bank? A microfinance institution?' Meanwhile, the linguist is looking at the same scene and thinking to himself: 'I wonder if the old woman and the customers speak the same first language? And if not, I wonder what language they are using between themselves to bargain over those vegetables . . . or maybe they are using a mixture of languages?'

We view the world through the prism of our own experience and our own interest; we pay most attention to what seems most important to us at any given time. For an economist it is perfectly natural to focus on the economic aspects of a particular scenario without giving a thought to other aspects such as, in our example, the clothes the people are wearing, the pattern on the blanket or, indeed, the language or languages being spoken. Linguists notice language, because they are fine-tuned to do so. (The linguist in the anecdote above was one of the present authors, of course). They notice not just what is said, but how it is said. They also have at their disposal a set of terms and concepts that make it possible to talk precisely about language. With this book we would like everyone to become a *noticer of language*, armed with some understanding of the insights that linguistics can provide; this, we hope, will encourage readers to engage with language-related debates and issues and enable them to do so from an informed position.

Background to the book

The idea of linguistics often makes people shudder, and as linguists, we sometimes wonder why. For many years we ran an MA course in language teaching and applied linguistics at a university in London. The course explored questions such as:

- Does everyone speak with an accent?
- Why is it so difficult to sound like a native in a foreign language?
- Why do teachers tend to use red pens?
- When is the best time to start learning a language?
- Will English always be a global lingua franca?
- How many different speech sounds are there in the world's languages?

These types of questions fascinated our students and led to engaged and excited debate. However, even though not one of these questions can be answered – or even properly talked about – without the technical and theoretical underpinning of linguistics, when the actual word 'linguistics' was uttered, almost all of them would pull faces and groan. The question we asked ourselves was: How could they, as language professionals, not be interested in linguistics? The answer, we discovered, lay in their previous experience of the subject.

What do we mean by linguistics?

The kind of linguistics that our students had been studying, wherever in the world they came from, seemed to follow a very circumscribed approach to the field which tended to focus on the technical description of language as a set of structures. This approach to the subject tends to view language as an abstract system, a view originating from the pioneering work of Ferdinand de Saussure, in which he made a fundamental distinction between 'langue' (language as an abstract system) and 'parole' (language as it is actually spoken by an individual). Syllabuses of this kind typically set out to describe language in terms of the principles around which it is structured (e.g. Chomsky's influential theory of Transformational Grammar), often at the expense of any substantial discussion of language as it is actually *used*. Add to this the forbidding-looking apparatus of the International Phonetic

Alphabet (IPA), and one can understand the students' unenthusiastic response.

Linguistics, however, is a much broader field than this might lead one to suppose, invaluable though such work has proved in contributing to our understanding of how human language is structured. There are different kinds of linguists, just as there are different kinds of geographers and different kinds of biologists (for example). There are historical linguists who are interested in how languages develop over the course of time; neurolinguists who study language and the brain; linguists who work on regional dialects; linguists who study how children learn to speak; field linguists who analyse and codify previously unrecorded languages; linguists who advise on language policy; others who work with language in the school curriculum; linguistic ethnographers who are interested in observing and understanding communicative activity. The list could go on.

In this book we discuss many of the areas encompassed by linguistics, but especially those which have a direct relevance to explaining or understanding communicative interaction from a social, multilingual and intercultural perspective. In other words, we are primarily interested in the kind of linguistics that incorporates what Halliday calls the 'messy' bits (1978: 38); that is a *social* linguistics. Our approach uses linguistics as the enabling framework with which to describe, analyse and understand the phenomena we observe, even if these phenomena are not all characterized by language in the sense of words and sentences. That is to say, we also take into consideration other communicative modes (such as visual representation), specifically where they fulfil a communicative function in a language-like way. We recognize that this approach might not accord with everyone's opinion of what is meant by linguistics but, as we will explain shortly, our aim with this book is to encourage our readers to see the enormous potential that linguistics holds for explaining the scope and complexity of human communication.

Above all, this is a book about noticing. It aims to show how a linguistic lens can offer insight into the communication that surrounds us every day and everywhere. We hope that readers of this book will not only become linguistically informed, active observers of language for its own sake, but also be equipped to take on and challenge some of the misconceptions, assumptions and prejudices that so often skew public discussion of language issues.

We hope to engage readers' interest by posing questions about real-world language phenomena of the kind that we experience in our day-to-day lives. To this end we use examples of communication that we have collected ourselves, ranging from such things as a fragment of overheard conversation in an east London café, to a footballer's post-match interview on Sky TV, via a postcard sent from the Costa Cálida to a sign displaying the name of a restaurant in Tashkent, Uzbekistan. These, along with our many other pieces of raw, naturally occurring data, serve as material for analysis as well as a springboard to discussion of the wider issues that they raise.

The book is for anyone who has an interest in language and who wants to know more about how we communicate in everyday social interaction. We envisage our reader as someone who may have questions about language-related phenomena that have concerned, puzzled or even amused them and who would like to develop a deeper understanding of the subject.

It is worth emphasizing that the title of the book is *Why Do Linguistics?* and not 'How To Do Linguistics'. This book is not an introduction to linguistics, nor is it a linguistics textbook or course. There are other books available which fulfil this purpose, and we will recommend some of them later on. Rather than attempting to teach you linguistics, we want first, to show you that a linguistics lens can offer you new perspectives and insights and second, to persuade you that knowledge about language should be an integral part of everyone's knowledge about the world.

How the book is organized

We have organized the book into three sections, each consisting of five chapters. Part I, **Reflective Linguistics**, comprises a series of exploratory chapters that survey the ground and pose questions about language, language practices and how people perceive and think about language. We use this part of the book to establish a set of themes which run through both academic and popular debate about language and to which we return in later sections of the book. We label these themes 'noticing', 'correctness', 'belonging', 'diversity' and 'difference'.

Part II, **The Study of Language**, focuses on the 'stuff of communication' itself (Kress 2003: 47). We outline the basic tools of linguistic description and explain the analytical approach we use in discussing our data, namely discourse analysis. Drawing on these principles in helping us to draw out what we have found linguistically interesting, we analyse examples of communicative activity in the following three chapters, each under a different rubric: speaking and spokenness, writing and writtenness and choosing our words.

In Part III **Why Do Linguistics?**, we argue for wider appreciation of linguistics and its relevance to real-world experience. Given increasing globalization, urbanization and movement of populations we argue that a linguistics lens can aid understanding of social and cultural complexity encountered in contemporary societies worldwide. In arguing for a more prominent role for the study of language in the school curriculum, along with greater language awareness in the workplace and more generally, we show how what often appear to be problems of language are in fact problems of perception which can be attributed to a lack of linguistic knowledge.

About the material

As already noted, most of the examples we use in the book are from our own observations. They comprise photographs of signs that we have come across in our travels, notices that we have seen in and around our places of work, personal correspondence, comments overheard, snippets from newspapers, publicity materials and other such examples of what we have noticed and found interesting from a linguistic point of view. All images have been reproduced in black and white because of the limitations of print, but are available in full colour on the accompanying website. We have also drawn on conversations with our students, whose own linguistic observations and experiences have helped us to see things through fresh eyes. By using such data, typical of the different kinds of communication that everyone encounters, every day, wherever they are in the world, we hope to show that doing linguistics is not just for professional academics, but can also be something that everyone can engage in.

About naming

There are two aspects to the issue of 'naming'. The first concerns how we label the kind of linguistics we do. Are we linguists? Are we social linguists? Are we sociolinguists? Are we social semioticians? Are we applied linguists? In fact, we could argue that we are all these things. We are linguists because we use the descriptive tools and insights that the discipline provides. We are social linguists because we study linguistic data from the perspective of communicative activity. We are sociolinguists because we look at language and communication in society. We are social semioticians because we explore communication as meaning and meaningful in the social world and we are applied linguists because we believe the study of language and language-related fields is relevant to real-world issues. However, for the purposes of this book, and for simplicity, we intend to use the term *linguistics* as a general term of reference and *linguists* when referring to ourselves and others interested in language phenomena. We will, of course, use the other terms when referring more specifically to particular frames of knowledge or analytical approaches.

The second point concerning naming is that sometimes we draw on examples from our own individual experience. In such cases, we use the pronoun 'I' followed by the relevant name (Tim or Fiona) at the start of each example so that readers are aware of whose experience it is. Otherwise we use the pronoun 'we'.

A final point: we are native English speakers, writing in English for readers who have English as part of their linguistic repertoire. Hence, while we use examples from other languages wherever this seems appropriate, English naturally occupies a prominent position throughout the book. However, we wish to stress that this is a book about language and the study of language, not about English, and we hope it will encourage reflection on other languages and linguistic contexts with which readers might be familiar.

PART ONE

Reflective linguistics

Introduction to Part I

We begin the book with a collection of reflective chapters arising out of the sort of questions that often crop up in the media and in day-to-day conversation. Some of these questions might stem from curiosity, a simple desire to know – How many languages are there in the world? Are some languages more difficult than others? Others might arise from a particular observation or interaction – Why do young people all speak like that? Why is that word spelt that way? In this way we hope to invite readers to reflect on these questions themselves, in the knowledge that they are much more complex and hence much more interesting than might at first be understood.

We use this first part to show the appeal of noticing language phenomena and the value of making strange what we usually take for granted. Jan Blommaert and Dong Jie, in their book *Ethnographic Fieldwork: A Beginner's Guide*, set out very well what it means to use an ethnographic approach for the study of language (linguistic ethnography) and use the phrase 'collecting rubbish' (2010: 58) to describe the practice that linguistic ethnographers develop of never rejecting anything that might, one day, prove useful in shedding light on communicative activity in some way or another. For instance, many of the materials in this book comprise 'rubbish', that is, linguistic data that may seem insignificant, even worthless, that we have collected over several years in the anticipation that one day we might be able to make something of it. We take photographs of shop signs, we note down comments overheard, we keep hold of students' essays, junk mail, newspaper reports, recordings of conversations, in fact anything that might have something to say about language, communication and social-cultural practice.

Sometimes the phenomena observed instigate questions. For instance, why would a clothes shop in a French provincial town call itself 'Top Fun Boutik', using a kind of 'mash-up' English? And why in the same region would an assistant in a bakery not understand a request for a particular kind of bread (baguette) when the masculine article, *un*, is mistakenly used (un baguette) instead of the correct feminine, *une* (une baguette)? Why do Nigerians often sound like they're having an argument when they clearly seem to be getting along? Why do girls tend to write longer text messages than boys? What is it about that email supposedly from the bank that makes me feel suspicious?

It is through noticing and asking such questions that we begin to explore, not only the objects of our observations themselves, but what might lie behind them. And inevitably, what lies behind them is always to be found in the *social*; that is the cultural, the ideological, the political, the historical, the geographical factors that affect our linguistic choices and our communicative activity.

In Chapter 1 we use four examples of language phenomena that we have observed and collected to show the kinds of discussion that such phenomena can promote. These discussions go well beyond the limits of the examples themselves by raising further questions about how and why people communicate in the ways they do. The following four chapters each focus on a particular issue of the type referred to at the beginning of this introduction and draw on language examples, conversations, comments and other resources that help us to reflect on the questions that they give rise to. Chapter 2 examines the question of 'good' language, clarifying the concept of correctness itself and considering how it is perceived in different social and cultural contexts. Chapter 3 looks at how different communities develop their particular ways of communicating both socially and culturally, while Chapter 4 explores the challenges that multilingual societies present, the strategies that are developed and the benefits that emerge. Chapter 5 responds to the question of how similar or different to each other languages actually are, and in so doing shows some of the extraordinary variety of linguistic configurations among the languages of the world.

Our ultimate aim with Part I is to entice readers by showing how far-reaching reflective linguistics can be and how even small observations can lead to much larger discussions which offer insights, not only into language and communication, but into societies and our own interactions within those societies.

1

About noticing: Becoming a linguistic ethnographer

Linguistics is everywhere because language is everywhere.

M. A. K. HALLIDAY[1]

1.1 Introduction: The lift on the left

If you go to the Holloway Road Underground station in London you will hear a recorded message, in a woman's voice, as you wait for the lift to take you down to the platform or up to street level. The station, along with several others on the London Underground, is served by lifts as well as a fixed staircase. These stations lack the necessary space to accommodate escalators and their platforms are often very deep underground. In order to manage the queues of people that build up, Transport for London (TfL, the body that runs the stations on the Tube) tells passengers which lift of the two or three available is due next. The message says: 'The lift on the left shall be the next lift.'

Why have we chosen to start this book with such a random utterance? The simple answer is that there is nothing random about it at all. It is, in fact, an example of what we mean by *noticing*. We have frequently used this example with our students to encourage them to become active noticers of language, telling them to pay attention when they are waiting for the lift and to report back to us anything they find odd. We now ask you to do the same. So, does anything about this message seem odd or out of place to you? If you don't notice anything at first, try saying it as if you were telling it to a friend who is waiting for the lift with you. If you didn't notice anything odd about it before, do you notice something now?

Our aim with this chapter is to demonstrate what it is that we mean when we talk about *noticing* and in so doing show what it means to become a linguistic ethnographer. We have organized it around examples of linguistic phenomena which stood out for us as having something useful and interesting to say about communication and linguistic interaction. We have already introduced the first case which we discuss in more detail below and add three further cases which focus on particular questions of linguistic and communication relevance.

1.2 Paying attention

So let us now take a closer look at the TfL announcement to see why we noticed it in the first place and to try to understand what we can learn from what is, as we will show, a rich piece of linguistic data.

Example 1.1

The lift on the left shall be the next lift.

This is an example of the familiar genre of recorded public announcement messages. These are generally heard where routine activity takes place, such as public transport contexts, but where certain difficulties, dangers or inconveniences may be avoided if the message is heeded or where public reassurance is considered necessary. Hence we have messages such as 'Mind the gap' warning people about the gap between the train and the platform, now made famous on tee shirts, or warnings in shops about potentially dangerous equipment on the move; for instance, 'Please be aware, fork-lift trucks may be operating in this area'. These messages either run on a loop or are triggered to play at relevant moments. They are generally quite short and to the point and they are often filtered out as the result of what is known as 'habituation' (e.g. Phansalka et al. 2010). However, some messages, such as the one in our example, are listened to mainly because they are directly addressed to people who are in a state of waiting for something to happen and that something is the topic of the message itself. Although habituated to the message, we take note because it tells us something immediately relevant which affects our actions. However, what some people may not notice (while others clearly do, judging by reactions on blogs and discussion boards, as we show below) is a rather strange choice of expression used in the message; that is, the use of the auxiliary *shall* as a marker of the future tense. Why does the speaker use *shall be* instead of the standard *will be*?

When we analyse this usage, what sort of tools do we need? For example, we might need to know what accent it was pronounced with, and what the social features of the accent might be perceived to be. We also need grammatical knowledge – we know that it is grammatically correct, or as we would term it, well-formed (see Chapter 2). In order to truly *understand* it, though, understand where it is right and where it goes wrong, we need to speculate about the intentions of the speaker, why they consider this usage to be appropriate and how this might have come about.

The first thing we might suggest is that there is a certain uneasiness among some speakers of modern British English about how to sound formal, or rather, as we would say in linguistics, about how to use formal register. An example of this is the insurance salesperson on the telephone who uses the reflexive personal pronoun *yourself* as in: 'We'll send the policy out to yourself.' Similarly, 'Have you got your licence on yourself, please?' (Police officer to car driver on the Channel 5 reality TV programme, *Emergency Bikers*[2]). Where this usage has come from is something of a mystery, just as the use of *shall* is in our tube station example. In neither case is the usage necessary or correct in grammatical terms; it seems rather to have something to do with feelings about politeness and formality. In the case of *yourself* the speakers perhaps feel that the phrases *to you* or *on you* somehow sound too direct, even abrupt. Or they might feel that *yourself* has a more official tone or quality about it, resonant of the language of legal documents, which both the insurance agent and the police officer would no doubt be familiar with. Seen in this light, we can speculate that whoever scripted the London Underground message felt that *shall be* sounds better – more formal, more authoritative, more official – than the workaday *will be*.

So, now we've identified that it is the use of *shall* for *will* that makes the message sound odd, let's explore it in a little more detail.

Part of the problem lies in the grammar of English which, unlike highly inflectional languages such as Russian or Spanish, does not have a fully articulated future tense. (see Chapter 5). English employs other means to express the future as in 'I'm (I am) going to do something'[3] or 'I'll (I will) do something'. These are known as auxiliary verbs because they help form tenses when connected to other verbs (e.g. *will* write; *have* written; *am* writing). The auxiliary *shall* has a dual function in English, however, and exists somewhere between what is called a modal auxiliary verb (e.g. *could* write; *may* write; *should* write) and a temporal auxiliary verb like *will*. Modal auxiliaries modify the verb in some way; they say something about the status of the verb's meaning. In the case of *shall*, there is some transition in its use. It can be used as a temporal auxiliary for the first-person singular and plural – 'I shall write a poem!' 'We shall discuss it later!' – though this usage has come to sound slightly archaic and quaint. Using *shall* with other subject forms (you, she, they) is associated with authority or special power, and often has a declamatory note. For instance, in the King James version of the Bible, *shall* is used for proclaiming the Ten Commandments, notably in the negative and archaic form ('Thou shalt not', or in more modern versions, 'You shall not'). It is also popularly associated with a judge's handing down of the death sentence: 'You shall be taken to a place' and in fairy tales, usually in conjunction with a magic wand, we find: 'Cinderella shall go to the ball.' More prosaically, a notice on the back door of a supermarket in north-east London proclaims to delivery drivers: 'Bread shall be delivered to the front door only' as if it were an instruction written on a tablet of stone. The only other occasion on which standard English tends to employ *shall* is in the interrogative form for suggestions but again, only with the first-person singular or plural – 'Shall we go to the ball?'

We might speculate, then, that the TfL people who scripted the message in Example 1.1 made an error of linguistic judgement in thinking that the difference between *shall* and *will* was one of register rather than one of semantics. In other words, they seem to have deduced from the contexts in which they have encountered *shall* that it is essentially a more formal, prestigious and authoritative-sounding alternative to *will*. At heart, the real strangeness of *shall* is connected to what is known in linguistics as perlocutionary force (Austin 1962); that is, the power of an utterance to enact or prohibit something. By dint of this authority such utterances are only spoken (or proclaimed) by those who are entitled to speak them in certain, often ritualized, situations. There is as far as we know no King Solomon at London Underground; a disembodied public announcement tape is not a magisterial authority; a tube station is not normally considered a ritual space: therefore the effect is odd, even rather comical.

As a postscript to this example, we might mention that at Russell Square, another of the lift-serviced stations, new lifts have been installed. The first of these became ready quite recently, and to our interest, the odd-sounding usage has now been reproduced in writing on a digital light board. Indeed, the usage seems to be being employed right along the Piccadilly Line, and has been sighted at Northern Line stations, resulting in letters to local newspapers and mocking posts on blogs and chatrooms. 'Oddly pompous', said one commentator. 'They want to sound important and are afraid of using ordinary words', said another. It was language blogger Mark Forsyth, though, who captured the incantatory quality of the phrase, which we noted above, observing: 'It sounded as though the voice were trying to *make* lift number two the next lift, as though it were an imperative, as though Harry Potter were pointing his wand and *willing* that lift to come and get me.'[4]

1.3 Naming what you notice

Our second case (Figure 1.1) involves a different kind of communicative phenomenon, one which can be found anywhere in the world and which can appear, often overnight, and disappear equally swiftly. We use this example

FIGURE 1.1 *Graffiti in Tottenham, London.*

to introduce and unpack the term that we use in this book when referring to a 'piece' of communication. The term is *text*[5] and, as is obvious from our example, we are using it differently to the everyday use of the word. We discuss this in more detail below, but first let's take a closer look at Figure 1.1 to see whether and how it can be considered a text. It appeared one day along my (Fiona's) route to work and, enticed firstly by its strong lines and its use of colour (see accompanying website) and then the realization of its textual quality, I stopped to photograph it.

The graffiti is striking for several reasons, some immediately obvious, others perhaps less so. There is the contrast between the colours involved in the composition: the black used for the drawing, the red for the heart, both painted against a vibrant turquoise background. There is the strong outline of the figure, the oversized hand with the finger pointing, the one eye, the stance, the single word. These aspects alone ensure its noticeability. However, the serendipity of the combination of two key elements, the blank canvas of the turquoise-painted board, which encloses an overgrown bit of waste ground below a railway embankment, and the parking meter on the pavement right in front of it, is what gives it *communicative* salience. It speaks to you. Clearly this was too good an opportunity for the graffiti artist to let pass.

1.4 Text – 'the stuff of communication'

As we have previously explained, throughout our discussion we use examples of communicative phenomena such as the graffiti in Figure 1.1 or the recorded message from London Underground to draw out issues that linguistics is concerned with and to develop discussions around those issues. The general term we want to use for these phenomena is, as we have already indicated, *text*. This is a term that is used in linguistics, particularly in *social semiotics*, to refer to what is produced (or co-produced) in the process of communication (see also Chapter 7). For something to be a text it must be meaningful, or be intended to be meaningful, have what Halliday (e.g. 1978) calls 'meaning potential'. For instance, a text can be a single word such as 'Help!', an interaction of words and gestures in a conversation, an architect's drawing of a planned building. What these have in common is their intention to mean and communicate something specific within a given contextual frame. The word *help*, for example, has an inherent meaning which you might find in a dictionary. However, this does not necessarily make it a text. What turns the word into a text is where, when and with whom it is uttered, how it is uttered and whether it is uttered in combination with other communicative (or *semiotic*) resources. The word 'Help!', cried out, accompanied by an arm raised above the water intends to mean something quite different to the word 'Help!', whispered behind a hand, eyebrows raised, to someone sitting beside you.

The word *text* comes from the Latin *textus*, meaning something that is woven together (from *texere*: to weave). This makes it a particularly suitable term for referring to communicative phenomena as it emphasizes the point that communication involves the combination, or weaving together, of different resources. The further association with the English words *textile* and *texture* enhances not only the sense of a text having substance (or materiality) and of its being layered but also the implication of making something by combining different elements. Whenever we engage in communicative activity this is precisely what we do. We choose different elements, which from a social semiotic perspective are known as *semiotic resources*, to communicate our meaning in the most effective possible way. For example, if you are out walking along a busy street in a foreign country where you don't speak the language and you want to ask the way, you will need to approach someone and attempt to engage them. But how do you do it? The resources you choose for this purpose will depend on what you consider most appropriate for the situation and, indeed, what you happen to have available. They might include a gesture, holding out your hand, for instance, accompanied by a facial expression such as raising your eyebrows and smiling. You might also hold up a street map, if you had one, in order to indicate the kind of communication you want to engage in. If these strategies don't work you might draw on other resources, and if they don't work either, you might give up and try someone else. Communicative success or failure will depend on the fit between what you choose as your communicative strategy and your co-respondent's interpretation. Not speaking the language suggests a poor fit, but if you use other resources such as the map, the chances of success are increased.

By now it will be clear that our use of *text* differs from the way most people use it, to mean something that is written down. For instance, people talk about the text of a play, meaning the written script as opposed to the performance, or text messages to distinguish them from voice messages. The term is also used in association with authoritative and established or 'undisputed' knowledge, be it disciplinary, as in textbook, or religious, as in the Bible or the Koran. However, for our purposes, text is 'the stuff of communication' (Kress 2003: 47).

1.4.1 *When is a text not a text?*

Kress (2010) suggests there are two aspects that are involved in making a text, representation and communication. Representation concerns the act of making something, of giving 'material realization' to your meaning(s). What would turn a representation into a text, though, is if there were a communicative dimension, the intentionality to communicate something specific that we suggested above. As Kress says: 'Communication . . . is to make my meanings known to my assumed audience' (2010: 51). Our example of being lost in a strange city is a case in point. A street map simply held in your hand is not necessarily a text (although some enthusiastic passer-by might take it as such and start giving you unwanted advice). However, if you're holding it opened out and looking around with a beseeching expression on your face, the combination of these elements produce a text which is intended to mean something like 'I'm lost. Please help me!' Of course, a map is a text in its own right. It has been produced, using a variety of semiotic resources (colours, lines, shapes, words, etc.) to communicate spatial arrangement, location and direction. The map in our example, however, is used as one of several semiotic resources itself in the production of a different kind of text, with a different meaning. By contrast, a map simply held in the hand, neither being looked at nor used in any gestural way, is not, at that moment, *intended* to be understood as a text in its own right.

1.4.2 *Why is our graffiti a text?*

We now return to ask why the graffiti in Figure 1.1 can be considered a text. First of all, the artist has made clear choices about what resources to use in what combination and in what arrangement in the representation. The turquoise boarding and the parking meter are not the artist's productions in themselves, unlike the image she or he paints, they are enlisted resources, though they may also have given the artist the idea in the first place. It is, though, the graffiti itself that brings the elements together so as to make it meaningful as a cohesive whole. There is the strong directive produced by the combination of the word *pay* and the finger (could it also be a gun, 'gangsta' style?) pointing to the parking meter. We know that the word is meant as an imperative and not a noun precisely because of the way in which these elements sit in relation to one another. Halliday and Hasan, writing about verbal communication, argue that cohesion is fundamental to the making of texts in that it activates meaning:

> Cohesion . . . is part of the text forming component in the linguistic system. It is the means whereby elements that are structurally unrelated to one another are linked together, through the dependence of one on the other for its interpretation. (1976: 27)

This linkage of disparate elements produces what Liu and O'Halloran call, in their discussion of multimodal texts, 'intersemiotic texture' (2009). This is the way in which different elements (the visual, the verbal, the locational, etc.) combine to produce a desired meaning, something that our graffiti exemplifies. From this there can be no doubt that our graffiti is a text!

But, what about the bright-red heart and the single eye? How are they meant to mean in relation to the rest of the text? Perhaps the eye tells us that we are being watched, though its shape does not speak of surveillance. Does the heart adjust the hard meaning of the directive to 'pay' in the same way that modal verbs do, as we explained earlier in the chapter? Maybe it tells us that the directive is not so strong after all. Whatever it means in the context of the message in hand, the heart turned out to act as a kind of graffiti tag,[6] or perhaps better, a refrain. Having noticed this one, I began to spot more of them around the area. There were hearts painted on walls, on street furniture, on advertising hoardings, some encompassed by a similarly drawn figure, others alone. The 'heart' graffiti, as I came to call it, had become a conversation.

As is the nature of most graffiti, this one is no longer in view. There is a ghostlike remembrance of the original, the parking meter, a fragment of turquoise board, both appearing lonely without their co-text. Was the board with its drawing dumped somewhere, or did someone take it and put it on display? If so, not only would its status have changed (now a piece of art?), but also how its meaning, its communicative affect, removed from its context and separated from resources that formed part of that meaning.[7] Could it still be considered a text in the way we have discussed here? The answer is that it probably could be, though it would be a different text communicating a different meaning or set of meanings.

Can a shoe be a text? In Iraq or Egypt, when held up by one or a thousand people with the sole facing away towards another person (either present or absent) that shoe becomes a text. Simply holding up a shoe or even drawing it on a wall denotes the meaning of disregard or disgust for someone. This meaning, which used only to be understood within the culture of the Arab world, is now known worldwide as the result of news media reporting of the aftermath of the overthrow of Sadaam Hussein.

This is not to say that the shoe is intrinsically a text, but rather it is a text if it is used in this way in this context. The shoe worn on the foot is not a text, it is a shoe (though you might be able to imagine circumstances where people consciously use shoes to communicate meanings such as 'I am rich', 'I am cool', etc.).

1.5 How language encodes relationship

We used our example of the graffiti to introduce our use of the term *text*. Our third case focuses on the interpersonal dimension of communicative activity: the relationship between the participants involved in a given textual interaction and the relevance of context. In this case the text is an email recently received by me (Fiona) and written by someone we will call 'Sadia'.

> Fiona
> Kindly fill and send the attached referee document to the email mentioned in the document.
> Regards
> Sadia

Without knowing anything about the participants or the circumstances the email can be understood as a clear directive from one person to another in which the recipient is expected to carry out the task. There is a strongly authoritative tone about the email, expressed in the choice of the imperative form of the verbs *fill* and *send* and further confirmed by the use of the adverb *kindly*. Used alongside the imperatives, *kindly* asserts the status of the writer as someone who has the right to make such a demand; someone in a position of superiority. There is also something of the formal and formulaic about the email, almost as if it had been sent by a stranger working in a large organization. This impression is produced by the choice of the passivized phrase, 'the attached referee document', which expunges any sense of the identity of the 'attacher' and creates a further interpersonal distance between the writer and the reader. This is despite the fact that the two participants are on first-name terms, though it is worth also pointing out that the absence of a salutation (dear, hi) and the use of the rather remote closing (regards) further adds to the sense of entitlement apparently claimed by the writer.

When I received this email, my immediate reaction was to think 'What a cheek!'. But why did I react in that way? The answer lies in the context of the email – what kind of action was being expected and by whom? – and the reason for my reaction lies in the writer's misjudgement of register. In this case the issue is not a misjudgement of formal use, as in the case of TfL announcement above, but rather of how register encodes power relations. We tend to notice register more easily when there has been a register transgression, as a little context will now demonstrate.

The writer of the email was a former student who had originally written asking whether I would be willing to provide an academic reference for her. I replied saying that I was happy to do so, despite being rather busy, and almost immediately received this email in reply. Its peremptory tone stood in stark contrast to what should, in my view, have been a grateful, polite and friendly request. It did not fit the interpersonal context in which I, as her former university teacher and the person of whom the favour was being asked, should have been in the 'senior' position whereas the former student, as the supplicant, should have been in the 'junior' position. Instead the opposite was implied, due to the linguistic choices the student made. From the student's perspective, however, the email may well have appeared perfectly polite and even friendly. She is a South Asian speaker of English and, in our experience, very courteous. It is, therefore, likely that she mistook the word *kindly* to be a marker of friendly politeness which might soften the request, rather than a marker of presumed authority to command. Despite being a very able user of English, she did not realize that *kindly* juxtaposed with the imperative form of a verb serves to categorize a message as a demand rather than as a request. This is rather similar to the way *polite notice* is used in signs which are designed to warn people off doing something, such as parking in front of a private garage, in a way that is far from being friendly or even polite. There is a tension between the apparent politeness of the request and the real force of the writer's intention, illustrated by the following handwritten notice displayed, in obvious frustration, in a common area of a British army base in Afghanistan: 'A NICE NOTICE: USE THE FUCKING BINS NOT THE FLOOR OR GROUND'.[8] The subtlety of meaning communicated by 'polite notice' or the explicitly ironic 'nice notice' is something that non-native speakers are not always likely to appreciate, as the example of a notice pinned to a fifteenth floor balcony door in a five-star hotel in Tashkent (Figure 1.2) suggests.

FIGURE 1.2 *Notice in a Tashkent, Uzbekistan hotel.*

We can be pretty certain that the hotel manager really did intend to write a notice that was polite rather than a 'polite notice' particularly because this notice was designed to help rather than prohibit with its message warning against locking yourself out.

Returning to our misjudged email, we might ask how she could have written it differently; what alternative textual choices she could have made. Perhaps something like the following would have been better received.

> Dear Fiona
>
> Thanks so much for agreeing to do the reference. I've attached the reference form which you need to fill in and send to the email address provided.
>
> Thanks again
> Sadia

In this version, the appreciation is foregrounded and the interpersonal relationship is maintained as friendly. This new version has a lighter tone than the original and instead of the formulaic and formal register of the passive construction (attached referee form) chosen for the original, here the writer takes responsibility for attaching it (I've attached). The directive, for me to fill in and send the form, is still there but in this version it is expressed not as an imperative, but rather as a modalised version of an imperative (you need to). It could have been softened even further by choosing, for instance, 'they need you to' thereby removing responsibility for the request from Sadia herself to the people who asked for the reference in the first place. Furthermore, such a shift in responsibility (or agency) moves it away from me, the intended referee: 'they need you to' rather than 'you need to'.

Register is something that we mostly take for granted and, as already pointed out, tends to become an issue when the 'rules' are transgressed. We learn about register through our social interactions. The wider the variety of interactions, the greater our register repertoire becomes. It is useful to be aware of register when talking with or writing to people whose native language is different to your own (see Chapter 5). It is also useful when discussing public debate around issues such as the supposed falling standards of language use. For instance, as we discuss in Chapter 13, the difference between how children talk in the playground and how they talk in class is not one of correctness, as it is often misrepresented in the media and by politicians, but one of register. Our fourth case, which is based around an overheard fragment of conversation, picks up the point about context, appropriacy and choice of semiotic resources.

1.6 Styling as an act of identity

A group of schoolchildren were being led along by a teacher in north London, evidently on a school trip or outing of some kind. Catching sight (presumably for the first time) of the imposing bulk of Arsenal Football Club's Emirates stadium, one boy excitedly nudged his friend and gasped:

'That's the Emirates, innit. Dat is sick, man!'

What can we say about an utterance like this, in terms of the boy's choice of linguistic resources and their relationship to the context? What made Tim, who noted it down, take an interest in this remark and why is it worthy of comment?

First, let's detail some of the context: this was a group of a dozen or so boys, a fairly standard London demographic with a mix of cultural and ethnic groups. The speaker was black, his friend white. All were about 11 years old, and the ones whose voices could be heard were clearly Londoners. Now, let's look more closely at what is said, and how it is said, starting with the first sentence:

That's the Emirates, innit.

As long as you know that Arsenal Football Club's ground is called 'The Emirates Stadium' and you know where the stadium is, the statement *That's the Emirates* is unremarkable and easily interpreted. The tag, *innit,* looks as if it could be a question or a question tag, like *isn't it?*, but it was said with a flat, slightly falling tone. So what is it doing there? It is clearly not meant as a question seeking confirmation, or expressing doubt, as might be the case had *isn't it?* been used with a questioning intonation (and therefore we do not write it here with a question mark). It does not seek any acknowledgement. In fact, as many British speakers are aware, *innit* has become widespread throughout the London region, fulfilling a variety of functions. Sometimes it is used as a catch-all tag to serve for the more grammatically explicit or complex variable tags such as *wouldn't we?* or *don't they?* as discussed in Cheshire et al. (2008). Sometimes it is used as a marker of approval in response to something someone else has said, and sometimes, as in our example, it is used to add emphasis and authority to a statement.

Now let's turn to the second part of the utterance, which seems to us to have been drawn from what we would call a different repertoire; one which affirms a certain individual and group identity. This is represented in the vocabulary, the pronunciation and the rhythm of the utterance as we will now show:

'Dat is sick, man!'

This statement was said in a higher voice than the first statement, with the highest pitch on the word *sick*. These prosodic features, that is the name given to aspects of speech such as pitch, stress and intonation, together with the shift from the standard *that* to the variant pronunciation *dat*, along with the use of *man*, might appear to give the whole utterance a Caribbean flavour. Some might assume that the boy was proclaiming his ethnic heritage by reproducing the speech patterns of the Caribbean – but this is unlikely. In fact, *any* of the boys could have said these words, in this way, regardless of ethnicity. Borrowing speech styles across supposed ethnocultural boundaries is a well-documented phenomenon in youth speech (e.g. Rampton 1995, 2006; Kerswill et al. 2007; Cheshire et al. 2008).

If we now focus on the vocabulary, the two words that stand out are *sick* and *man*. *Man* has a long history in English as an address term, rising and falling in popularity over successive generations. It has had a resurgence in recent years particularly among young urban speakers and is used as a 'vernacular vocative' as in Rampton (2010) to acknowledge mutual membership of an urban, predominantly young, multi-ethnic, multicultural group. In our example the boy does not pronounce *man* in the Jamaican way (which would be something like 'mon'); the link he makes is not with the Caribbean but with his own London peers. The other word, *sick*, is widely used among this group and means something like 'excellent'. It is derived through the device of 'inverted meaning' and, according to the Oxford English Dictionary, originated in North America. Such usages can be dated back the nineteenth century century and possibly further.

The final feature of note concerns the use of the word 'is'. Rather than using the contracted form (*dat's* for *dat is*) in line with his earlier '*that's* the Emirates' he uses the full form *is*. This might seem a very small detail, but it is worth noting because it draws attention to what is a particular rhythmic pattern often found in modern London youth speech. This pattern is characterized by a staccato rhythm typical of French, Welsh and, perhaps more pertinently, many African and South Asian languages, where individual syllables are given more or less equal stress (and they are hence known as syllable-timed languages). This differs from stress-timed languages such as English or Arabic, which have a high number of reduced vowel sounds and therefore have a rhythmic pattern which moves from one dominant syllable to the next. For example, if we take the word 'banana' as pronounced with an English rhythm, it would go something like 'baNAna' whereas if a French or Nigerian person were saying it (in English, of course) it might go something like 'BANANA'. What is interesting in our example is that the boy uses a more normal rhythm in the first sentence *That's the EMirates, innit,* where *that's, Em* and *in* are stressed, but with the primary stress on *Em*, whereas in the second sentence he shifts towards the alternative rhythm described above where each syllable is stressed almost equally. Our guess is that the second sentence could be understood as a pre-fabricated utterance, that is, a chunk of language which is available for use as a stand-alone item. As such, not only are the words pre-fabricated but also the way they are said.

Ultimately, what our example really shows is what Rampton (e.g. 2010: 2) has called 'stylized performance' which can be seen in the shift from a more or less standard style, in the first sentence, to a style which references, or indexes, a mixed, inner-city, multicultural, young London identity in the second sentence (see Cheshire et al. 2008). It is not an attempt to mimic Caribbean speech, as people often assume, or a sign that he does not know how to speak standard English (see Chapter 12), it is an unselfconscious act of identity. From a linguistics perspective, we might say that the boy is not just admiring the Emirates or encouraging his friends to admire it: he is admiring it using a speech style which affirms who he is and who they are. If he had been talking to his mother he would surely have said it differently!

1.7 Conclusion

With the four cases discussed here we have tried to show how, through observing and analysing textual choices and communicative interactions, we can gain insights into things like social relations, identities and attitudes. The invitation to notice is an invitation to look again at communicative phenomena which are often taken for granted or simply pass unnoticed. However, noticing is not enough in itself. What turns noticing into understanding is the kind of unpacking that we have demonstrated in this chapter using the tools that linguistics makes available, and it is this which enables us to engage in debates on language from a position of knowledge rather than simply of opinion. In the next chapter we explore the idea of what constitutes 'good' language, with particular reference to standards, dialects and notions of prestige and correctness. We consider how received, 'common-sense' ideas are not adequate to explain how language actually works, or always helpful in understanding that language is a fluid and ever-changing resource.

Suggested reading

Blommaert, J. and Jie, D. (2010), *Ethnographic Fieldwork: A Beginner's Guide.* Bristol: Multilingual Matters.

This slim volume does precisely what it says on the cover in a very readable way. With examples from their own work, the authors guide readers through the experience of researching first-hand observations and the questions that those observations give rise to. It offers both theoretical insights and practical advice on doing ethnographic work particularly in relation to linguistic and sociolinguistic phenomena.

Mooney, A. S., Peccei, J., LaBelle, S., Henriksen, B. E., Eppler, E., Irwin, A., Pichler, P., Soden, S., (eds) (2011), *Language, Society and Power Reader.* Abingdon: Routledge.

This edited collection provides a clear overview of key concepts in social linguistics. But it does more than that. It explores such questions as: What is language? How does it represent meaning? How does it affect and reflect things such as identity, gender, age or ethnicity? It is a very good read, full of thought-provoking discussion.

2

About correctness: What is 'good' language?

2.1 Introduction

In this chapter we look at a number of themes related to the notion of 'good' language. First we try to pinpoint exactly what is meant by correctness in language, introducing the concept of well-formed and ill-formed utterances. We then examine some data in the form of a set of election campaign posters, and ask if we can go beyond the idea of the well-formed and the ill-formed utterance to develop an awareness of how correctness and appropriacy can be viewed quite differently by different groups of speakers, especially in highly diverse contexts. This leads on to a discussion of standard and non-standard language varieties, and the emergence of new languages and language varieties. Finally, we discuss notions of 'good' in the context of prestigious or highly valued language. Throughout all of this we will try to show that there is very little that is fixed in matters of language, and that prestige, standardness and even correctness itself are often in a state of shift and flux.

2.2 Standard and non-standard varieties; well-formed and ill-formed utterances

Over many years of teaching linguistics and sociolinguistics to English language teachers, we have found that one of the hardest things for our students to accept is that non-standard forms of language, linguistically speaking, are as good and as grammatical as standard forms. It is understandable that they should be resistant to this notion: many of them are non-native speakers of English, and have invested a lot of time, energy and money in making themselves expert users and teachers of the language. They also, naturally enough, have a vested interest in ensuring that only 'correct' English should be regarded as acceptable. But native speakers too, who themselves often speak non-standardly, can be nearly as resistant, and indeed can be disparaging even about their own speech ('I don't talk proper').

Modern linguistics, though, holds as a fundamental tenet that standard languages (that is, the kind of English or Italian, for example, that you would find in an English or Italian dictionary and grammar book) are, in essence, no more than dialects which happen to have become socially privileged as the result of historical processes. This can seem counter-intuitive, as most of us have been educated to believe – and in some language communities much more than others, as we see in Chapter 5 – that the standard form of our language is a special and enduring entity, governed by fixed rules, and that any other dialect or variety is an inferior version of it. But the rules of standardness are produced, so to speak, after the event, a fact observed as long ago as 1511 by John Colet in his preface to William Lily's Latin grammar:

> In the beginning men spake not Latin because such rules were made, but, contrariwise, because men spake such Latin the rules were made. That is to say, Latin speech was before the rules, and not the rules before the Latin speech. (Cited in Ostler 2007: 253)

Of course, Colet did not go all the way and point out that one dialect of Latin is as good as another, in terms of linguistic form. It is striking, though, that he made this point – that in some sense it is the *speakers* of a language who collectively determine what is right and wrong, and not an external source of authority – at a time when, as we shall see later, the ideology of the standardization of language was beginning to take shape in Europe (Milroy 2001).

You can test your own notions of 'rightness' and 'wrongness' in English by comparing different kinds of utterances. Look at the ones below: What can you say about them in terms of grammatical correctness and/or acceptability to you as a speaker? Could you rank them in an order of 'rightness'? Do some of the ones you find unacceptable feel more so than others? Why? And what do you base your opinion on?

1 It were a right good night, weren't it?

2 She is a woman fair-haired with features attractive.

3 You know how it go. Muthafucka gots ta have all the finest things in life.

4 Leaves, like the things of man, you/With your fresh thoughts care for, can you?

5 Arrested their in needs it which code fill bad better of.

6 If you'd told me about this earlier, I might have been able to do something.

7 Happy birthday, innit.

8 Was you on deck at the time the colours were struck?

9 Get out of here, you stupid bastard!

Let's now look at them in a little more detail. Number (6) would be agreed by most native speakers to represent standard English, and to be 'correct' in its grammar. Utterance (9), too, must be reckoned standard English. The fact that it uses low register (we will discuss this term later), and contains what might be considered offensive language, is neither here nor there in terms of linguistic form. Both (2) and (5) must be deemed incorrect. Sentence (2) is perfectly comprehensible, but could only ever have been produced by a non-native speaker, presumably a speaker of a language, like Kiswahili or French, in which the adjective generally follows the noun rather than preceding it. Sentence (5) is incomprehensible, and might have been produced by a random word generator; the fact that it is incomprehensible is not necessarily enough to make it unacceptable, but the fact that it has no grammar certainly is. Both (2) and (5), then, are examples of what we call *ill-formed utterances*: they do not conform to the rules of any native-speaker variety of English.

The others deviate in greater or lesser degree from the standard, but this is not the same as saying that they are incorrect. Number (1) corresponds to a specific geographical variety. *I were* and *it were* are common dialect formulations in much of northern England (compare the modern standard German *ich war* and *es war* – *I was* and *it was*); *right* is a northern dialectal alternative to the standard intensifier *very* (and was once common in mainstream English, where its fossilized remains can be observed in phrases such as *right royal* and *the right honourable member*). Number (3) is a participant observer's rendering of the speech of an African-American gang member in a US prison,[1] and might be described as an ethnic, group-defining or identity-establishing variety of speech. This is also partly true for number (7), overheard in a shop in east London, where *innit*, as we saw in Chapter 1, is typical of the usage of young Londoners living in ethnically mixed inner-city areas (from which it is fast spreading); we might also therefore think of it as a geographical or age cohort-related variety. A usage might be recognizably from a past era of English, as in (8), the words of a judge taken from the transcript of the court martial of Lord Cochrane in 1801.[2] A judge would not be likely to say *you was* nowadays, though note that it is still common in basilectal (i.e. less standard, and generally more working class) speech in the London area and beyond. Or it might be recognizably poetic in style, as in Gerard Manley Hopkins's couplet (from the poem *Spring and Fall*) in (4). What is vital to note about all of these last-named, though, is that (with the possible exception of (4), and poetry is very often an exception to the normal rules of language – that's part of the point of poetry), they are well-formed utterances in a way that (2) and (5) are not. They are rule-governed, even if the rules concerned are not those of standard English; they are not sub-standard, they are merely non-standard.

As we have already suggested, one of the great insights of the discipline of linguistics in the twentieth century was to establish that everyone speaks a dialect: a rule-governed variety of a language which differs regularly from the varieties around it. That dialect might be the socially privileged one that we call 'standard English', 'standard Korean' or whatever, but it is still a dialect. In terms of linguistic structure, sentence (1) above is just as good, in every way, as sentence (6), and as linguists 'we don't draw a distinction between what is grammatical and what is acceptable' (Halliday 1978: 38). In other words, the social standing of dialects, or whether or not they are generally viewed as being 'good' or 'proper', has nothing to do with it. Keep this fundamental fact in mind as we go beyond ideas of correctness and incorrectness, standardness and non-standardness, and complicate things a little by considering whether, in fact, correctness in language is in a constant state of flux.

2.3 Correctness, context, community

We turn now to a set of examples which raises questions about correctness and appropriacy: specifically, the question of how linguistic norms operate in different environments and how (or even *if*) they are perceived. Cameron (1995) points out that ordinary speakers tend quite often to have a more hard-line or prescriptive view on the matter of correctness and 'good' usage, even if they often speak non-standardly themselves, than professional academics trained in descriptive linguistics. (The descriptive approach sets out to describe how people speak, as opposed to the prescriptive approach of telling them how they *should* speak.) As she (1995: 12) notes, drily: 'Linguistic conventions are quite possibly the last repository of unquestioned authority for educated people in secular society.' This has a good deal of truth in it, at least if we are talking about the supposed monolith which is standard English. And yet, within any given speech community – this term is of course a rather slippery one, and we will look at it more closely in the next chapter – there may be a range of views as to whether a usage is acceptable or not. Some speech communities are more cohesive than others; some are more easily able to agree than others on what is good, correct or merely appropriate in a particular context. It is therefore probably to be expected that when we take English as a whole, spoken by a vast range of people as a native and non-native language, across a vast range of cultures and contexts, and London – perhaps the best exemplar on earth of the 'super-diverse' (see box) environment – there can be jarring outcomes.

The phrase 'super-diversity' (Vertovec 2006, 2007) was coined in an attempt to highlight the fact that migration to Britain since around the turn of the twenty-first century has been radically different in both scale and character to what came before. Whereas migrant communities traditionally were characterized by their historical links to Empire and Commonwealth, more recent migrants are increasingly likely to be of non-Commonwealth (and often multiple) origins, more mobile, more scattered and more globally connected. Britain has become more socially complex than ever before, and this super-diversity is reflected in language use. The 2011 Census revealed Polish to be the second most spoken language in England, ahead of 'traditional' immigrant tongues like Urdu, Punjabi and Cantonese. The seventh most spoken language in England and Wales is Arabic (159,000); there are 70,000 speakers of Tagalog, 76,000 of Persian and nearly 100,000 of Turkish. It also showed regional concentrations: there is, for instance, a large community of Lithuanian speakers in Boston in Lincolnshire, and one of Korean speakers in New Malden, Surrey, while you are most likely to come across Somali in Brent in north-west London (ONS 2011b). In London as a whole, the census confirmed the impression of growing diversity, with at least 100 languages spoken in nearly every borough of the capital. In the borough of Newham, in east London, 41 per cent of residents do not have English as their first language, and 9 per cent are unable to speak it at all. (*Evening Standard*, 30 January 2013).

Here, then, is a small study of a case in which differing normative values and models of acceptability might seem to be operating. It draws on a selection of campaign posters for a students' union election. The posters, from which we have extracted the salient linguistic features, were pinned up around the campus at a large university in central London which has a very high proportion of international students.

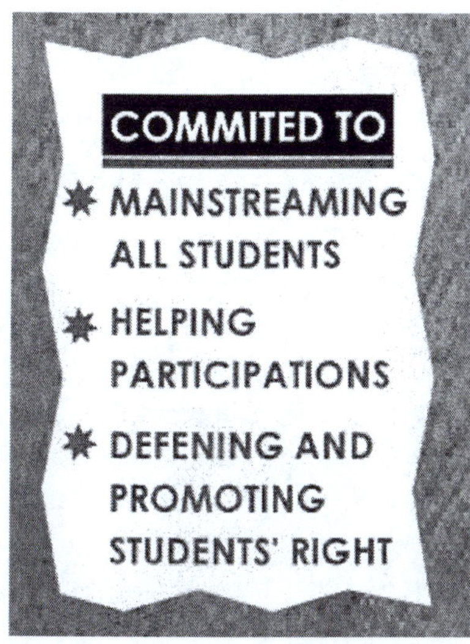

"VOTE FOR THE REASON"

"YOUR VOTE WORTH TO ME"

FIGURES 2.1–2.4 *Student election campaign posters.*

What puzzled us, when we came across these posters, was why the candidates, all of whom were originally from the Indian subcontinent, appeared not to have ascribed any great importance to the need for linguistic accuracy or even meaningfulness on such publicly displayed documents. They were, after all, putting themselves up for election to official student union posts, in a university, in the city and country often considered to be the very home of the

English language. It is not that the candidates themselves lacked high levels of literacy: we knew one of the candidates well, had taught him at postgraduate level and knew him to be an academically able and articulate student. In fact, it is this that first made us wonder what lay behind this seeming carelessness. We say 'seeming' carelessness because the candidates had, for the most part, paid considerable attention to the visual impact of the posters, drawing on a variety of visual resources in designing them. The choice of fonts, the spatial arrangement, the carefully posed candidate photographs[3] all indicated this. Furthermore, because the productions conform visually to the genre, broadly understood, of the election campaign poster, we can safely conclude that they were not on new and unfamiliar territory, or at least they did not *think* they were. What is more, they would have spent time and money on getting them printed in large quantities; we learned from our own student, who we will call Rafi, that he had had his posters printed at home in Bangladesh and sent back to him in London.

This being so, was it then a case of a non-native speaker printer's error, as in Blommaert's (2010: 31) discussion of misspelt English in a Chinese restaurant menu? We think not, because the types of error could not be attributed solely to the misreading of a handwritten script, as in that case. Apart from misspellings, the posters contain linguistic elements whose meaningful interpretation is difficult if not impossible, and which are unlikely to have been introduced at the printing stage. Nor is this a case of subcontinental English following established norms which happen to be different to those of standard British English (see e.g. Pennycook 2010; Kachru 1994). The errors are simply errors. The question that intrigues us was, why would the producers of the posters not have bothered about 'getting it right' even to the extent of having the text quickly checked over by a native English-speaking fellow student?

A possible, partial solution to this puzzle might lie in what these student election hopefuls considered to be the most salient aspects of their posters. Consider the attitudes and assumptions contained in the following extract from a paper entitled 'English – the Communicative Pinnacle' in the collection of abstracts for an academic conference held in a southern Indian university in 2011:

> There are many reasons as to why studying English is important. One is being that we sound more educated and literate, two is to communicate properly with others, and three because it is important for career advancement and respect in the business world.

The fact that English can be invested with such power is not in itself any great surprise; this aspect of the discourse surrounding English in the Indian subcontinent and beyond has been discussed in detail for many years now (see e.g. Kachru 1998). More striking is the way that 'we sound more educated and literate' is given as the very first reason for studying English, foregrounded and given priority over the idea of communicating 'properly' with others. The emphasis on the value of how one *sounds* to others suggests that the importance of accuracy or meaningfulness in English is here subordinated to the importance of English as a symbolic resource. That is to say, for this writer at least, the primary purpose of using English is to present oneself, and be perceived by others, as 'an English speaker'. In this sense the strange phrases of the student union posters could be thought of as meaningful, but with linguistic meaningfulness taking second place to the symbolic meaningfulness carried by English in South Asian societies. As Figures 2.5 and 2.6 (relating to a national election in Pakistan) show, the creative use of English language as just one communicative resource among many is a characteristic feature of South Asian public discourse. The fact that the English phrases used ('your choice for vote?' and 'Say Yes to Vote') do not correspond to any normative variety of English is not, in terms of communicative intention, of any great importance.

FIGURES 2.5 AND 2.6 *Pakistan 2012 election posters.*

The French theorist Pierre Bourdieu's influential account of language as symbolic capital (Bourdieu 1991) assumed that a speaker needed to be well versed in (probably educated in) the *langue légitime* or hegemonic language of a particular society in order to reap the benefits associated with it. In the case of South Asian electioneering, though – and within some other South Asian contexts, too – it might be enough to use a 'kind of' English. Indeed, we must assume that the majority of the population to whom the political candidates and authorities are trying to appeal are, in fact, unable in any case to read the English words – and many of them unable to read at all. Linguistic accuracy is hence not the number one priority. The larger point is to use words that people will *recognize as* English: to some extent at least, the value of the words is semiotic rather than linguistic; or emblematic rather than denotational, to borrow Blommaert's (2010: 29) formulation. (And see Edwards 2012: 190–1 for a useful discussion of this peculiar role of English in the world.) As Rafi himself said when we asked him to comment on the inaccuracies: 'In Bangladesh, this would not matter. No one would care about this.' We look at this very important aspect of language use in some detail in Chapter 11 ('Translanguaging').

Is this conception of the value of English as a symbolic resource what underlay the students' lack of attention to linguistic detail? If so, then it is unfortunate that such conceptions do not tend to travel well. What might be acceptable on a public campaign poster in the subcontinent, where English has both symbolic and linguistic value, appears sloppy, to say the least, in the British context, where the symbolic value of English *as English* is zero. In essence, then, it might be argued that these posters represent a misreading by the South Asian students of the norms of the speech community they were inhabiting. They perhaps thought that they had acted appropriately because they employed the high-scale, supralocal code – English; but in the way that they used it, applying their local norms or 'local diacritics' (Blommaert 2010: 189), they failed to recognize that other norms are present in 'our' locality (i.e. the native English-speaking social and geographical space), and they ended up indexing themselves as careless or uneducated – quite the opposite of what they had intended. If they had been producing such posters using their own language in their own locality, they would undoubtedly have applied the same attention to linguistic accuracy that would be expected by an English speaker of a public poster in London. To produce semi-literate Bengali in Bangladesh would be, to use Rafi's word, 'inexcusable'.

But if this is indeed the case, then the argument leads us straight to another knotty question: In what kind of speech community did these students think they were? It does not really seem likely that they had, as Blommaert suggests about the '419' fraudsters whose attempted scamming email texts he analyses, 'no awareness of the difference between their variety of English and the normative varieties known to their addressees' (2010: 130). After all, they were living in Britain and were exposed to such normative varieties day in, day out. Perhaps they were persuaded that it didn't really matter, as the university contained so many international students using English as their lingua franca – a super-diverse speech community in an already super-diverse city. Or is it that we, middle-class, middle-aged native speakers, are out of step with what kind of norms are acceptable in London? Did they in fact know perfectly well that their 'local diacritics' were out of step with native norms but nevertheless consider them still to be valid? The Indian conference abstract referred to above also contains the following:

> English is no longer the white man's language. . . . Today, when a non-native speaks in English, he hardly ever remembers it as a foreign tongue. The users of the English language today are viewed as makers of meaning rather than learners of the language.

This chimes with Rafi's response when we asked him why, in his opinion, he and the other student union candidates had not gone out of their way to ensure that the English they used was grammatical and meaningful to English speakers:

> *Power relationship should be noted here. As a non-native speaker obviously you feel shy and you feel less empowered, in the sense of: well, I know English, [but] a native speaker is definitely going to say 'here is a mistake, there is a mistake'. It's a kind of thing that what you have learned so far is not good enough. Again, it's a power struggle, I think, in a sense, it's as if . . . you're not my teacher. . . . It's a kind of thing that you develop within yourself. . . , it's a kind of relationship that I know what I'm doing, my message is quite clear, I'm not going to go to you for checking, because you're not my teacher. It's a kind of arrogance.*

Canagarajah (2013a: 163–70) is explicit in pointing out that some people who think of themselves as 'post-colonial' are often more than willing to defy and resist what they see as linguistic norms being imposed by native speakers of English, and that this can lead to the development of new norms, perhaps even arrived at with the active or tacit co-operation of native speakers. If such self-assertive, defiant attitudes actually do underlie the linguistic behaviour of some non-native speakers in London, then it is obvious that an overarching, authoritative and normative 'standard' English might have only limited traction in their minds. It would not just be that the students misunderstood the norms with which they were working, but that the high-status norms which one would assume to be operating in a university in Britain's capital city were actually no longer doing so, given that the students would perceive the space to be 'transnational, supralocal, and cosmopolitan' (Canagarajah 2013a: 163).

Potentially, we are dealing here with new, unstable or unpredictable varieties of the language. Potentially, too, this would apply equally across the border which separates native speakers from non-native speakers – a border which, in highly diverse London, is a fuzzy and porous one. It has been amply demonstrated that 'crossing', where elements of a range of non-British language influences are incorporated into 'street' speech, has long been a feature of young Londoners' communicative repertoires (Rampton 2006, 2010; Harris 2006). Indeed, perhaps the most noticeable sociolinguistic development in London of the last several decades has been the decline of traditional 'cockney' speech and the advent of what has been dubbed 'Multicultural London English' (see Cheshire et al. 2008), characterized by such pronunciation features as 'laahk' (/la:k/) for *like* and 'dis' (/dis/) for *this*, a shift from stress-timing towards syllable-timing, and lexical innovations such as the use of *bare* as an intensifier in place of *very* or *a lot* ('there was bare police there'). As Cheshire et al. argue, usages like these could have been drawn from a very large range of non-British sources.

Assuming that the notion of a speech community has any real validity in a globalized, super-diverse city, then, in order to understand the student union candidates, we would need to consider what the norms of London speech might be, or rather, might appear to be. That is, we would need to ask how correctness and appropriacy are perceived and judged in highly diverse, highly complex societies where the 'speech community' is in reality a conglomeration of speech communities, resulting in what Blommaert (2010) calls 'polycentricity'. So, following on from the sociolinguist Joshua Fishman's classic (1965) question, 'Who speaks what language to whom and when?' we might ask: 'What forms of language are acceptable to whom, when, and where?'

2.4 The transience of standardness: Or, in Lisbon do they speak good Portuguese or bad Latin?

One way of approaching this problem is to look at the nature of 'standard' languages. Think back to the nine utterances, well-formed and ill-formed, with which we began this chapter. As we suggested then, often when people refer to speaking and writing correctly, it is not *correctness* per se that is meant (for any dialect is linguistically just as correct as any other), it is adherence to *standardness*. It is easy to assume that the standard is solid, immutable, somehow ordained, a natural feature of linguistic life. But as many commentators have pointed out, the idea of a fixed and normative language, which is distinguishable from all other languages and the correct speaking and writing of which can and should be taught, is a deeply ideologized one. It has been linked to the apparatus of the modern nation state and even to the practice of colonialism (Pennycook 2010: 81–3; Milroy 2001; Blommaert 2008). It is perhaps worth being reminded of the genesis of the best-known and most influential language academy in the world, the Académie française.

Founded in 1635 under Louis XIII, its first head was not an eminent linguist, a poet or a man of letters, but the king's first minister, Cardinal Richelieu, his chief crusher of opposition and enforcer of royal power – a man with an 'obsession with order, discipline, regulation, and control' (Cooper 1989: 11). Enforcing the standard is an eminently political act.

Importantly, the standard, apart from being an ideologized and artificial construct, is also transient. As Crowley (2003) reminds us, the term 'standard' referred historically to the monarch's standard – the flag on a battlefield which constitutes a visible reference point that all can rally around (and see also McArthur 1999). From there it came to be applied to the idea of an exemplary, authoritative measure against which others can be tested. Unlike a flag or a measure, though, a standard language is necessarily something of an abstract concept. It may be reified in the form of an officially sanctioned grammar and lexicon: but all that this provides is a snapshot of the language at a certain point in time, and in the considered opinion of a select (and quite possibly self-selecting) group of speakers of the language. Living languages, by their very nature, are in a constant state of flux and change, and have their primary existence in the minds and mouths of speakers rather than in dictionaries and grammars, no matter how up to date these may be. What Milroy (2001: 534) calls the 'ideology of standardisation' did not really take root throughout Europe until the eighteenth century (though in places it began much earlier); even now, few people speak standardly, and virtually no one speaks standardly at all times. Even when they do, they might not use what is often thought of a standard accent. The United Kingdom's near-iconic Received Pronunciation (RP), used as a model by millions of non-native speakers of English worldwide and enshrined in British dictionaries as *the* pronunciation, has probably only ever been used by at most 5 per cent of the British population, and at least one linguist thinks it is 'effectively, dead or dying' (Milroy 1999: 33). Certainly, its once unassailable prestige is in decline, though there is, of course, a continuing social prejudice against non-RP accents in some quarters. British comedian Jimmy Carr's nice little joke about accent relies on British people's awareness of this: 'I'm from the Home Counties, so I don't have an accent. This is just how words sound when they're pronounced properly.'

To see how even supposedly standard languages develop and shift over time, take as an example another international lingua franca at an earlier historical period: the Latin of the western Roman empire, which developed into what we now know as the Romance family of languages (French, Portuguese, Romansh, Spanish, Catalan, Romanian, etc.). We can be reasonably sure what standard Latin is or was, essentially for the reason that it is no longer spoken. What we think of as this standard Latin was an elite written code. It is very unlikely that most Roman citizens, whether in Rome or beyond, often spoke like this; Cicero remains the touchstone of Latin oratory, in grammatical elegance and correctness, but at home probably even Cicero did not speak like Cicero. While the written standard appears at a certain point to have become frozen in time, the speech of ordinary speakers, especially in the provinces, changed and evolved, leading to a distinction between *lingua latina* (the metropolitan standard) and *lingua romana rustica* (the Roman speech of the countryside).

It is possible to pinpoint some of the linguistic changes to Latin as regional habits of speech took hold (though they must have been there all along, under the surface). To take a very few: the hard /k/ of Latin *cantare* (to sing) became a palatalized /ʃ/ in French *chanter*, but remained hard in Spanish *cantar.* (For the slanted brackets and the phonemic symbols, see Chapter 6). In both, though, the final vowel dropped away. You can compare different regional dialects: the Lusitanian /r/ parallels the Hispanic /l/ in word-initial consonant clusters, as in Portuguese *prato; praia* ('plate', beach'; compare Spanish *plato; playa*). French, meanwhile, acquired the habit of deleting /s/ in certain contexts: *école* for *escola*, itself developed out of Latin *schola.* Almost everywhere, elaborate case endings of nouns withered, and prepositions took their place. The demonstrative or deictic *ille* ('that one') and its variants became *els, il, la, le, las* and so on – definite articles, where none had existed in Latin. In similar vein, but perhaps reflecting a different local word order preference, in what was to become Romanian, formations like *homo ille* ('that man') became *omul* (the man), while *lupus ille* became *lupul* (the wolf). Regional words were borrowed from sub-stratum languages to the Romance overlay: hence, for example, Spanish *izquierda* (left), from Basque, which finally displaced the Old Spanish *siniestro* (Latin *sinister*), and must have co-existed with it for a long time. There was also absorption into the mainstream vocabulary of what had previously been slang, perhaps that of Roman military units; for example, *testa* – meaning a pot or vase with ear-like handles – for *caput* (head), leading to French *tête* and Italian *testa.* The formal Latin *equus* (horse) gave way in many areas to the popular *caballus* (with a meaning more like 'nag'), hence Occitan *caval*, Romanian *cal* and French *cheval.* Around the fourth century, too, word order began to change, perhaps under the influence of the speech of Germanic tribes (Ostler 2007: 119), and the verb crept from the end of the sentence, where it had often sat in standard Latin, towards the second place in it.

As Anthony Burgess has it, the Romance languages grew out of 'the people's Latin' (1992: 156). The process might have begun as early as the first century, and gathered pace with the decline of Roman power in western Europe. Many educated speakers, we must imagine, would have been horrified by what they would surely have perceived as a decline in standards. Ivan Illich describes the Spanish scholar and grammarian Antonio de Nebrija as having being 'distraught' at the degeneration of classical Latin when he wrote his groundbreaking grammar of the Castilian language (cited in Scollon and Scollon 2003: viii).[4] Perhaps we might guess too at the existence of a defiant feeling of ownership or appropriation on the part of people who wanted to speak in their own way, and not be beholden to the arbiters of correctness. At some point, though, in this long, slow process of language change – or more precisely at a variety of points, depending for example on the existence of literature, translation of religious works and so on – in each of the Romance-speaking territories, people stopped thinking of the vernaculars as debased Latin, and began to consider them as languages in their own right: whole, grammatically consistent, lexically rich and properly pronounced. This process of vernacularization becomes visible to us in about the twelfth century, when books began to be published in the new languages. We can see one turning point in the French mystery play *Le Jeu d'Adam*, (The Play of Adam), whose anonymous author wrote the text of the play in the vernacular, but inserted stage directions and sung choruses in Latin.

The ideology of standardization, in turn, it has been suggested, really took hold during the period of eighteenth century European nation-state building, though in fact there had certainly been attempts to standardize and thereby to lend prestige to the vernaculars some centuries before that, most notably in the compilation of grammars (Milroy 2001). Perhaps, what really changed from the eighteenth century is that regional varieties other than the newly anointed standard then began to be regarded as debased versions of it, rather than as legitimate local tongues in their own right. This must have been a curious and unsettling experience for very many people: at the independence of Italy in 1861, it has been estimated, only about 3 per cent of the population of the unified country spoke what we would now call 'Italian' (Lewis et al. 2013).

Can we discern here the future of English, with increasing divergence leading to the birth of new languages? It seems to occur again and again to modern English speakers as a possible, if not inevitable scenario when they think about Latin (Ostler 2007; Edwards 2012), rather as American presidents were traditionally supposed to have read Gibbon's *Decline and Fall of the Roman Empire* with an eye to its lessons for the United States. Perhaps language break-up begins when differing norms begin to be not only accepted, but ideologized as natural and inevitable, even desirable. The change is not just in the language, but in the way that speakers think about the language. After all, nobody in Lisbon or São Paulo thinks that they speak bad Latin: they think that they speak good Portuguese. The standard changes according to where you view it from, and perhaps our student union campaigners and their peers think that their use of English is appropriate to the super-diverse context in which they find themselves, and feel comfortable with it, even if their teachers are not (see Graddol 2006). (The idea of multilingual speakers mixing and combining the norms of different speech communities in order to create new kinds of language is one that we shall revisit in Chapters 4 and 11). The sheer reach and spread of English is, anyway, such that the history of previous dominant languages is no longer any kind of guide to what might happen to it in the future; there aren't really any precedents (Crystal 2006: 422). And if English does diversify radically into a new family of languages, this might, as Crystal suggests, force the development of a more nuanced and complex notion altogether of what standard language actually is. To quote Rafi once more, musing on the phrase 'Your vote worth to me':

> *Probably he got the phrase from someone else, not a native speaker. . . . If you're talking about global English, in a multilingual situation, I understand, you understand. It's not a native way of expressing it, but I know what it means.*

Some linguists (e.g. Seidlhofer 2001; Jenkins et al. 2011; Jenkins 2013) have in fact suggested that non-native speakers of English often do not (or even should not) feel that they need to cleave to the norms of traditional, standard English, particularly when they are speaking to other non-natives. The resulting variety, if that is what it is, has been labelled 'English as a Lingua Franca' or ELF – an English which belongs to no one in particular and has no native speakers of its own (and in that sense at least is rather similar to a pidgin, though a pidgin is typically a very reduced form of language, with little in the way of grammar and a very basic vocabulary). The proponents of ELF have in turn been criticized, not least because, as with the notion of 'World Englishes' (i.e. locally recognized variants of English), this kind of approach of necessity assumes that language is an objective 'thing' in itself and that 'languages' are separate or separable entities (Pennycook 2010; and see Mackenzie 2013; Canagarajah 2013a, for varyingly critical discussions of ELF). ELF is in any case something that happens, rather than something tangible and which can be taught. It is hard to imagine it having a life of its own as a defined variety, given that most learners of English would presumably prefer to study standard English – ideologized social construct though it may be – than to spend time and money learning what might be judged a sub-standard 'foreigners' English', even if this is what they finally end up speaking. Whatever the case, in the end what is important to remember is that English, even standard English, is not and never has been immutable: 'The language in its multitude of guises has at any stage in its history varied socially and geographically, and any notion that there has ever existed a uniform version is a fallacy.' (Dewey 2007: 349).

It is therefore incumbent upon speakers and students of language to expect, and indeed to respect, a measure of diversity in usage, perhaps especially in highly diverse contexts. This means accepting, too, that there is nothing inherently 'good' or innately prestigious about any one language, dialect or variety as opposed to another. As we have already noted, the prestige of standard languages derives from social context and ideology, not from inherent linguistic superiority (Milroy 2001). So let us now turn briefly and finally to the question of language prestige, and the importance of social attitudes to language and language use.

2.5 'Even the beggars speak English': Language prestige and subjectivity

In some social contexts, a particular language might become so indelibly associated with (expensive) education, social and economic power, high culture and so on that it takes on an aura, as if it were the language itself, rather than the works and actions of its speakers, that represented 'civilization'. Ovid in exile in Tomis (modern Constantza, on the Black Sea coast of Romania) bemoaned in his *Tristia* or *Poems of Sadness* the fact that he had to live among barbarians, and listed linguistic deprivation among the other deprivations of his reduced lifestyle:

> Not just a climate cold,
> A soil shrunken under hoarfrost;
> Not even a Latinless land, or one of garbled Greek:
> But because of how I live
>
> (*Tristia* 5.10. English translation cited in Williams 1998: 58)

But Ovid had at least the insight to see that the tables had been turned on him, and that while command of Latin had been for him, the proud Roman, prima facie evidence of his social status and for his claim to be a civilized man, for his hosts it held no special significance. In fact, they regard him as lacking in social accomplishments because he cannot speak the local, Getan tongue:

> What conversation! They in local lingo, I in gestures.
> Here *I* am the barbarian [*Barbarus hic ego sum*], understood by none.
> At Latin words the Getans simply gape and giggle.
>
> (In Williams 1998: 56)

Latin, rather remarkably, retains a good deal of its prestige even today, centuries after it last had native speakers. All speakers, though, of whatever language, know instinctively that certain languages or language varieties enjoy greater societal prestige than others. However, this prestige varies according to the social, geographical or historical/temporal space in which the speaker is situated, and therefore any shift in time or space (and hence in social context) can result in a dramatic and unpredictable shift in how the language is perceived (Canagarajah 2013a; Blommaert 2010). The conquest of Peru in the sixteenth century resulted in a situation of diglossia (see Chapter 4) wherein the imperial language of the Incas, Quechua, abruptly lost its associations with power and prestige, and Spanish came to be seen as the language of civilization and culture. Half a millennium later, a man from a Quechua-speaking family in the Andes, now a virtually monolingual Spanish-speaker resident in Lima, talks semi-jokingly about how Quechua is little heard back in his village:

> 'Ya están perdiendo ya. . . . Como se dice, ya se están civilizando. . . . La civilización está llegando allí.'
>
> [They're losing it now. . . . As people say, they're becoming civilised. . . . Civilisation is reaching there.]
>
> (Marr 2011: 229)

Where Quechua would once have been seen as a mark of social attainment, in Peru it is now the very opposite. This essential subjectivity holds of course for English as it does for other languages. English was once thought of as carrying little prestige, having none of the associations with education and access to elite communication that it today carries virtually worldwide. Indeed, as late as the medieval period in England it was assumed that educated people would naturally prefer to read and write in Latin or Norman French. Robert Mannyng's introduction to his English language work of 1303, *Handlyng Synne*, is quite explicit:

> For men unlearned I undertook
> In English speech to write this book.

As suggested above, a shift in space rather than time can produce equally dramatic effects. If the social and educational context you were brought up in has encouraged you to subscribe to the notion of language prestige, like the idea of the standard language, as being something objective and unchanging, then these effects can be very difficult to digest. A pair of Indian students of ours, both professional teachers of English back at home, told us of the surprise, turning to disappointment and then distress, that they felt on first arriving in London in order to undertake their postgraduate course. In India, they had enjoyed unchallenged social status and automatic respect because of their excellent command of English. But most people in Britain speak English, of course, whatever their social status, and the students found that the value of their hard-won and much-prized sociolinguistic resources had simply evaporated overnight. As one of them put it: 'Here even the beggars speak English!' Well, yes. English has social value in certain contexts, and not in others: and even then, the value will vary according to the variety of English spoken and local attitudes to it. Similarly, the prestige generally accorded to Spanish in, say, Britain or France is apt to be greater than that accorded it in Texas or New Jersey, where Spanish is as likely to be associated with the housemaid or the plumber as it is with Cervantes or the Museo del Prado. If the social capital represented by language has value in a social market, as Bourdieu theorized, then our globalized world is a 'messy marketplace' where 'patterns of value and use become less predictable and presupposable' (Blommaert 2010: 28).

2.6 Conclusion

Unpredictability can be frustrating and puzzling when we try to analyse language. Indeed, as Cameron (2012b) points out, some people just feel very uncomfortable with language change, feeling it to be somehow indicative of other kinds of (unwished-for) change in society itself. And yet change must be embraced, for non-fixedness is not just something that complicates matters, it is a defining feature of language itself. Ideas about language prestige, appropriacy, quality, standardness, even grammatical correctness itself are in a state of flux, whether this is immediately visible or not, and it is the job of the language noticer to try to work out what is happening beneath the surface. In super-diverse contexts such as London, or Toronto, or Marseille, or Johannesburg, and in an era of instant communications and global movement, the tendency towards non-fixedness becomes even more marked, as speech communities appear, disappear, evolve and mutate. In the next chapter we look more closely at this notion of speech and discourse communities, and consider the ways in which community can be said to be enacted or created through language.

Suggested reading

Cameron, D. (2012b), *Verbal Hygiene*, 2nd edn. Abingdon: Routledge.

A new edition of a work that has attained the status of a modern classic, this accessible, level-headed and persuasive book looks at popular attitudes towards language use, including such areas as 'politically correct' language and the importance of 'correct' grammar. Without condescension, it argues that the urge to regulate language can be explained as a symbolic attempt to impose order on an unruly social world.

Paffey, A. (2014), *Language Ideologies and the Globalization of 'Standard' Spanish.* London and New York: Bloomsbury.

The question of how and why the ideology of language standardization developed and is maintained is here examined from the perspective of Spanish, rather than the more familiar one (to many) of English. The author uses textual analysis of newspapers alongside critical discussion of the role of the Real Academia Española (the supposed guardian of the language), and the notion of an 'international' Spanish to show how language ideology is institutionally maintained on a global scale.

Pennycook, A. (2010), *Language as a Local Practice.* Abingdon: Routledge.

In this entertaining and challenging book the author takes the three themes of language, locality and practice, showing in a series of geographically diverse discussions (e.g. India, the Philippines) how each informs the others. The point is made insistently that language is primarily an *activity*, something that emerges through practice and at a local level, rather than an abstract, external structure or system which is drawn upon by its users.

3

About belonging: How does language enact community?

3.1 Introduction

Some time ago, after several weeks of being in London, one of our international students asked whether she looked unwell or unhappy. We told her she looked fine and asked her why she wanted to know. She explained that it was because people kept on asking her if she was alright and she didn't know why and she didn't know how she should respond. When we explained that this was a common greeting and that the normal response was to repeat *alright* with a falling tone, in assent, and possibly an added *you* as a question, she was bemused but much relieved.

This chapter offers a series of reflections on how the contexts and cultures we find ourselves in affect our language practices. Because we adopt an understanding of culture that includes but goes beyond the national/ethnic/linguistic frame, we use the term community (e.g. Wenger 1998) in considering how interactional norms and linguistic repertoires (Hymes 1996; Blommaert 2010) can impact upon communicative effectiveness. We look at questions such as why communicative strategies work in one context and not in another, how acts of greeting or apologizing, for instance, are differently constructed and interpreted and how the use of particular communicative resources confirm and/or affirm identity and belonging and vice versa.

3.2 Small talk

The anecdote with which we started this chapter serves to illustrate the point made by Halliday and Hasan (1989: 10) to which we referred in Chapter 1: language is made up not of words and sentences but of *meanings*. The problem for our student was not an issue of familiarity with the English word *alright*, but rather a lack of familiarity with its cultural meaning as a general, informal greeting, often used instead of *hello*. Such interactions, known as phatic communication,[1] typify the kind of small talk that we engage in every day. These kinds of interaction mean more and less than the actual words used and serve as a way of expressing things like presence ('I'm here'), engagement ('You're here'), ice-breaking ('Let's not feel awkward') even solidarity ('We're in this together'). They develop in particular ways within particular communities and new versions emerge (e.g. *alright*) as old ones (e.g. *good-day*) fall away. They are largely ritualized and so anticipate a specific kind of response, which is equally phatic in nature, and together they serve to maintain a sort of social cohesion. To give an unexpected response can disrupt this in both serious and trivial ways. For instance, to go into an explanation of how you actually are in response to an *alright* would lead to a bemused tolerance or, more likely, to being ignored. Example 3.1, an entry from an online discussion following an article on the BBC website (Evans 2011) about 'small talk', bears this out.

Example 3.1

> **blog Comment number . . .**
>
> **(username)**
>
> **3 HOURS AGO**
>
> Interesting article. Cultural differences like these can be quite amusing . . . a few years ago I remember chatting to a German girl who'd spent the previous summer in the USA as an au pair. She was saying 1 of the reasons she'd found it hard to adjust was that she couldn't understand why the Americans she met would ask how she was doing but then didn't seem interested in her (detailed) response!

The cultural differences referred to in this blog post stem from the original BBC article which sparked off what turned out to be a lengthy discussion involving 718 posts about national variation around small talk and other pragmatic aspects of communication such as politeness which can cause incidences of interpersonal confusion and even rupture. The article itself discussed differences between German and British phatic practices, using the example of a German translation of the popular British children's book, *Paddington Bear*, as the starting point. Evans gives the following example from the original English,

> 'Hallo Mrs Bird,' said Judy. 'It's nice to see you again. How's the rheumatism?'
>
> 'Worse than it's ever been' began Mrs Bird. (Michael Bond 1999: 12)

explaining that in the German version it was simply cut out. This is because, according to sociolinguist Juliane House, who was interviewed for the article, the Germans 'don't really do small talk'. Her research into communicative interactions between Germans and Anglo-Americans (House 2007) provides examples of interactional awkwardness arising from the differences between the English-speaking participants and their German counterparts with regard to acts of politeness, including small talk.

From the same blog another post asserted that it was not just Germans who responded inappropriately, from the English point of view, that is.

Example 3.2

> **blog Comment number ...**
>
> **username**
>
> **2 HOURS AGO**
>
> Not just germans, my husband's italian & never says 'fine thanks' to the question 'hi, how are you?'. I always have nudge him to be quiet as he launches into a description of how he's feeling.

The sociologist Irving Goffman discussed this in terms of the 'rules of conduct' based around the notions of 'obligations' and 'expectations'.

> Rules of conduct impinge on the individual in two general ways: directly, as *obligations*, establishing how he is morally constrained to conduct himself; indirectly, as *expectations*, establishing how others are morally bound to act in regard to him. (Goffman 1967: 49)

Using the greeting *alright?* falls into the category of 'obligation' and an *alright* with the downward tone of confirmation or a *yeah thanks* with even possibly the add-on *you?* represents the category of 'expectations'. Unexpected responses, like those mentioned in the blog, fall outside Goffman's 'rules of conduct' and would, he argues, 'characteristically lead to feelings of uneasiness' (1967: 48) just like those described by the bloggers. In Britain, the expression *alright?* is used essentially as a 'passing-in-the-street' acknowledgement. It communicates (or indexes) 'I know you're there. I want to let you know I know, but I don't intend to get into a long conversation with you right now'. If both parties share the same understanding of this 'rule of conduct', they will each be perfectly content for the interaction to last only a matter of seconds.

In Thailand, people kept asking Tim, 'bpai nai?' (Where are you going?) but were uninterested in his detailed, albeit bemused, explanations. The anticipated reply is 'bpai tee-ow' (I'm going around/out). In China people ask 'Have you eaten?' which, for non- Chinese, could be disappointing when they realize that it is not actually an invitation to supper or breakfast.

The fact that so many people engaged in this discussion demonstrates the strength of feeling about these practices. Their role in maintaining social equilibrium within communities and between individuals is often unrecognized until what is seen by a given community as transgressive behaviour disrupts that balance. Small talk, despite its apparent smallness, clearly occupies an important place in showing mutual recognition and creating solidarity between participants in specific communities. However, deciding whether the Germans are more or less polite than the English based on the absence or presence of small talk, or whether the British and North Americans are deceitful because they ask you how you are even though they are not interested in finding out, is unhelpful. Such views promote easy stereotypic thinking and in so doing prevent a more enquiring approach to difference which recognizes that some communities might do things differently to 'us' (see also Chapter 5). Canagarajah (2013b: 213) has suggested that we should expect 'to take difference as the norm and negotiate it, rather than flag the differences'. In fact, for the most part, we do learn to live with our differences and incorporate them into our social-cultural lexicon, especially now as transnational interactions become increasingly common.

What underlies many of the comments in the blog referred to above concern, not just small talk, but politeness. It is one of the hottest flashpoints in everyday human interaction and because of its relevance to maintaining social cohesion, it is a much researched and highly contested area of study. Blommaert has pointed out:

> Movement of people across space is . . . never a move across empty spaces. The spaces are always someone's space, and they are filled with norms and expectations, conceptions of what counts as proper, normal (indexical) language use and what does not count as such. (Blommaert 2010: 6)

The fact is that whenever we move from one space to another we need to be aware that different norms of interaction might be expected and, equally importantly, we need to be aware that people entering our spaces from elsewhere may have different norms and expectations. However, difference is not confined to the boundaries of languages, nations or even cities, but rather is an intricate network of highly nuanced ways of doing (and saying) things 'around here' which develops over time and within specific communities.

3.3 Performing politeness

As we learned above, what constitutes an appropriate response to a simple greeting in itself can cause confusion when the rules of interaction are not shared by the participants. When it comes to notions of politeness, what we take for granted, whoever we are and wherever we are from, may be very different to what others understand as markers of politeness. As the British blogger in Example 3.2 went on to write about her Italian husband:

> He's very direct asking questions or favours from friends though while i just cringe with embarrassment. He would be totally fine with them saying 'No' whereas i would NEVER ask unless i was sure they'll love to!

Embarrassment, bemusement, discomfort and downright annoyance are all potential reactions when different ways of enacting politeness come into play and it is easy for us to think of incidences in our own experience. What we are interested in here is politeness expressed linguistically, rather than acts of thoughtfulness such as someone helping you carry a heavy bag up a series of steps in a station, or not letting a door swing back onto someone behind you. We start off with an example from a study on intercultural communication undertaken by a Brazilian woman who was doing an MA in Applied Linguistics in London.

Example 3.3

> The first week of instruction on my MA course and we were told the university was offering free language courses to the students. I promptly enrolled in German 2 believing the few lessons I had had in Brazil would enable me to follow. After 2 weeks, however, I realised I was misplaced and went to the Learning Centre in order to ask to be transferred to the beginner level. I requested the group change to the man behind the counter who straightforwardly informed me it would not be possible anymore because the deadline for transfers had been 3 days before.

> Without delay, I employed the most effective Brazilian strategy for getting what is apparently 'impossible', the so-called 'jeitinho brasileiro'. I looked at him, threw a big smile and in a somewhat begging and whining tone of voice said:
>
> 'Oh, come on, Pleeeeease, do it for me.'
>
> He frowned and stared at me for seconds, and ignoring my seemingly 'alien' behaviour, turned to the queue and said: 'Next, please.'
>
> (Sarno-Pedreira 2004: 7)

If you are a member of the same community as the man in the learning centre, then you will probably understand his reaction to the whining tone. If you belong to a community where a whining tone is an effective strategy for getting what you want, then you might consider the man's response to be unfriendly, even rude. In explaining the *jeitinho brasileiro* referred to in her anecdote, Sarno-Pedreira goes on to note that parents in Britain, when teaching their children to be polite, offer a very different kind of instruction compared to their Brazilian counterparts. She points out that British parents would ask their children something like 'What do you say?' or 'What's the magic word?' when the child has omitted *please* when asking for something, whereas a Brazilian parent, focusing on the tone rather than the words themselves, would say '*How* do you say it?' In other words, in Britain it is the word that performs politeness[2] whereas in Brazil it is the manner of the performance.

Our second example concerns the time a Japanese university colleague asked for help with what we might call a 'begging letter' to an Anglo-Japanese Foundation in London seeking funding for books for a Japanese language teaching library she was setting up. She wanted me (Fiona) to check the letter for errors of English and style. On reading through it became clear that though there was little wrong with regard to accuracy of language, there was an organizational problem which might well have affected how the letter might be received. For a native English-speaking reader the letter as it was drafted would appear, at best, slightly irritating, and at worst, insincere. The effusive remarks that the writer made about the Foundation and its work in supporting educational projects with which the first half of the letter was taken up would most likely be viewed as flattery used to 'butter up' the potential sponsors and the fact that the actual request did not appear until the end of the letter would be seen as annoying procrastination. The advice I gave was to reorganize the whole letter by bringing the favour request up to the top, clearly stating how the money would be used and the benefits that it would provide while any flattering remarks should be placed at the end of the letter. The colleague found it extremely difficult to abide by this advice. For her, using such a direct approach, particularly for a favour, would be considered extremely impolite in Japanese.

These two examples show that politeness strategies do not necessarily travel well and that an understanding that politeness can be performed differently in different cultures is useful knowledge to have. However, it is important not to overgeneralize into such remarks as 'All Brazilians/Japanese/British are or do or say such and such' in ways that objectify and essentialize practices that are, in reality, dynamic, shifting and often dependent on the specific circumstances in which they are performed.

3.4 The case of 'sorry'

Newcomers to the United Kingdom from abroad often remark on how polite the British are and, when pressed, tend to point to the frequent (even excessive) use of the word *sorry*. However, the kind of *sorry* that most are referring to is not necessarily indicative of extreme politeness but rather is the kind of phatic communication we discussed earlier. Try walking along a busy street in Britain or standing squashed on a train. Every time someone touches you accidentally you will probably hear a muttered *sorry*. It is instinctive and in most cases simply acknowledges that an interaction has taken place. However, despite this apparently automatic use, if someone bumps into, or even just jostles the arm of a British person and omits to say *sorry* they are more than likely to receive a dirty look or a disgruntled 'hurumph', being considered impolite.

In his *Apologising in English*, Mats Deutschmann (2003) investigates the uses and contexts for apologizing in British English. Using the British National Corpus of Spoken English which consists of around ten million examples of informal spoken conversations from around the United Kingdom representing different ages and different social groups, he shows that *sorry* occurs most frequently, used in 60 per cent of the cases involving apologizing (2003: 64). The most common use was for what he calls 'hearing offences', as in 'I didn't hear what you said' (or 'I don't believe what you said'), followed by 'lack of consideration offences' including things like not hurting someone's feelings, being late or causing inconvenience. Other uses include slips of the tongue, social gaffes or mistakes and misunderstandings. He also identifies further uses such as when seeking attention as in 'Sorry, can you help me?' used in a shop, or when about to disagree with someone in an argument 'Sorry, I can't accept that!'. In fact, these last examples could be seen as anything but apologies. Of course, the corpus would not have collected the phatic kinds of *sorry* we have just been discussing, as these, by their very nature, do not occur as part of a conversation. It is interesting to note that Deutschmann, a Swede, is an 'outsider' with regard to the community he was studying and as such would himself probably have been more sensitized to apologizing in English than a local 'insider' would be. It is often only when we move across social and cultural spaces that we start to pay attention to phenomena the natives take for granted.

For instance, we have noticed that Nigerians, when speaking English, tend to use *sorry* when someone else trips up, drops or bumps into something, even though they have no responsibility at all for the mishap. The explanation for this usage is that in languages such as Yoruba, Igbo or Hausa, Nigeria's three principal languages, there are formulaic phrases for showing empathy that do not have an exact correspondence in English. Hence *sorry* tends to be used as the nearest approximate expression where English speakers may say things like 'Oh dear!' or 'Are you OK?'.

Another example of a mismatched *sorry* can be found when South Koreans speak English. Their practice tends to be the use of non-verbal apology strategies such as smiling or bowing for small offences, acts which performed in Britain, for instance, are likely to be misunderstood. Smiling could be interpreted as sarcasm; bowing, which is associated with deference and formality, would be considered strange or excessive. On the other hand, a Korean may appear to under-apologize, using a simple *sorry* when a fuller apology would be expected. This mismatch is explained by Kim (2008: 258). She points out that:

> Many South Korean learners of English fail to perform the speech act of apologizing effectively. For example, they might say sorry in situations where the Korean *mianhada* is appropriate, regardless of whether sorry is appropriate in such situations (mianhada is translated as sorry in most bilingual dictionaries).

Apologizing across and between cultures is hard, not because we don't like to admit we're wrong, but because we may perform it wrongly. For an English speaker, the French word for sorry, *désolé(e)*, seems excessive because of the association with the English word *desolate*. Equally, imagine how surprised and even embarrassed a Korean must feel when an English speaker says *sorry* for some minor offence instead of simply smiling or bowing!

We have selected the following instances of *sorry* from a random search of the word in the British National Corpus of Spoken English. Consider how it is being used in each case and what it can/could mean.

- Sorry he didn't look very pleased, did he.
- Sorry?
- So sorry just a moment.
- Sorry, sorry.
- Oh dear I'm sorry, I'll give you the other hundred for February.
- I'm sorry, I'm moving on to the next paper.
- I mean I'm sorry to hear you're keeping some bad company
- Do what, sorry?
- No so' no I think it, no sorry, sorry, not it's not, it's two days one night.

Although behavioural norms of politeness exist for speakers of all languages and in all cultures, they are not necessarily linguistically marked as such. House, referred to above (who is German), illustrates this point with an example from her own experience. 'While an utterance like "Go down to the basement and get it for me" may appear like an impolite order to my British husband, it may be perceived as perfectly polite by myself when I talk to him in that way' (2007: 262). All cultures have strategies for performing politeness, sometimes encoded verbally and sometimes not, and while some may appear linguistically fussy and over-complicated and others may come across as bordering on rudeness, we have to remember that as outsiders we may misread the cues. Being aware of such differences and how they play out linguistically can mitigate feelings of annoyance even though, as we saw from the blog comments above, those feelings are very difficult to eradicate completely.

Before we leave this particular discussion, we want to reiterate that whenever we talk about norms of interaction in relation to cultures or languages or even communities of practice, we must be careful to recognize the potential for overgeneralizing. The norms of interaction are just that, norms. That does not mean that everyone abides by them or even values them. Deutschmann himself found this out first hand when making his way to the bar of a packed pub in the North West of England. He writes:

> I negotiated my way through the crowd while delivering a seemingly endless stream of 'sorries', 'excuse mes' and 'pardon mes', and proceeded to try to

> catch the barman's attention in a similar manner (unsuccessfully, I may add). A man standing next to me enquired why I was apologising all the time. I apologised again (for apologising) at which he explained that 'in there they were all mates and if I wanted a beer I'd better cut the crap, put my fiver on the bar counter and state loudly and clearly what I wanted.' He demonstrated what he meant by addressing the barman with a 'John, you dozy bastard. Give the man a pint.' The result was instantaneous; before I could say 'face work',[3] a cold and well-needed lager stood before me. (2003: 23)

With this anecdote, Deutschmann shows that things are not always as straightforward as the motto, 'when in Rome do as the Romans' suggests. What the Romans do is often difficult to put your finger on. Moreover, not all Romans are the same – and not all of them are even Romans.

3.5 Community of practice – identity and identification

So far we have been discussing issues associated with transcultural or translingual interactions, particularly in relation to the kinds of interactions that oil (or seize up) the wheels of social harmony. In this part of the chapter we move away from the idea of culture connected with national or regional characteristics and consider instead the idea of community, particularly in relation to the concept of a community of practice.

If we were to ask you what culture you belong to, you would probably say something about your nationality or ethnicity. This is certainly an important aspect of identity and influences the ways we do things and shapes the kinds of things we know, believe and understand. However, it is less likely that you would mention your profession, your hobbies or even your family. That is because we do not normally connect such affiliations with 'culture'. It is for this reason that the term *community* can be helpful as it enables us to view more local or narrowly defined contexts such as our line of work, our interests, our households and so on, which all have their own practices with their own norms of interaction. All of us belong to many different communities, so that to say 'I'm Nigerian' or 'I'm British', for instance, offers only a partial view of who we are.

The concept of community was first used in sociolinguistics in the 1960s by scholars such as Dell Hymes, William Labov and John Gumperz. The term has been used to reflect different analytic interests: linguistic community, speech community, community of practice and discourse community. We briefly summarize each in turn before discussing an example in more detail.

In a general sense a linguistic community (Gumperz 1962) refers to a group of people who share a common language (which may be different to that of the wider community). A good example of this is of migrant communities who use language X when they are together, but language Y when they are with others who do not speak language X. The term also allows us to differentiate between speakers of different languages within multilingual countries such as India or Nigeria, where most people have at least two languages that they can use as they wish or as appropriate (see Chapter 4).

A speech community (Hymes 1967, 1972; Labov 1972) refers to a group of individuals who make linguistic choices in order to identify with each other. This differs from a linguistic community in that it does not necessarily mean that they speak a different *language*, in the sense of Hindi, Spanish, Japanese and so on. Rather, it refers to ways of speaking (sometimes called codes) which denote association with a particular social group. Examples might include the choice of a particular regional dialect of a given language, where someone may choose to speak with a relatively 'neutral' (i.e. less marked) dialect or accent at work, but may choose a more marked version when in the pub. The language of a speech community can be used as an 'act of identity' (Le Page and Tabouret-Keller 1985) to show membership of that community, as in the case of teenagers using whatever the current youth speech style happens to be, as we showed in Chapter 1, or desired membership of that community.

A community of practice (Lave and Wenger 1991) refers to a group of individuals who, by being together over time, experience or construct particular relations and practices. Such communities include professional groups such as teachers, computer engineers, social workers, plumbers, taxi-drivers and so on. They can also include special interest communities such as goths and trainspotters or communities based around leisure activities such as digital games or gardening. Within these communities, members have particular ways of talking about things, developing and using terms which have particular meanings within the community. This is also what Bizzel and Herzberg (1990) have called a *discourse community*. The kinds of talk that group members engage in are often seen by outsiders, who feel that they are being kept outside, as jargon or gobbledegook. For the insiders, however, the discourse has developed in order to maximize communicative effectiveness. If you know what the terms mean both conceptually and in practice, then information and ideas can flow more freely and activity can be undertaken more efficiently. Let's now look at an example.

3.6 Being a physicist

When we have shown the extract in Example 3.4 to various groups of people, it has elicited a range of different reactions. Some give a wry smile, others grimace, some look aghast, no doubt dreading that they might be asked to engage with it, while others appear to be entirely unfazed. So what accounts for such diverse reactions? With apologies to any readers who happen to be physicists, we will look at it from a linguistics perspective.

Example 3.4 (from Cohen-Tannoudji et al. 1977:28)

4. Time evolution of a free wave packet

Until now, we have been concerned only with the form of a wave packet at a given instant; in this paragraph, we are going to study its time evolution. Let us return, therefore, to the case of a free particle whose state is described by the one-dimensional wave packet (C-7).

A given plane wave $e^{i(kx-\omega t)}$ propagates along the *Ox* axis with the velocity:

$$V_\varphi(k) = \frac{\omega}{k} \qquad \text{(C-24)}$$

since it depends on *x* and *t* only through $\left(x - \frac{\omega}{k}t\right)$; is called the *phase velocity* of the plane wave.

Most people will recognize this as a scientific or mathematical text because of the specific semiotic resources that it uses. It is a multimodal text which combines verbal (written words organized into clauses) and mathematical (numbers and symbols) modes of communication. It belongs to a particular domain (science/maths) and, if you know something about science or maths you may even be able to further identify it as a physics text. The degree of familiarity or comfort you have with the text tells you about your own status in relation to it; that is your degree of belonging to the relevant community that it emerges from.

For people who are not physicists, or who have very little knowledge of the field, the title of the extract itself could seem mysterious, even poetic.

Time evolution of a free wave packet

Just as the student at the beginning of this chapter understood the word *alright*, as an English word with its dictionary meaning, we can, if we are competent readers of English, understand the individual words in this extract and see that they are organized meaningfully in relation to each other. We can understand that there are two noun phrases, *time evolution* and *free wave packet* each consisting of adjectives or nouns acting as adjectives (*time, free* and *wave*) and the noun the adjectives are qualifying (*evolution* and *packet*) and that they are linked with the relational preposition *of.* We can understand what these words mean in their own right and we can even try to make sense of them as they are used in this arrangement. We might, for example, be able to get the idea of *time evolution* as something to do with change or development over time but what on earth is a *free wave packet*? Presumably the rest of the extract will tell us.

In fact, what we learn is that a wave packet is a phenomenon in physics that has a form and that earlier on in the book this has been discussed; this section considers it in relation to its time evolution, also related to form, one might assume. But, for most of us, the invitation to 'return to the case of a free particle' in order to move forward is the point at which we can go no further. From now on, in this extract, everything depends on both prior knowledge of terms of reference and the ability to work with the mathematical formulae that comprise the explanation of the new state, or rather, value, to use the proper physics term, being introduced – *phase velocity*. The term can only be understood if you can recognize the formulae's terms of reference, $V(k),\varphi = \omega/k$, and that you know what t represents. Without that knowledge, there is little more that the lay reader can do. From the writers' perspective, the assumption is that their reader knows the formulae, perhaps because they have already been introduced earlier on in the book, and armed with that knowledge, the reader will now go on to understand what *phase velocity of the plane wave* is.

All disciplines use language in this way, not to make things difficult for outsiders or to keep them outside, but rather to make things easier for insiders and help them talk to each other without having to constantly explain everything over and over again. When physicists use the terms *free particle, wave packet* or *phase velocity*, they take it for granted that other physicists know what they mean, even if there is disagreement over the finer details. Being a member of a community means not only being able to take part in the relevant activities, but being able to talk about them to other group members. Being able to do these things is a way of performing a particular identity – in this case being a physicist – and a way of showing your membership of a particular community of practice.

When we showed this extract to a group of young scientific researchers, they correctly identified it as having come from a standard text on quantum mechanics, and in so doing demonstrated their own membership of that particular community. It is worth noting that none of them were native speakers of English. Membership of a discourse community transcends linguistic or language community.

We can think of all sorts of communities of practice that develop their own ways of talking about their particular 'things', in other words, their own discourses. Medical practitioners are an obvious example, as are IT professionals; but what about drug dealers, World of Warcraft fans or people who regularly use the gym? Just look at the next example (Example 3.5) which is taken from a video game discussion forum.

Example 3.5

> **Re: (The fully cured) Gen. FF Trivia thread!**
>
> In Final Fantasy VI, the Relic Tintanabar replenishes your HP as you walk. In Final Fantasy VII, there is a similar accessory, the Cat's Bell. =3 Where can you obtain this item?

The terms of reference that Final Fantasy fans use and share, with the special meanings that they accrue in the course of the developing community, can be as opaque to the outsider as the physics text above is to non-physicists. Culture, with its associated linguistic practices, develops from the activities a community (or even a nation, come to that) engages in, and the 'way we do things around here' becomes deeply embedded in the minds of the members of that community, as we saw with the blog comments on the issue of politeness.

3.7 Conclusion

Throughout this chapter we have sought to raise the issue of difference. This has been a tricky path to negotiate as the potential for stereotyping always lurks below discussions of this kind, particularly in relation to what are often thought of as national characteristics. It is for this reason that we have used the concept of community, and specifically community of practice. Our aim was to show that culture as a categorizing term is problematic because it implies singularity; but none of us inhabits a single culture. Part of the problem is the fact that the term *culture* is used in two main ways – 'big C' culture to refer to cultural products such as literature or music, and 'little c' culture used to refer to practices (see Holliday 2011). The term community offers a way out of this terminological ambiguity. We can say 'I'm a Moroccan', 'I'm an Italian' or 'I'm a Pakistani', but within each of these there are many different communities; linguistic communities, speech communities, regional communities, each with their own practices. If we then add others such as religious or secular communities, professional communities, age communities, gender communities, then we can see that we are much more complex than a singular understanding of culture might lead us to believe. We participate on different levels in many different communities, all of which have developed and continue to develop their particular quirks of behaviour, as it might seem to the outsider, but which to the insider are perfectly normal. We all operate within a wide variety of different communities and in so doing develop different linguistic repertoires (see Blommaert 2010) as we go along.

In the next chapter we revisit some of these ideas from a sociolinguistic perspective, focusing on how communities organize themselves (or are organized) linguistically. Using a linguistics approach there, as we have done here, enables us to unpack the complexities of communication in relation to identity, belonging and participation in multilingual settings.

Suggested reading

Holliday, A. (2013), *Understanding Intercultural Communication: Negotiating a Grammar of Culture.* Abingdon: Routledge.

Holliday's framework for analysing intercultural communication offers an interesting and usable approach to unpacking this complex area of social interaction. The book uses a series of observations and narratives to explore key themes in a way that is authentic, engaging and deeply insightful.

Hua, Z. (ed.) (2011), *The Language and Intercultural Communication Reader.* Abingdon: Routledge.

What makes this such an interesting collection is its international scope which includes discussions on such diverse topics as the pragmatics of the expression *Insha' allah*, politeness strategies in modern Chinese, community affiliation and identity in Tanzania, all framed by discussions on some of the most influential theories in the field of intercultural communication. It is a fascinating read.

Riley, P. (2007), *Language, Culture and Identity.* London: Continuum.

This book provides an excellent overview of key literature in this area which, along with specific examples, offers a discussion that is not only well grounded in theory but also presented in a practical and accessible way.

Spencer-Oatey, H. (ed.) (2008), *Culturally Speaking: Culture, Communication and Politeness Theory,* 2nd edn. London: Continuum.

This edited collection, which focuses specifically on politeness and intercultural pragmatics, offers contributions from scholars across a range of different cultural and linguistic backgrounds. Issues such as 'face' in international business interactions or how different communities respond to compliments are analysed and discussed showing how the approaches and tools provided by linguistics, and pragmatics in particular, can shed light on everyday social interactions.

4

About diversity – how do societies organize language?

4.1 Introduction: *The Big Fight* on NDTV

The presenter introduces the panellists, the audience settle down in anticipation, and the theme for the evening rolls across the bottom of the screen: 'WILL LANGUAGE UNITE OR DIVIDE US?' It's NDTV of India's flagship discussion programme,[1] and things are about to get heated. The debate begins with the issue of a recent incident in the Legislative Assembly of the state of Maharashtra, and a video clip of the incident is shown. A Hindi-speaking Member of the Legislative Assembly (MLA) takes his oath in the Hindi language, whereupon an MLA of the Maharashtra nationalist MNS party seems to run at him and hit him, protesting that he should have taken the oath in the state language of Marathi. The video shows a scuffle, a crowd of men pushing and shoving at each other, there are raised voices; it's difficult to see exactly what's happening. In the studio, the presenter asks the MNS representative, party Legal Vice-President Akhilesh Chaubey, to explain the incident. Chaubey indignantly denies that anything untoward was going on: it was simply a protest against the use of Hindi and a defence of the Marathi language. He adds that anyone is free to speak whatever language they like in the Assembly. Sanjay Arupum of the Congress party intervenes:

> *Who has given [MNS leader] Raj Thackeray the authority to say you have to take oath in Marathi? We never accept it. No-one is going to accept it. . . . He always behaves like a dictator. He wants to behave like a dictator. . . . Please, go ahead, go on, we don't mind it. But you have no right to impose any thought of yours on us or anybody else. If you want to issue any dictates, issue dictates to your own MLAs. Ask your MLAs to take oath in Marathi language or whichever language you want. But you cannot ask Samajwadi Party or Congress MP or anybody . . .*

The rolling screen caption now reads 'WHAT SHOULD BE OUR LINK LANGUAGE?'

Professor Kancha Ilaiah, a writer and dalit or 'untouchable' activist, now points out that most MLAs, from whichever of the 'linguistic states' (see below) in fact tend to put their own children in English-medium schools. There is loud agreement from the audience. They encourage the use of the regional languages, he says, only for 'mere poor people'. He goes on:

> *In all airports I see majority of the elite mothers talking to their children in English. Is it not their mother tongue now?*

In order to even things out, English, he suggests, should be the first language nationwide. Some of the other panellists vie to disagree with him, and all are now trying at once to get their voice heard.

The caption goes to 'SHOULD ENGLISH BE USED FOR EMPOWERMENT?'

Seemingly trying to diffuse the tension a little, the Hindi-speaking writer Rajendra Yajav, asked his opinion by the host, replies in that language, and a translation appears on screen:

> *If I speak in Hindi, I hope you won't hit me?*

This gets a laugh from the audience. But he then goes on to speak in Hindi at some length, there is no translation, and the audience become increasingly restive. Finally the presenter asks the Tamil MP and campaigner M. K. Kanimozhi to respond, which she does in the Tamil language, to delighted laughter and applause from the audience. Point made, she switches back to English:

> *I could not understand a word of what he [Yajav] said. I thought this is an English-language show.*

She points out that less than 40 per cent of the population of India speak Hindi and asks rhetorically:

> *And 60 per cent can be left out? They don't matter? And if you think it is right to speak in one language which 60 per cent does not understand, then I think it is . . . that is what we oppose. That is what we cannot accept.*

The panellists continue to talk and shout across each other, the audience murmur among themselves, and there is still a good half-an-hour to go. The production team must be congratulating themselves on having chosen such a controversial subject for their programme, as well as such combative guests. Not for nothing is it called *The Big Fight*.

4.2 Dealing with diversity

India shares a problem of language with many multilingual nations, but its very size and diversity mean that the problem, inevitably, is magnified. The States Reorganisation Act of 1956 found a partial solution to the question of what rights should be accorded to different language groups by reorganizing the patchwork of states and territories bequeathed by British colonialism into what are known as 'linguistic states'. Hence, very broadly speaking, each state has a majority population speaking a particular language which has official status in that state: Oriya in Odisha, Telugu in Andhra Pradesh, Kannada in Karnataka, and so on, with Hindi being the official language of several states, especially in the north and centre of the country, and also the pan-Indian official language. Other languages may also be recognized at state level, and English is recognized as a secondary or associate official national language. As *The Big Fight* shows, though, such attention to linguistic detail does not guarantee harmony.

As we will see in Chapter 5, people tend not to notice anything unusual or noteworthy about the language that they grow up speaking. In just the same way, people tend to assume that the way their own country or society organizes language is the natural way of doing it. India's linguistic states are one way of approaching the issue of language in a highly multilingual polity, but countries vary greatly in both their linguistic make-up and the way in which they deal with it. In this chapter we look at some of the different ways in which language is configured in societies around the world, and how people in these societies perceive and use the linguistic resources available to them.

If you were to ask someone at random, somewhere in the world, what language is spoken in the United Kingdom, it is a fair bet that they would reply 'English'. And so it is: but the leaflet distributed to English and Welsh households in preparation for the 2011 census (ONS 2011a) informed the public that they could also request the census questions in any one of 56 other languages, including Welsh, Tagalog, Yoruba, Yiddish, Vietnamese, Kurdish, Lithuanian and two dialects of Punjabi. Schools in many areas of Britain – some semi-rural and rural as well as urban – are quite accustomed to dealing with children from a range of linguistic backgrounds, and in London 100 or more 'home' languages might well be represented in large secondary schools. While there is no such thing as a 'typical' society in linguistic terms, most people in the world live in multilingual societies, and multilingualism must therefore be considered the norm. Within this broad norm, some countries have very little linguistic variety, and others have a lot more than their fair share.

At one end of the spectrum lie countries like Cuba, which, with no geographically contiguous neighbours, few recent immigrants, no indigenous linguistic minorities, and a history of centuries of Spanish colonial occupation, is as close to being a monolingual country as we are likely to get. Pretty much all Cubans speak Spanish, and apart from foreign languages learned at school, few speak any other language. In the same way, for various historical, geographical and political reasons, countries such as Poland, Japan and the Koreas (especially the North) score relatively low down on the diversity index. Contrast this with Nigeria or India – countries containing hundreds of different language groups, and within which it is perfectly common for people to use two, three, four or more languages on a daily basis. The most extreme example of multilingualism is probably Papua New Guinea, home to something like a quarter of the world's languages (though of course, in theory, an individual Papuan might speak only one).

There is little obvious need for countries such as Cuba to think about language policy, except in the sense of foreign language education policy; but for many countries, language is something which needs to be taken into consideration at various levels. What language or languages should people speak at school? What about in law courts or government offices? On television and radio? Is it necessary to legislate for some or all of these contexts, or none of them? Should the state in fact take a hand at all, or is it just a question of custom and practice?

We might also note, then, that there is no such thing as a typical attitude towards multilingualism, or a typical way in which states deal with multilingualism. China recognizes a single, nationwide official language, Putonghua (roughly, Mandarin Chinese), and insists that the other major language groups of the country are simply dialects of this, linguistic evidence to the contrary notwithstanding (see Chapter 5). State employees in positions of linguistic influence, such as teachers and broadcasters, are required to pass an examination in Putonghua before they can take up their posts (Marr 2005). When we tell our Chinese students that neither the United States nor the United Kingdom in fact has an official language, they are typically amazed (though it surprises more than a few Britons and Americans, too), and express disbelief that modern, complex countries can function without one. The underlying perception of multilingualism in many countries is that it is inefficient – but demonstrably, this does not seem to have harmed Switzerland, for one, with its four national languages (the fourth one, after German, French and Italian, is Romansh, spoken in the canton of Graubünden).

4.3 Language and state control

Given this diversity, states have come to their own conclusions about how to manage language distribution and use: their responses are what we call language planning, or as a classic definition has it, 'the organised pursuit of solutions to language problems, typically at the national level' (Fishman 1974: 79). While virtually all governments practise some kind of language planning, the amount of interest shown in questions of language varies widely for political, cultural and historical reasons. Some polities are highly directive and explicit when it comes to what language can be used where, and for what purposes; others, far less so. In Turkey, where public use of Kurdish was prohibited until late in the twentieth century, while restrictions on broadcasting in Kurdish have now been relaxed, the language still cannot be used in 'official' contexts, where Turkish is still obligatory. In Canada, meanwhile, the Quebec government employs its own unit of inspectors, the *Office québécois de la langue française*, to enforce the regional laws making the use of French mandatory in public signage, advertising and the like. Wales, too, has strict rules about the public display of language (public signage has to be in both Welsh and English, for example) but its neighbour England, like the United States, is very much laissez-faire – not least, presumably, because most speakers of English do not tend to feel their language threatened.

Most countries probably lie somewhere between the two extremes, and a variety of approaches exist. States might make languages official, or joint-official, or official for certain things, or official in certain places. The state might encourage and promote certain languages, discourage and marginalize them (the notorious 'Welsh Not' or 'Welsh Collar' was used in some schools in the 19th century to shame Welsh-speaking schoolchildren into speaking only English), tolerate them or simply ignore them. In extreme cases, languages might be proscribed: the speaking of Gaelic was outlawed in the Scottish Highlands after the Jacobite rebellion of 1745, and following Spain's Civil War, General Franco banned the public use of Basque (see below).

As with any other aspect of politics, it cannot be assumed that governments always mean what they say about language. The Soviet Union's official policy on 'national' languages and cultures (basically, those of the individual 'national' republics) was a model of progressive inclusiveness: in practice, the state's approach was quite different. In Estonia, to take an example from the smallest republic of the USSR, while officially there existed a policy of Estonian-Russian bilingualism, in fact this meant that Estonians were required to learn Russian, while no serious effort was made to encourage ethnic Russians to learn Estonian. The same principle operated in many other former Soviet republics, including Lithuania, Latvia and Ukraine. As the historian Norman Davies (2011: 717) has remarked, this skewed approach to language planning was one of the factors which helped plant the seeds of conflict to come later, after the dissolution of the USSR. Language was certainly one flashpoint in the civic turmoil which broke out in Ukraine in 2014.

State policy towards language can differ radically even between countries that are in many other ways rather similar. In Haiti, the French-based Creole that is the native tongue of most of the population was declared a joint-official language (alongside French) in the 1980s, and is used in increasing numbers of contexts, including in writing and in basic education. Warning notices about what you can and cannot take on a flight from Miami airport in the United States are rendered in Haitian Creole as well as several other languages, possibly because Haitians, who make up a good percentage of the people passing through Miami, are now used to reading it. In neighbouring Jamaica, though, the similarly widely spoken, English-based creole language known as Patois is still heavily stigmatized in many contexts, and the official language of the country remains, emphatically, standard English.

Of course, if a fundamental aspect of language planning is to decide on what your language is, inevitably you have to decide what it isn't. In 2001, I (Tim) bought three dictionaries from a bookshop in Sarajevo: Croatian-English, Serbian-English and Bosniak-English. A decade earlier, I would doubtless have found only one, to render English into the official Yugoslavian language, Serbo-Croat. The war which consumed Bosnia-Herzegovina in the early 1990s, though, had one specifically sociolinguistic outcome: the three 'communities' of the country decided that they spoke three different languages, where previously they had been in agreement (officially at least) that they spoke variants of the same one (see Greenberg 2004).

This kind of planning, dealing with matters of the relative status of languages, is known by sociolinguists as status planning. It is to be distinguished from corpus planning – the actual design and implementation of policy on words, script, spelling, 'correct' usage and so on. Script reform, like the urge to 'purify' languages of foreign words, tends to be a by-product of social upheaval. The most famous twentieth-century example of such reform, the substitution of the Roman alphabet for the Arabic script previously used in Turkey in the 1920s, was a highly symbolic affair which advertised the repositioning of the new Turkish republic as a western-leaning, modern, secular and Europeanized state.

Acquisition planning, as opposed to status and corpus planning, refers to policy and practice relating to the teaching and learning of language, which in itself can be a heavily contested area (see e.g. Heugh 2013 for South Africa, where 11 official languages are in play, but English is privileged in the education system). Some linguists refer furthermore to 'acceptance planning' – a tacit acknowledgement that it is one thing to issue decrees and edicts about how people should speak or write, and quite another to ensure that they comply. Apart from anything else, language planning, as with planning for any other social activity, often needs to assume a degree of co-operation that is not always apparent:

> Though many Cameroonians have become bilingual, the majority are monolingual. Some of these monolinguals speak the only language they know to any other Cameroonian and if the interlocutor is also a monolingual,

the speaker will say, 'Cameroon is a bilingual country, so you have to understand what I am saying'.

(Jikong 2000: 117)

Stubbornness and resistance to being told what to do are common human traits, and it is therefore important not to assume that state approaches to languages automatically achieve the results they seek. Compare the fate of Basque in Spain, where it languished under a blanket 'Spanish only' policy during the Franco dictatorship, and in France, where grudging tolerance of, or perhaps indifference to, the language was the default position for much of the twentieth century. It is in the Spanish Basque country now that proficiency in Basque is increasing, to over 30 per cent of the population in 2006, while in the Basque provinces of France the proportion of people proficient in the language is only just above 20 per cent and is in steady decline (Cenoz 2008: 15). There are doubtless of course other factors contributing to the relative vitality of Basque in Spain, but this example shows that state attempts to marginalize or even exterminate a language might not only not succeed, but might actually result in a re-entrenchment or revival of the language concerned. The role of language as a marker of identity is powerful, complex and above all, unpredictable (see Edwards 2009; Ostler 2005).

By the same token, 'official' attempts to encourage minority languages that are perceived to be valuable are doomed to failure if speakers themselves do not share the state's view of the language, or that of (typically self-appointed) language nationalists. Irish is held by the state of the Republic of Ireland, and by many ordinary citizens, to have unique symbolic importance as an emblem of nationhood. The reverse of the Irish five-pound note (see Figure 4.1) which was produced up until the advent of the euro, shows two schoolchildren gazing in rapt attention at a verse written in Irish script on a blackboard (from *Mise Raifteirí an File* by Antoine Ó Raifteiri), while a third pores with a dreamy half-smile over an Irish-language textbook.

FIGURE 4.1 *Reverse side of the former Irish £5 note*

Not only is Irish important, is the none-too-subtle message, but it belongs to the next generation. However, outside the linguistic heartland of the Gaeltacht, Irish is rarely used as a medium of everyday conversation; and while the government ensures that all primary school pupils receive some instruction in the language, standards of proficiency are falling (Harris 2008). More important even than this, perhaps, is the underlying question of the 'heavy reliance placed on the education system to reproduce a basic competence in the language in each new generation' (Harris 2008: 50). What this means is that the state steps in to maintain at least a second language or foreign language-like competence in the language where the natural process of intergenerational transmission (the learning of the mother tongue in the home environment) has broken down. But this is of very limited value. Of course, learning the language at school, to at least a certain standard of proficiency, has to be considered better than nothing. But in terms of genuine minority language maintenance, as Fishman (1992: 400) states baldly, 'the school is too late'. Language shift is already under way.

4.4 Language shift, language prestige, language attitudes

Language shift – in essence, the process by which speakers over time stop speaking language A and start instead to speak language B – is a perfectly natural phenomenon, even if it is sometimes capable of provoking feelings of dislocation and even distress. As one writer nicely puts it: 'Throughout history, human societies have donned new languages like new cloaks' (Fischer 2005: 85). It has long been recognized in academic studies of language shift that the social and cultural associations of a language, the way it is perceived in and by the wider society, are often decisively important in the process. A fairly common scenario is that a language starts to become associated with elderly speakers and such undesirable things as illiteracy, poverty, a peasant lifestyle and rural isolation. At this point, naturally, younger speakers begin to avoid it; it therefore becomes ever more firmly associated with the elderly, even more younger speakers avoid it, and it thus enters a rapid spiral of decline. Observing shift from Tlaxcalan Nahuatl to Spanish in the fast-urbanizing Mexico of the 1960s and 1970s, Hill and Hill noticed that at a critical juncture in the process of shift Nahuatl became 'defined as a "village thing" which a forward-looking, ambitious person would do well to abandon' (1977: 59). This is the point at which efforts at language maintenance or reversing language shift (Fishman 1991, 2001) often begin to look doomed.

'Language Death' is a term used to describe what happens when whole communities undergo language shift, and there are no other extant communities speaking that language. The language, at least in its natural, spoken form simply becomes extinct. In the village of Mousehole in Cornwall, you will find a tiny cottage, marked with a plaque, which was the home of Dolly Pentreath (d. 1777), reputedly the last native speaker of Cornish. When Dolly died, the language died with her; from a communicative point of view, of course, it might be argued that the language died when the second-to-last speaker did, and there was no one left to speak it to.

In terms of an individual speaker's motivation, one way of looking at language shift is as a movement from one language or discourse community (as discussed in Chapter 3) to another. The process can occur within languages as well as across them, but the principle remains the same: through choice of variety, style or code, a speaker indicates the community to which they belong or to which they aspire – choice of language, like choice of clothes, being potentially a highly aspirational business. Consider this description, by his friend, of a young British-Syrian man who had been involved in street gangs in London and ended up in prison:

> With that customary Syrian charm, Ali always asked about my family and my boy. But prison seemed to have changed him. He became increasingly religious; the ghetto talk, the accent, the slang slowly disappeared. He became more articulate and he quoted Qur'anic verses
>
> *The Guardian*, 31 May 2013

To adopt a discourse style which features the quoting of Koranic verses is of course to place oneself firmly within an Islamic frame of linguistic-cultural identity. More subtly and interestingly, though, the friend is struck by how Ali distances himself from his former social identity by becoming, as he perceives it, 'more articulate' and dispensing with the 'ghetto talk' of inner-city London youth. This is a highly explicit example of positioning of the self in relation to surrounding speech or discourse communities through speech style: of demonstrating, to yourself and to others, where you belong and where you do not belong. Ali was subsequently killed while fighting alongside anti-government rebels in Syria in 2013.

By the same principle, it has long been established that someone trying to learn another language is more likely to do well if they have, among other types of motivation, strong integrative motivation (Gardner and Lambert 1972). That is, you are more likely to be a successful learner of language X if you identify with and have positive feelings towards the X-speaking language community. English of course is often identified not with a particular native-speaking country or population but with a transnational, globalized community of speakers who might be, and be from, almost anywhere. In this case, it has been suggested, some learners of the language might aim to acquire for themselves a bicultural identity – one which would incorporate their internationally oriented, English-speaking self as well as a local self (Lamb 2004). There is no obvious limit to the number of different speech, language or discourse communities that one might belong to, and speakers may move between such communities several times in a day, or countless times in a lifetime.

Importantly, while language serves as a means to index the kind of communities that the speaker belongs to – or the 'personae' that she or he inhabits, as Blommaert (2008: 83) puts it – that does not necessarily mean that you can always choose for yourself how this works: sometimes the indexing will be done by others, whether you like it or not. To this extent at least, identity is something which is ascribed to a person by other people (see Riley 2007), and language shift may well be the individual's way of escaping the societal indexing that marks speakers of a particular language negatively. At the extreme, this may mean that people simply deny that they speak, or have ever spoken, a particular language. In Peru, for example, it is possible to come across Quechua-speaking children who, having migrated from the Andes to Lima, simply 'become' Spanish speakers, and refuse to acknowledge anyone who addresses them in Quechua (see Marr 2011). As this suggests, to a large extent the motor of shift is the individual's and the community's attitude to the language in question. This can be very difficult to negotiate within families, especially migrant families where parents wish to bring their children up in their 'own' cultural-linguistic context, while the children want to assimilate to the society around them. The concept of language prestige also helps explain why some speakers can be reluctant to place much value on their own linguistic competence, or sometimes even acknowledge that their own language or variety is as good, whole and correct as any other. Ideas about language, in the end, tend to come from the society or societies which surround you.

Soon after graduating, I (Tim) worked for a while in a government office in east London. One of my workmates was a young British man, Raj, of about my own age, but from an Asian background. He asked me what I had studied at university, and I told him: French, German and Linguistics. He whistled in admiration, and said something along the lines of: 'You must be clever. I'm useless at languages'. Curious, I asked him whether, then, he only spoke English. 'Oh well', he replied, 'I speak Hindi, obviously, and Urdu – that's easy if you speak Hindi'. Anything else? 'Well, Gujarati. Oh, and Punjabi sometimes, when I'm with my Punjabi mates'. Many years later, we had a Jamaican student called Marlon in our undergraduate class on Language and Society, a young man with a good command of standard English and a barely noticeable Jamaican accent. Asked as part of the class what languages other than English he spoke, he replied that back home, he often used to speak Patois. Another student asked what this was, and he instantly replied: 'It's just broken English'. We pressed him as to what he meant by this. 'Sort of English words, but without any grammar'. Asked for an example, he said: 'Instead of *I'll be back soon* we'd say *Mi soon come back*'. So could we say, for example, Back come mi soon? 'Oh no', Marlon answered. 'That wouldn't make sense'.

What these two cases have in common is that in both, prevailing societal attitudes towards language and language varieties have become internalized and accepted as normal and natural, even when a few moments' thought, given the two young men's knowledge of their own situations, must surely have suggested to them that the societal views could not possibly be right. For Raj, the low status afforded in Britain to so-called minority ethnic languages such as Urdu and Punjabi meant that his command of them did not really register as learning languages at all. Being 'good at languages' meant mastering for example French or German – traditionally high-status languages, taught as academic subjects in the context of a school or a university – or perhaps 'difficult' non-European languages like Chinese or Japanese, when learned by someone of a non-Chinese or non-Japanese background. In the Jamaican case, the similarly low status accorded to Patois, compared to the standard English demanded in formal situations, is realized in the generalized view that Patois, unlike 'proper' English, does not have any rules of grammar. The linguistic fact that every language variety on Earth has grammatical rules, including rules about word order – in fact must have grammatical rules, in order for anyone to have any hope of making themselves understood – is obscured by ideologized prejudice against 'non-standard' varieties. The prejudice is then often internalized by speakers themselves who, having had little or no exposure to the discipline of linguistics, are not in a position to recognize linguistic fallacies for what they are. Here, of course, is where the question of 'why do linguistics?' comes in: in part, it is to give ordinary speakers the resources they need to defend their own, perfectly legitimate, language usages and language skills against a too-often uninformed and hostile public discourse.

Traditionally, it has been through the education system that 'correct' language (what Pierre Bourdieu called the *langue légitime* – the 'legitimate language', by which he meant the language legitimized by authority) has been instilled. While some schools in Britain, the United States and other parts of the traditionally anglophone world do now take a somewhat more usage-focused, language awareness approach to the teaching of English (as we discuss in Chapter 13), in terms of worldwide practice and the practice associated with languages other than English, this is still uncommon. At its worst, the approach which sets out to instil 'correctness' or standardness at any cost can end by making a child feel that his or her accent, dialect or language is worthless, risible, shameful. The gross unfairness of this was summed up memorably more than half a century ago:

> A speaker who is made ashamed of his own language habits suffers a basic injury as a human being: to make anyone, especially a child, feel so ashamed is as indefensible as to make him feel ashamed of the colour of his skin.
>
> Halliday et al. (1964: 105)

4.5 Language configuration and social structure

To acknowledge that languages enjoy different levels of prestige is to accept that there are always asymmetries: to some extent at least, language configurations are reflections of power relations. In situations of diglossia (a term first suggested by the American linguist Charles Ferguson in 1959), it is usual for certain more formal or high-prestige contexts, topics or speech events to be the domain of the 'high' (or H) language, while the lower-prestige ones tend to be the province of the 'low' (or L) code. (A 'domain' in sociolinguistics refers to the environment which favours or demands a certain language to be spoken as opposed to another one: it might be an actual physical space, or it might be to do with who is speaking, or what is being talked about, or the degree of formality and so on). Hence, for example, in German-speaking cantons of Switzerland, secondary school students would write (and speak) standard German (*Hochdeutsch*) in the classroom, but this would be an odd choice of code in which to text one's friends – such a text message would almost always be the domain of Swiss German or *Schwyzerdütsch*.

Of course, Switzerland is a relatively egalitarian sort of a place, virtually all Swiss German speakers are also able to use Hochdeutsch, and there is little stigma attached to using Schwyzerdütsch in a wide variety of contexts. This is 'diglossia with bilingualism', and no German-speaking Swiss citizen is likely to be or to feel excluded by it.

We also have 'bilingualism without diglossia', such as in Cameroon, Belgium, Canada or Switzerland as a whole, where which language one habitually uses depends basically on where one happens to be in the country. There may be tension between the languages – there certainly is in Cameroon, as we saw above – but there is no suggestion of one language being more suited than the other to formal contexts, important topics of conversation or high-status speakers. Your interlocutor might not like the code you choose to speak in – in fact she might object to it strongly – but there is no social stigma attached to using it.

Sometimes, though, the outlines of naked power in a country break through the surface in the form of its sociolinguistics: this is the case with 'diglossia without bilingualism'. Diglossia without widespread accompanying bilingualism might be characterized as an extreme form of uneven power and language distribution, often associated with war, conquest or colonialism. In this situation, the 'H' domains of a society – government, education, formal commerce, the media, the law, 'high' religion and the like – are the province of a particular elite language. For the bulk of the population who do not speak that language and are not in a position to learn it, these areas of national life are effectively rendered off-limits. This pattern of language distribution was very common in nineteenth and twentieth century European colonialism, as indeed it must have been in earlier, less commented-upon contexts, and its afterlife can be seen in large tracts of Africa and Latin America, among other places. Only about half of all Mozambicans speak Portuguese, for example, even though this is the official language of their country.

The fossilized remains of a diglossic system of this kind can still be seen in modern English. Native English speakers often tend to think of their lexicon in terms of unpretentious, 'easy' words and flowery, 'difficult' ones. Often there are pairs of such words with broadly similar denotative meanings (*talk* and *converse*, *build* and *construct*, *ask* and *request*, and so on) and speakers who choose the H in a situation which might be thought to require the L or unmarked variant will be accused mockingly of having 'swallowed a dictionary' or laughed at for clumsy pompousness, like the stock figure of the policeman who talks about having *apprehended the perpetrators*. (Other authority figures seem to feel the same urge: 'Unfortunately we did locate two deceased persons in the premises' said a senior fire officer on BBC London News). The source of this lexical division is in essence the events of a single, violent day in 1066, when speakers of the (Germanic) English language were conquered by speakers of (Latinate) Norman French. The ruling class suddenly spoke a different language to that of the peasant and the labourer. While it has been suggested that a good deal of administration must have continued to be carried on for some time in English (Ackroyd 2011: 101), still an English speaker would have to be expensively educated simply in order to make themselves understood to the new Norman lord, baron or king. Thus even though, over the next 300 or so years, the two tongues gradually melded together to become one (what we now call 'English'), the system of dual vocabulary – one part high-flown, formal and educated, the other down-to-earth and associated with the common person – continued and continues to mark the diglossic faultline bequeathed by a traumatic conquest.

Diglossia and domains are potentially rather rigid and unyielding concepts, though they are not intended to be; the above is certainly not intended to suggest that everyone always and only uses or used language A in context X and language B in context Y, whether in post-colonial Mozambique or in post-Conquest England. These terms remain useful to our broad understanding of the underlying frameworks of how language is configured in societies, but they cannot always account for 'the messiness of actual usage' (Heller 2007: 13), or what has been characterized, following Bakhtin, as 'heteroglossia' (e.g. Creese and Blackledge 2010). In order to deal with the complexity of small-scale, real-world code choice, a more nuanced approach is required, and one which acknowledges that, particularly in the super-diverse (Vertovec 2006, 2007) contexts generated by mass migration and globalization, the variety of linguistic resources available to an individual speaker is, potentially at least, practically limitless.

4.6 New perspectives on code choice: Using the available resources

In theory, of course, people are free to use whatever linguistic code they have available to them. In practice, communication is essentially a co-operative endeavour, whether or not you like the person you are speaking to; hence a certain amount of consensus is usually sought, consciously or subconsciously. This implies a process of negotiation to be gone through, again consciously or subconsciously, explicitly or implicitly. Harvey (1987) relates a telling episode in which a Peruvian peasant is being investigated by a judge in a local court in the Andes, charged with beating his wife. The wife tells her story in Quechua, and the (Spanish-Quechua bilingual) judge then calls the man forward to give his side of the story. The man begins by addressing the judge in Spanish, only to receive for his pains a sharp 'Manachu runasimita yachanki?' – 'Don't you understand Quechua?' This can be read as an attempt by the accused to place himself on a higher social footing than his wife, and implicitly to position himself closer to the judge, who might be expected to prefer Spanish, especially in this formal context. It is a linguistic claim for higher social status, but one which is slapped down with some force.

Code choice, then, is a socially conditioned event which is constrained by any number of factors related to prestige, appropriacy, effect, identity and so on. This brings us on to the question of how people perceive the linguistic resources available to them in multilingual contexts, and how they then choose to use them. Traditionally sociolinguists have described the alternate use of two or more languages by a single bilingual speaker in terms of code-switching and code-mixing (some commentators distinguish between the two, others do not). However, while the notion of code-switching remains a helpful one (as with the theory of diglossia, outlined above), recently more holistic approaches have been developed, drawn from highly complex multilingual environments, leading to a more fine-grained view of how people perceive and use language, one which considers all the extant codes in a speech community as potential communicative resources, even where an individual speaker is not able to use all the codes with fluency or accuracy, or is even essentially monolingual.

Umberto Eco's medieval murder mystery *The Name of the Rose* contains a curious character called Salvatore. He is a monk who has, we are told, lived in monasteries in many different parts of Europe and thereby acquired, in varying degrees, various different languages and dialects. Instead of suiting his speech to the region or company in which he finds himself, he has developed a strange idiolect (the term used in linguistics for a form of speech which is peculiar to oneself). It is composed of fragments of all the different varieties in his linguistic repertoire, including Spanish, English, Italian, Latin, Catalan and Provençal, mixed seemingly at random. This is from the 1983 English translation:

> Penitenziagite! Watch out for the draco who cometh in futurum to gnaw your anima! Death is super nos! Pray the Santo Pater come to liberar nos a

> malo and all our sin! Ha ha, you like this negromanzia de Domini Nostri Jesu Christi! Et anco jois m'es dols e plazer m'es dolors. . . . Cave el diabolo! Semper lying in wait for me in some angulum to snap at my heels. But Salvatore is not stupidus! Bonum monasterium, and aquí refectorium and pray to dominum nostrum. And the resto is not worth merda. No?

Most of his brother monks are of the opinion that Salvatore is not quite right in his head, and tend to regard his pronouncements as incoherent ramblings. Not the narrator of the novel, though, and certainly not its author, a semiotician of course of international renown. As Salvatore says himself here, 'Salvatore is not stupidus!' – and it turns out that he has understood what lies behind the gruesome events in the novel's monastery setting better than most of the others.

Eco's Salvatore was perhaps an extreme proponent of a practice which is now being theorized by educationalists and sociolinguists under the rubric of translanguaging (see e.g. García 2009; García and Li 2014; Canagarajah 2013a prefers the term translingual practice). Linguists have been discussing code choice since at least the 1950s; within this discussion, as noted above, the notions of code-shifting and code-mixing are well established. However, translanguaging, at least as thought of by these commentators, both encompasses these practices and goes beyond them, in an attempt to describe how bilingual and multilingual speakers use the full resources of their repertoires to express and reflect their culturally diverse realities in new, creative ways. The usefulness of translanguaging as a concept is that it aids us not only to understand shifting between two systems, but to begin to see the diverse networks of multilingual and multimodal communication built up by language users in diverse environments as single, unique, integrated and creative systems:

> Translanguaging is both going between different linguistic structures and systems and going beyond them. It includes the full range of linguistic performances of multilingual language users for purposes that transcend the combination of structures, the alternation between systems, the transmission of information and the representation of values, identities and relationships.
>
> Li (2011: 1222)

As Canagarajah (2009) and other South Asian sociolinguists were quick to spot, a translanguaging approach is very helpful for analysing countries such as India, where English occurs even in the speech of many of those who would think of themselves basically as non-English speakers. Apart from anything else, the ubiquity and penetration into local speech norms of English are on a scale that cannot be explained merely by the idea of local languages 'borrowing' from English.

To categorize the use of English alongside local languages in India simply as 'borrowing' or 'code-switching' cannot fully explain what has historically sometimes been derided as 'Babu English', but which we would perhaps now acknowledge as creative use of the available stylistic resources, as in a newspaper advertisement for a chain of Montessori schools: 'We claim that the . . . schools are second home for the children and ours is definitely maiden attempt yet to be challenged' (*The Hindu*, 15 May 2012). Or a roadside advertisement for a holiday resort near Kochi which promised *A delightful beacon in the heavenly destination*. As Pennycook (2010) rightly insists, this is not merely 'English as a Lingua Franca' or 'World Englishes', but English accommodating itself to local norms and practices.

From here, naturally, it is a fairly small step to questioning the very idea of borders between languages. Scholars researching the speech behaviour of bilingual speakers in linguistically diverse communities such as urban school classrooms have been arguing for some time that the concept of separate, discrete and identifiable languages is no more than an ideologized, societal construct (see e.g. Blackledge and Creese 2008; Makoni and Pennycook 2007), though not everyone agrees with them (see below).

It has of course long been unremarkable in sociolinguistics (though it can be unsettling to newcomers to the subject) to point out that, in the last resort, the decision as to whether a certain variety should be labelled a 'language' or a dialect of another language is more often than not a cultural, political or ideological rather than a linguistic one. ('A language is a dialect with an army and navy', the linguist Max Weinreich is famously supposed to have quipped). This is relatively painless when we are talking about closely related and structurally similar pairs of languages such as Galician and Spanish, or Dutch and German: but what if we were to start thinking in this way about *all* languages? For some, this is clearly a step too far. Edwards (2012: 43) while agreeing that languages are of course in a sense merely social constructs, regards the attempt to then 'disinvent' them as 'merely an attempt to be provocative. . . . For all ordinary intents and purposes there *are* separate languages, and there *are* distinct varieties within them'. This is perhaps right. But even if we do not immediately accept the view of a language as nothing more than an ideologized construct, it would appear to be unnecessarily limiting, to say the least, to analyse an individual's overall linguistic capabilities solely in terms of their formal competence in Language A, Language B and so on. Should we not also pay attention to the way in which the individual might use bits and pieces of the various languages in their repertoire, and combine and refashion the languages in order to increase or even multiply the affordances which lie within them?

As Edwards (2012) trenchantly argues, this approach does not in itself tell us anything new (and he is surely right to observe that 'translanguaging' is an unattractive word). But it does bring a shift of emphasis: it is a perspective which regards code choice in highly diverse contexts as primarily a creative activity and a way of maximizing communicative potential by using the available resources, rather than as primarily a process of choosing the appropriate set of linguistic structures for a given domain. In that sense, it might of course help us to make sense of the student union posters that we looked at in Chapter 2, and the campaigners' seemingly blasé attitude to notions of standardness and well-formedness. Their priority, it appears, was not to adhere to the structural conventions of standard English as such, but to use *language* in a way that was consistent with the highly diverse environment in which they found themselves.

4.7 Conclusion

We revisit the whole idea of language as a societal and individual resource in some detail in Chapter 11, where we also look at some more examples from different parts of the world. For now, we might finish by noting that in considering the many and diverse ways in which societies organize language, we find ourselves inexorably drawn into the question of how speakers themselves organize language. More even than this, close observation of super-diverse 'hybrid urban multilingualism' (Pennycook 2010: 83), and for that matter hybrid non-urban multilingualism, leads us in the end to the question of to what extent our traditional notions such as those of separate, discrete languages, of native and non-native speakers and so on, are actually still helpful when we wish to think about how language works in the modern world. Once we begin to really *notice* language, the way language is actually used, it becomes apparent that ordinary speakers do not always maintain the strict conceptual separation between languages that the existence of written grammars and dictionaries, official languages, 'national' languages and so on might lead us to assume. But to begin with, in the next chapter we look at some of the ways in which languages are indeed 'the same', and some of the ways in which they can be said to differ.

Suggested reading

Edwards, J. (2012), *Multilingualism: Understanding Linguistic Diversity*. London and New York: Bloomsbury.

A book in this author's characteristically down-to-earth style which addresses the whole concept of diversity in language from a range of viewpoints (multilingualism in society, the question of translation, endangered languages, etc.) and which, among other things, launches a entertainingly brutal attack on the whole notion of 'translanguaging'. A very good read.

Vigouroux, C. B. and Mufwene, S. S. (eds) (2008), *Globalization and Language Vitality: Perspectives from Africa*. London and New York: Bloomsbury.

This is an original and well-chosen collection of chapters which addresses a large range of sociolinguistic contexts across Africa, from Morocco to South Africa and from Senegal to Mozambique, surveying both African and European languages and focusing in particular on the question of how smaller, local languages can survive the twenty-first century in the face of competition from larger, regional and even global languages.

Mesthrie, R., Swann, J., Deumert, A. and Leap, W. L. (2009), *Introducing Sociolinguistics*. Edinburgh: Edinburgh University Press.

There are many introductions to the discipline of sociolinguistics available, mostly covering much the same ground. This one covers the basics thoroughly, but adds some extras in the form of, for example, chapters on regional and social dialectology, some useful case studies and a whole chapter on the sociolinguistics of sign language.

5

About difference: Do all languages work the same way?

5.1 Introduction

Some years ago, at the university where we taught postgraduate students, we had a small incident in a seminar which delighted those present at the time (bar one unfortunate person) but had the later effect of leading on to a serious discussion about the way languages work. A 30-something Bangladeshi man, whom we shall call Zahir, found himself in the position of arguing against a point that had been made by another student, a statuesque Scandinavian woman of striking appearance, whom we shall call Kristina. Zahir got off to a bad start by saying: 'He says that . . .' at which his friends sitting next to him laughed and corrected him: 'No, no, no. You mean *she*'. Flustered, he tried again. 'He says that . . .' Now all the students were laughing and Zahir's friends were beside themselves. Once more he tried. 'Sorry. I mean – he says that . . .' As the room erupted with laughter at poor Zahir's evident embarrassment, Kristina finally reacted. Looking coolly at Zahir, she drew herself up, swept back her long, blond hair with a flourish and asked him in Garboesque tones: 'Is it *so* hard to tell the difference?'

The foreigner who keeps making mistakes in a second language is a stock comedy figure. In the 1970s there was a British television programme called *Mind Your Language* set in an ESOL (English for Speakers of Other Languages) classroom, which essentially relied on this one situation for its comedy effect, such as it was. This was in the early days of mass migration, and the programme would not be made now: its relentless stereotyping, essentializing and patronizing of comical foreigners was very much of its time, and would hardly be to the taste of most of modern Britain (or so one hopes). But one authentic note was struck. It is in such settings as multilingual classrooms and workplaces, the interface where linguistic and cultural systems meet, that the contours that reveal how languages and cultures work are at their sharpest and most visible (Gunnarsson 2013; Clyne 1994; we will have more to say about this in Chapter 14). And the kind of errors you tend to make in a foreign language do of course stem partly from the ways (structural, phonological, sociocultural) in which that language and your own language differ. If Bengali speakers (or Chinese, come to that) so often confuse *he* and *she*, it is because their language's pronoun system does not differentiate between genders. Similarly, speakers of Russian, Polish and other Slavic languages often have difficulty in using the articles *a* and *the* correctly (when they remember to use them at all). But of course, if your language does not have articles, as theirs do not, then they present a fearsomely complex challenge.

A flyer taped to a lamp post in east London appealed for any information about a lost pet in the following terms: *'Cat has been lost. Cat is called Charlie. . . . Cat does not have collar. If anyone finds cat, please call (number).'* It's a reasonable bet that Charlie's owner is a speaker of a Slavic language.

Some knowledge of, or at least about, other languages is therefore an invaluable resource for teachers of ESOL and teachers of any discipline who wish to understand why their students make the mistakes they do: but it is equally vital for language learners, and indeed anyone who has to negotiate social interaction in a multilingual context. The need has often been supplied by books such as *Learner English: A Teacher's Guide to Interference and other Problems* (Swan and Smith 2001). This offers the reader a whirlwind tour of the essential features of a selection of languages or language groups (Russian, Greek, Farsi, Spanish and Catalan, the Dravidian languages of southern India, etc.) and then lists an impressively large number of the interference problems that might crop up when speakers of these languages are learning English. To take a sample of such problems at random, they include the fact that Dutch speakers tend to devoice a voiced (see Chapter 6) word-final consonant (*leaf* for *leave*, *dock* for *dog*); that Dutch has a narrower intonation range than English; and that, as Dutch lacks the tags commonly used in English answers, its speakers might also inadvertently give an impression of abruptness or rudeness (plain *no* for *no, they don't, do they?*) (Swan and Smith 2001).

Understanding how other languages work is of self-evident cultural benefit. The *inter*cultural benefit in the study of linguistics, though, lies in taking the next step, and beginning to recognize the potential strangeness in one's own language when seen from another's perspective. Of course it is almost a truism that, just as we do not notice the culture we are born into, we seldom think there might be anything odd or curious about our mother tongue. There is an innate subjectivity in the way we think about language, especially as children, which amounts almost to a kind of subconscious solipsism. We assume that the way our own language does things is simply the normal way of doing things, and it is other languages that are strange. It is only with exposure to and knowledge about other languages that we come to realize what our language has in common with them, and what makes it different and potentially difficult. (And this is one of the strongest arguments in favour of the teaching of language and languages at school, something we discuss in Chapter 13). In this chapter, then, we consider some of the innate similarities and differences among languages themselves, whether grammatical, phonological or semantic (i.e. conceptual). What is 'normal'? Is there such a thing as logical word order? Are some speech sounds more common than others? Is it possible to talk about different 'types' of languages? Finally, moving from the innate properties of languages to the ways in which languages are ideologized, we consider briefly some of the different narratives that surround languages, and the qualities that their speakers attribute to them.

5.2 Saying what needs to be said: Grammar and conceptual systems

It may cause some slight awkwardness for an English speaker to be forced to choose between a formal 'you' and an informal 'you' when addressing someone in a language that differentiates between the two (German *du* and *Sie*, Spanish *tú* and *usted*, Russian *ty* and *vy*, etc.) There is ample room for embarrassment here. Equally, speakers of languages which have this so-called T-V distinction may find it odd to have to use the unvarying *you* when addressing anyone in an English-speaking context, regardless of status, age, kinship or degree of familiarity. In French, for example, using the term of address *tu* instead of *vous* is a question of category choice, as Guillot (2012) points out when discussing English subtitles of French films. How, she asks, can an English subtitle represent the hurt intended by someone using *vous* when the intimacy of the relationship would normally require *tu* or, indeed, the insult intended when it is the other way round?

But this is relatively small stuff. For speakers of languages (like Javanese, Japanese or Burmese) which have elaborate and finely graded systems of address, in which personal pronouns have to be selected according to exacting social criteria, to have a severely limited choice of how to address someone or how to refer to oneself can feel very uncomfortable indeed. Riley (2007) gives the example of one of his students, a Burmese speaker who, despite being a French specialist, felt that French was 'such an impolite language'. Asked to explain, he said:

> In my language, I have an 'I' for when I am superior or inferior to you, for when I am pleased with you or angry with you, so that when I speak French I always feel like a bull in a china shop, never respectful, never expressing my attitudes appropriately. (Riley 2007: 85)

The inevitable feeling of linguistic 'otherness' when engaging with another language can be fairly mild, or, as in this student's case, it can be genuinely disconcerting and unsettling. This is otherness that actually affects one's sense of identity and relations with others. And seen through the Burmese speaker's eyes, suddenly English, with its bare and unforgiving personal pronoun system, devoid of nuance or flexibility, begins to look like a very blunt instrument.

The T-V distinction used to be second nature for English speakers, too – but things have changed, to such an extent that most of us 'can no longer even follow, for example, the detailed subtleties and shifts which take place in the personal relationship of Celia and Rosalind in *As You Like It*, which is revealed by their sensitive shifting between thou and you' (cited in Halliday 1978: 89). I (Tim) was told some years ago about a teacher from the south of England who, having taken a job in South Yorkshire, commented to one of her new colleagues how charmed she was by the children using 'thee' and 'tha' to her. The colleague went without further ado to her classroom and gave the children a good dressing-down. Knowing the new teacher was not aware of how the T-V distinction worked, the children were cheekily addressing her as an equal. Even in South Yorkshire, though, this usage is disappearing.

Of course, all languages differ in the way they classify experience and order reality. This is perhaps most immediately obvious in the area of lexis (vocabulary), where things are divided up and identified in ways that can seem to outsiders bizarre or just unnecessary. Latin distinguishes between paternal aunts and uncles (*amita; patruus*) and maternal ones (*matertera*; *avunculus*); English doesn't bother. In other areas it might appear that it is English which is being fussy: there are 11 primary colours identified in English, while Hanunoo speakers in the Philippines make do with 4. One word, *beizi,* in Chinese suffices for 'cup', 'mug' and 'glass'. French, meanwhile, needs two words for 'river', *rivière* and *fleuve* (the latter flows into the sea).

There are even more subtle differences, though, than these. A key element of understanding language and how languages work lies in noticing what needs to be said within the structure of the language, and what doesn't. Sometimes this can produce startling results: take what is sometimes called, unscientifically, the Quechua 'drunk' particle. In Quechua, as in its Andean neighbour Aymara, the speaker has to encode the provenance of information, or its evidential base; so there are suffixes like *-mi* to be attached if you actually witnessed the thing you are talking about, and *-si* if you didn't. Then there is the ending *–sqa*, which is used for things which are outside the speaker's conscious experience. As well as being used for talking about what happened before you were born or when you were a baby, it is also used to relate myths and legends or to describe the strange customs of other groups of people. It is the way to talk about things that happened when you were asleep. With refreshing honesty, though, it is also used to describe things that happened, or might have happened, when you were blind drunk. (Anyone who has attended an Andean village *fiesta* will appreciate that this might be quite a useful aspect of language to have to hand.)

Thai is one of the group of languages (including many sign languages) which employ a system of noun classifiers – so when enumerating or specifying things, rather than simply use a noun like *car* or *policeman* you have to add a tag word to the noun, indicating to which class or group of things this noun belongs: in the case of these two words it would be *vehicle* or *person*. So 'three teachers' would be *ajarn sahm kon* or 'teachers three people'. This seems fairly straightforward, but the different entities which are grouped together under particular classifiers offer some tantalizing semantic puzzles and insights. The normal classifier for people, *kon*, does not cover those people considered to be above and apart from the rest of Thai society: specifically, royalty and Buddhist monks. *Chabup* covers such things as newspapers, letters and some other kinds of documents, which is immediately comprehensible, but slips of paper such as tickets come under *bai*, along with fruit, eggs and leaves. *Lem* includes books and knives, while the vehicle classifier, *kun*, excludes ox-carts.

This leaves us with a big question: Do we all experience the world in the same way, regardless of language, or is our experience filtered through the language we happen to speak? This is the field of argument associated with what is known in linguistics and anthropology as the Sapir-Whorf hypothesis, and we refer to it in (a little) more detail in Chapter 6. Certainly we can say that, in order to 'know' a language, cultural knowledge is needed as well as formal linguistic knowledge. Other language communities' ways of seeing and saying sometimes have the power to make the familiar suddenly unfamiliar (or vice versa) or to encourage you to see things in a new light. The nineteenth-century linguist and traveller William Burrow in his *Romano Lavo-Lil: Word*

Book of the Romany; Or, English Gypsy Language (1874) recorded the Anglo-Romany names for various English towns and counties. *Porrum-engreskey tem* or 'Leek-eaters' country' is Wales. That's reasonable enough, as is *Lil-engreskey gav* (Book fellows' town) for Oxford, and *Mi-develeskey gav* ('My god's town') for Canterbury. But what about *Dinelo tem* (Fools' country) for Suffolk, or *Rokrengreskey gav* ('Talking fellows' town') for Norwich?

The point, let us emphasize once more, is not just that other languages are odd or behave in unexpected ways, but that what seems odd to us is perfectly natural, normal and expected for the native speakers of those languages. As we suggested with the example of the Burmese student, one of the bigger challenges in thinking about language is to try to imagine, or to notice, what is strange, clumsy or difficult about our own language. Take a simple English utterance like *She went to the shop*: the information encoded goes well beyond the basic idea of going and the basic of idea of shop, which you would get away with perfectly well in, say, Thai or Chinese, if the context were clear enough (*bpai rahn* or literally 'go shop' could be a very acceptable Thai translation of the sentence, as it could equally be of *I'm going to the shops*). English tells us the sex of the person and the fact that there is just one of them, along with the fact that there is only one shop involved and that it's a specific shop known to all involved, and that this happened at some point in the past. And English *has* to tell us these things: they are not optional extras, and English speakers don't need to think consciously about specifying this information. It is just part of the way the language is structured, as obvious, necessary and uncontroversial to English speakers as the existence of noun classifiers is to Thais or the necessity of specifying provenance is to Quechua-speaking Andean people. Or indeed, we might add, as the notion of having to assign gender to nouns is to French speakers (two genders) or German speakers (three!). For English speakers learning French at school, the notion of compulsory grammatical gender is usually their first taste of the true 'foreignness' of 'foreign languages' – and it never really goes away. Hence Fiona's indignant refusal to believe that the lady in the boulangerie really didn't understand her when she asked for '*un baguette*' rather than '*une baguette*'.

5.3 Why Yoda sounds other-worldly: Word order and language types

One basic and highly noticeable way in which languages differ is in word order. Rigidity of word order varies from language to language. Some are very fixed, some very free, but there is usually a clear preference. In English the usual order is subject-verb-object, or SVO, as in *the postman delivered a parcel.* Welsh, like its cousin Gaelic, prefers VSO, as in *gwelodd y plentyn geffyl*, 'the child saw a horse', literally *saw the child a horse.* Latin has relatively very flexible word order, but in Roman times at least showed a marked tendency towards SOV, as in *Homo doctus in se semper divitias habet*, from Phaedrus's version of Aesop's Fables – 'an educated man always has wealth within himself' or, word-for-word, *man educated in himself always wealth has.* Hindi and Korean, for instance, work this way, too. We can say, then, that there is no obvious or logical word order in human language, no matter how strongly we may feel, instinctively, that ours puts things in the 'natural' order. Interestingly, though, object-initial (i.e., OSV and OVS) languages are the least common by far: in fact, for a time many linguists doubted they really existed at all. They are confined to little more than a handful of languages, many of them spoken in the Amazon basin (Olawsky 2006). The Hollywood scriptwriters who wrote *Star Wars* knew what they were doing, then, when they gave Yoda his characteristic 'fronting' word order, as in *'The dark side I sense in you'.* Although it is completely and immediately comprehensible, there really is, for most people on earth, something very strange about this kind of word order.

We can also think about 'types' of language by grouping together the ones which tend to form their words and sentences in similar ways (an approach known as morphological typology). In analytic or isolating languages words are single, self-contained units, with no inflection and few or no affixes; that is to say, you cannot alter the meaning of a word by changing a part of it or by adding a new part to it. This and the fact that the words tend to be monosyllabic gives Chinese political slogans and proverbs some of their characteristic punchiness and zip.[1] Samoan, Vietnamese and the Gbe group of languages spoken in West Africa, among others, are also of this type. Synthetic or inflectional languages, by contrast, have more or less elaborate morphological systems, whereby things such as tense, case, number or gender can be signalled by the use of internal modification or the addition of affixes (prefixes at the beginning of words, suffixes at the end, infixes in the middle). Arabic, Russian, Greek and Amharic are all inflecting languages, but a classic example is, again, Latin. While 'to show' is *monstrare*, the word *monstravisses* means 'you might have shown'. A Latin verb can in fact have some 300 different forms (Janson 2004: 200), compared to a Chinese verb's one. In such languages, as grammatical relationships are encoded within the words themselves, word order tends to be more relaxed.

Agglutinating or affixing languages (e.g. Turkish, Finnish, Japanese, the Indian language Malayalam and many of the Bantu languages of southern Africa) build up words by placing grammatical units into predetermined 'slots' corresponding not only to number, tense, possession and so on, but potentially also to cause, reciprocity, position, direction, agency, inclusivity and a host of other things. This can produce highly complex 'portmanteau' forms like the Aymara *hiwas-kam(a)aru-s(i)-kipa-si-p-xa-ña-naka-taki-sa* ('so that we are able to communicate among ourselves') (Brown and Ogilvie 2009: 109). For the non-native, learning such a language can be daunting. While it is a relatively straightforward process (albeit slow, if we are honest) to build up your own words, piece by piece, it is quite another matter to decode the words of others; that is, to work out what might be the overall gist of a rapidly spoken utterance containing a root followed by perhaps eight or nine suffixes. Lastly, polysynthetic or incorporating languages are characterized by their incorporation of the major elements of the sentence, such as noun and verb, into single words, which tend therefore to be very long and very complex. An often-quoted example (for good reason) is the Inuktitut *Qasuiirsarvigssarsingitluinarnarpuq* – 'someone did not find a completely suitable resting place'. Many Australian and Native American languages, such as Tiwi and Mohawk, are of this type.

Bear in mind that this is a broad-brush, idealized categorization rather than a rigid framework; often, languages can show different tendencies in different parts of their grammar. English, for example, presents as something of a mixture: it is partly analytic (*will* to indicate future tense, *more* to indicate the comparative); partly inflectional (*-er* also indicating the comparative; cat-*s*, foot/*feet* to indicate plural); and even partly agglutinative (*un-fortunate-ly*).

5.4 Easy sounds and difficult

Everyone thinks their mother tongue sounds 'natural': it would be strange if this were not to be the case. The corollary of this is that at an instinctive level we perceive some of the sounds of other people's languages as strange or difficult. The most common consonants worldwide include /p, b, t, d, k, g, f, s, m, n/: these and a number of others would raise few eyebrows anywhere. The rarer sounds, though, can seem quite extraordinary if they don't happen to figure in your own language's phoneme inventory (i.e. the list of distinct sounds in any language which can be used to differentiate meaning – we'll look at these terms in the next chapter). Arabic has a distinctive sound called a pharyngeal fricative, produced right at the back of the throat; many American and African languages, particularly, employ ejective consonants, in which air is retained and then released explosively, as if the speaker were spitting the sound out. And one of the small pleasures in teaching linguistics is to watch the faces of students who are hearing 'click' languages like Xhosa and Zulu for the first time. If you have never heard sounds like these used in language, it's well worth looking online for a video clip of Miriam Makeba singing the Xhosa traditional song 'Qongqothwane', otherwise known as 'The Click Song'.

Sounds might suddenly change, for reasons that seem opaque to non-native speakers. Turkish demands vowel harmonization, so when forming agglutinating suffixes you cannot mix front and back vowels, or rounded and unrounded. Welsh has initial consonant mutation, so in certain circumstances, the word for Wales, *Cymru*, can become *Gymru*, *Chymru* or *Nghymru*. (As in the signs on the motorway saying 'Welcome to Wales' – *Croeso i Gymru*). In the languages collectively known as tonal languages, as we have noted previously, changing the tone with which a word is said (e.g. from rising tone to rising-falling tone) will change the actual meaning of the word. To the outsider it might seem preposterous that a mere matter of getting the tone slightly off means that a Vietnamese or Igbo speaker will utterly fail to understand what you are saying: but for speakers of such languages, the difference between rising tone and rising-falling tone is as obvious and important as the difference between, say, /k/ and /g/ (and see our discussion of meaningful contrast in the following chapter). You would not say in English that you were 'going to get your goat' when you were actually 'going to get your coat'.

5.5 Brothers under the skin? Language families

If all languages have different sets of sounds, encode different things and work in different grammatical ways, is there actually a hard core that is common to all? In fact, for several decades linguists have worked in an effort to establish what the universal properties of language might be, a project often associated (not entirely accurately) with the American theoretical linguist Noam Chomsky's conception of the 'Universal Grammar'. This is a highly contested field, and there is relatively little that all can agree upon. We can say with some certainty, for example, that all languages have nouns and verbs, vowels and consonants. Beyond rather bare and not particularly helpful statements of this kind, it is probably safer to talk about tendencies in language rather than universals. Some linguists and cognitive scientists have argued that genuine, profound linguistic universals are in fact 'vanishingly few' (Evans and Levinson 2009: 429), and that describing these tendencies is really the limit of what we can say in general about language. Certainly typological research into the world's languages (there are perhaps 4,000–6,000 of them, depending of course on how you define 'language') demonstrates that there exists astonishing diversity at all levels: phonological, syntactic, morphological and semantic.

But as with the animal and plant worlds, so with language: extreme diversity is underlain by interconnections and kinship relations. Languages can be grouped together by 'genetic classification' into families if they share a common ancestor language. The big, overarching families have often evocative names like Macro-Chibchan, Ge-Pano-Carib or Palaeosiberian. The big families can be further divided into subgroups, for instance Germanic, Balto-Slavic or Indo-Iranian; and so on, down to the level of individual languages. In this way, language 'family trees' can be constructed for most languages, so it can be seen which languages are related to which, and how closely or distantly. Figure 5.1, for instance, is a family tree for the Celtic languages, some of which are now extinct while others are very much alive:

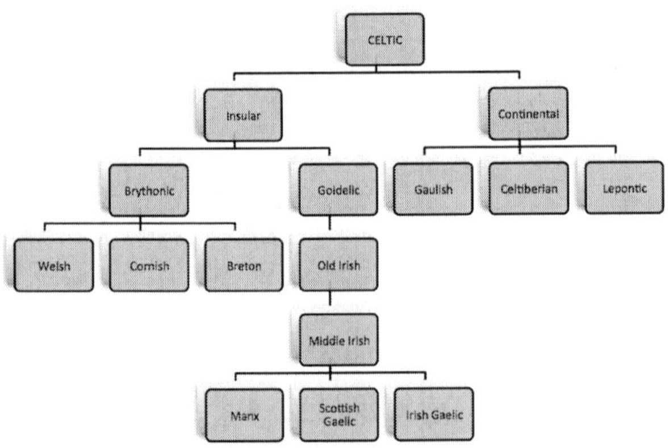

FIGURE 5.1 *A family tree of Celtic languages.*

Basque, uniquely in Europe, is an isolate – that is, it appears to have no relatives at all, or at least no living or documented ones. English's first cousin (besides Scots, Robert Burns's native language, spoken in the Borders and not to be confused with Gaelic) is Frisian, spoken in parts of Holland and Germany, just across the North Sea opposite the east coast of England. You would probably expect this; English, while it has a large store of vocabulary derived from French, is at root a Germanic language.

English, though, along with many other European and Asian languages, has descended from a single common source language known as Proto-Indo-European (PIE), which was probably being spoken in Europe, perhaps on the southern Russian steppes, by around 3,500 BCE. The existence of such a language was first publicly postulated by the British orientalist and polymath Sir William Jones in 1786, and since then historical linguists have worked painstakingly to piece together how the language was structured and what it might have sounded like. They do not always agree, to put it mildly (see Ramat and Ramat 1998 for a taste of how acerbic their arguments can be), and there are of course no written records to go by. What is beyond argument, though, is that over a period of some 5,500 years, Indo-European 'differentiated' into a host of daughter languages, intermingling with the languages which were already being spoken in the area to produce eventually an 'extremely rich and culturally significant superfamily of languages' (Fischer 2005: 81). It was the regular sound correspondences between Sanskrit and some European languages that first alerted Jones and his contemporaries to the possibility that a common ancestor language had existed: Sanskrit *bhrātr*, English *brother*, Latin *frater*, Greek *phrater* and so on. English is therefore related – if distantly – to more remote and, to the English speaker, exotic-seeming tongues such as Armenian, Persian and Albanian. This is an important point to bear in mind when thinking about languages other than one's own, or trying to learn them: if you look for difference you will certainly find it, but if you look hard enough for similarity you might be pleasantly surprised.

We have seen, then, that languages can work structurally and conceptually in a variety of ways, all of which seem utterly normal to the speakers of those languages. Now let's look finally at the different, but related question of the things that speakers *believe* about their languages – another area in which it is notoriously difficult for native speakers to step back from their own subjective experience.

5.6 'My language is special': Language narratives and ideologies

Linguists tend to agree that 'Chinese' comprises a core group of eight languages which are for the most part mutually unintelligible, plus many smaller dialects. Many Chinese people, though, do not. Over our years of teaching Chinese students, it proved an uphill task to convince them that descriptions of the Chinese linguistic context given in linguistics textbooks correspond to the Chinese linguistic reality. For in China, of course, it is an article of faith that there is 'one Chinese', of which the eight languages are actually dialects. This is taught with rigid emphasis throughout the education system, and the fact that the different languages are written using the same characters (see text box) is adduced as proof of the proposition (Wardhaugh 2010). Thus writing, which is of course a technology (see Chapter 9) is mistaken for language itself.

It is difficult to avoid the suspicion that the insistence on 'one Chinese' is more an ideological proposition than a linguistic one; a metaphor rather than a description of fact. That is to say, when the Chinese state, through its media and educators, insists (as has historically been the case) that there exists a single, indivisible Chinese language, what it really wants to impress upon its citizens is that there exists a single, indivisible China. The Hongkongese, for example, can already be disdainful of the Putonghua spoken by mainland immigrants to the region, expecting them to learn Hong Kong-style Cantonese (Gu 2011). If Cantonese-speakers as a whole were to absorb the idea that they did not actually share a common language with Beijing (and see Snow 2004 on this matter), might they not next wonder why they should be part of a Beijing-ruled state? Hence the determination of the Chinese government that political unity must not be threatened translates into a metaphorical insistence that Cantonese is a dialect of Chinese. But for those who have been assured since childhood that there is only one Chinese language, there is nothing metaphorical about it. It is a fact, and to begin to think otherwise is extraordinarily difficult.

The eight main Chinese language groups (Yue, Wu, Mandarin and so on, known collectively as Hanyu) are all written using the same characters in mainland China, even though the languages are on the whole not mutually intelligible, and pronunciation of the characters varies according to which language the reader speaks (Snow 2004; Wardhaugh 1998). This might seem rather odd to non-Chinese people, but the principle is quite easy to demonstrate. Write on a piece of paper $35 + 16 = 51$ or $a^2 = b^2 \times c^2$. Find yourself three friendly speakers of three different languages: let's say an Egyptian, a Bulgarian and a Korean. Have each of them read out loud in their own language what you have written on the paper. Each of them can read it without difficulty, can they not? But none understands the language of the others. Script is not language.

All language communities in some sense tell stories about themselves, and many of them cherish traditions, historical narratives, myths, semi-myths, received ideas and assumptions about their language. While for some societies the question of language is of fairly limited importance, for others it is central to identity-making. For Bangladeshis, Bengali has almost sacred status, being associated not only with a long poetic and literary tradition but most importantly with the birth of the Bangladeshi state itself. The so-called Language Martyrs were students whose deaths in 1952 while protesting against the imposition of Urdu as the sole language of East and West Pakistan helped catalyse the movement for secession and eventual national independence. The day of the Language Martyrs, or Language Movement Day is still commemorated as a public holiday in Bangladesh; for citizens of that country, language is felt as a profoundly emotional phenomenon, and also one which has true political resonance.

Emotional resonance might equally be derived from a language's associations with religion. Arabic is a good example of this, of course: for observant Muslims, classical Arabic is quite simply the language of God's revelation, and is therefore not to be considered as one language among all the others, but above all the others. If one is studying linguistics, this can obviously be problematic, for as we noted in Chapter 2, it is a fundamental tenet of the discipline that, in terms of linguistic structure (rather than social prestige), there can be no hierarchy of languages: any one language is just as good as another. But still we have taught some Muslim students who have insisted on the exceptionalism of Arabic, even in linguistics classes, and even while agreeing that of course all *other* languages are to be considered equal. One simply said: 'My language is special.' Some have pointed to the elegance and regularity of Arabic grammar as proof of its divine perfection. The distinctive 'root and pattern' system revolves around triconsonantal word roots which, when combined with particular patterns of other letters, generate a host of related meanings. Hence for example the root *d r s* can give *madrassa* (school), *yadrus* (to study) and *yudarris* (to teach). The linguist Guy Deutscher, in his account of how languages develop, *The Unfolding of Language* (2005), is eloquent in his appreciation of this elegance: 'If there is anything in language which still seems to cry out for a conscious invention, this is surely it. For if it was not invented, how could people ever have stumbled across such an unusual idea?' (2005: 172). However, he then goes on, with a hint almost of regret, to demonstrate exactly how the grammatical systems of the Semitic languages (of which Arabic is of course one) are likely to have developed, driven by the very human desire to impose order on the disorderly and to draw analogies between the way one part of language behaves and another. It is not that Arabic came into being, as it were, perfectly formed and without irregularities: it is that, over time, humans have ironed many of the irregularities out.

Language ideologies come in all kinds. 'Ce qui n'est pas clair n'est pas français', claimed the eighteenth-century French writer Antoine de Rivarol: French is just *clearer* than other languages, something which one still sometimes hears from admirers of that language today. Another of Rivarol's claims, that French is in fact not just French, but 'la langue humaine' – the natural language of all humankind – is now perhaps rather less often heard; but in its day it was meant seriously. Aside from the intellectual, speakers' beliefs about their language might encompass the aesthetic, as when Brazilians sometimes say that Portuguese is 'a língua dos anjos', 'the language of the angels'. As we mentioned in Chapter 4, in some communities language is seen as a natural and necessary candidate for political control and legislation; in others it is not. To many French speakers it seems strange that English has no *Académie* to regulate it; to the English speaker it may seem just as strange that French feels it needs one. Language communities can differ also in the importance they ascribe to such social matters as the use of complex grammar as a sign of educational attainment (French, again); or accent as a marker of social class (British English, of course). And there is no shortage of downright crackpot invention, either, such as the Turkish Sun Language Theory of the 1930s, whose proponents, including Kemal Atatürk himself, claimed that Turkish was the true ancestor of all human languages (Lewis 2002).

It can be genuinely challenging for, say, an Arabic or French speaker to accept that there is nothing special per se about Arabic or French; that Arabic is not really holier than other languages, and French is not really clearer (Bengali not more heroic, Portuguese not more mellifluous, German not more logical, Greek not more glorious . . .). To be able to separate in one's mind the linguistic and the social, the scientific and the ideological, is a fundamental part of becoming a practised observer of language. In fact all languages have their particular quirks and variations, but no language is a complete outlier, and the variation is not random. Linguistics gives us the frameworks and general principles by which we can see commonalities in language, and thereby begin to understand and appreciate difference in some sort of context. Developing an awareness of how different languages behave, including your own, an understanding of why they behave as they do and a tolerance for what seems 'other', is all part of becoming a noticer of language. As the Roman playwright Terence wrote, *Homo sum, humani nihil a me alienum puto*: 'I am a human being; I consider nothing that is human to be alien to me'. It's all human language: none of it is strange at all, really.

5.7 Conclusion

We have tried to demonstrate in this chapter that a basic knowledge of some overall linguistic frameworks can help ease the difficulty we all encounter when faced with another language or another way of 'doing things' in language. In essence, the more you know about language as a field of study, the easier it is to engage with any particular language and its speakers. This chapter concludes Part I of the book and prefigures Part II, where we introduce some of the key concepts and approaches in the field of linguistics and the study of language. The issues that we have raised in Part I and the explanations that we have offered are intended to whet the appetite for what is to come, as we turn from looking at broad-based language issues and concepts to the actual description and analysis of language itself.

Suggested reading

Dalby, A. (1998), *Dictionary of Languages: The Definitive Reference to More than 400 Languages.* London: Bloomsbury.

Descriptions of some hundreds of the languages and language groups of the world, alphabetically arranged, with notes about their history, dialects, range, literature and characteristic features. Includes useful maps and, often, examples of the languages and even the scripts in which they are written. Excellent as a reference book, or, for the language enthusiast, just for browsing.

Deutscher, G. (2005), *The Unfolding of Language.* London: William Heinemann.

An accessible and entertaining book which traces the development of human language from its first evolution to the present day and imbues it with a sense of awe and excitement. The author argues persuasively that creation and destruction are ever-present forces in language, leading inevitably and constantly to language change.

Swan, M. and B. Smith (eds) (2001), *Learner English, Second Edition: A Teacher's Guide to Interference and other Problems.* Cambridge: Cambridge University Press.

An established classic of a reference book, battered copies of which are to be found on the bookshelves of English language teachers all over Britain and, particularly, in language schools worldwide. As well as giving descriptions of the basic features (phonological, grammatical and so on) of a range of commonly encountered languages and groups of languages, it lists the common mistakes made in English by speakers of these languages which result from 'interference' from the native tongue.

PART TWO

The study of language

Introduction to Part II

As will be clear by now, linguistics is an extremely wide-ranging field of study. This is unsurprising given the centrality of communication in human experience and its fundamental expressive and reflective role. As we explained in our 'General Introduction', our focus is on the kind of linguistics that is concerned with communication in social interaction; on language and other communicative modes as can be observed in our day-to-day interactions.

In Part I, we considered different communicative phenomena that we ourselves had found interesting and even puzzling in the course of our daily lives. We used these to consider questions relating not only to language as an object of study in its own right but also as a social agent which plays a fundamentally important role in issues such as interpersonal relationships, identity and power. However, in order to discuss such issues, it is necessary to have access to some foundational linguistic tools of the kind that we, as linguists, often take for granted as being part and parcel of our analytical repertoire. The aim of Part II, therefore, is to introduce these tools and show how they can be used to develop readers' language awareness and analytical expertise.

First of all, we argue that language awareness is developed by observing, describing and understanding communicative activity in its natural environments. This is not to say that these environments are always informal or uncontrived. For instance, a political speech might be an example of contrived communication but, as Fairclough and Fairclough (2012) show, it can be a rich linguistic resource for analysis. We also want to reiterate that we consider language from a *multimodal* perspective in that we extend the meaning of *language* in language awareness to include non-verbal communicative modes alongside the verbal modes of speaking and writing. However, as we have already pointed out, in order to observe the language phenomena encountered, it is necessary to work with particular analytical and descriptive resources, those tools that we have just mentioned. So, to put it as simply as we can, for us language awareness is knowing what language looks like and how it works as a system (*linguistic* knowledge); it is knowing how to talk about language; the terms of reference and what they refer to (*metalinguistic* knowledge); it is knowing what language does and how it does it (*social semiotic* knowledge). With this tripartite approach, we can say that for us the term *language awareness* encapsulates what it is we hope this book helps readers to develop. With enhanced language awareness, as we understand it, readers will find themselves becoming more actively observant of the communicative phenomena they encounter every day, more critically engaged with these phenomena and ultimately in a stronger position to participate persuasively in debates which have language at their core.

We start off with an overview of the fundamental descriptive tools of linguistics (phonetics and phonology, morphosyntax and semantics) in Chapter 6 and then explain the frameworks that we use when analysing the different communicative phenomena we have chosen for this book (Chapter 7). The following three chapters demonstrate how these linguistic tools and frameworks can be used to explore such things as differences between the grammar of speaking and the grammar of writing or the etiquette involved in, say, signing a workplace leaving card. Chapter 8 is concerned with spoken and speech-like communication, Chapter 9 considers writing and writing-like communication and Chapter 10 explores how we shape our meanings by making particular semiotic choices. Although our interpretations of these examples may differ from those of other people, we make no apology for this as our aim is to show how a linguistics lens can open up how we think about the kinds of communication we practise and experience. In so doing, we hope to encourage readers to undertake analyses of their own in response to their own questions originating from their own observations.

6

Essential linguistic tools

6.1 Approaches to the study of language

In the essays in the first part of this book we have already used a number of terms from the field of discourse analysis, such as text, genre and register, that help us to characterize different kinds of language and communication. We also used terms borrowed from the broad field of sociolinguistics, such as code-switching, dialect, domain and diglossia, which help us as observers to talk with a certain amount of precision about how language works in society. We now turn to what might be regarded as the traditional core of descriptive linguistics, the study of language form and meaning. We should point out once more that the aim of this chapter, as with the whole of this book, is not to teach the reader linguistics. Rather, it is to introduce basic terms and ideas in order to illustrate the scope and field of activity of linguistics and encourage the reader to go off and read up for herself or himself the areas that seem most interesting and relevant. We hope that readers will be able quickly to start using these tools themselves, thus becoming better resourced when thinking about and debating issues connected with language.

One of the main difficulties in talking about linguistic tools and approaches is that it very quickly becomes difficult to separate them: some of the borders between the traditional terms of reference are very porous and very unstable. To give just one example: in languages like English, intonation is generally considered part of phonology (the sound system of a particular language – we discuss it below). By varying intonation, we can express attitude – anger, suspicion, delight, surprise – but we cannot change the dictionary meaning of a word, even though we may change its semantic value in context, as in a sarcastically drawled 'oh, *sorry*'. In tonal languages, by contrast, such as Igbo, Punjabi, Dangme or Vietnamese, intonation also has lexical value. This means that by changing the tone with which you say some words, for example from falling tone to falling-rising tone, you actually change the meaning of the word. In Igbo, for instance, the utterance *ike* can mean 'strength', 'buttocks', 'to tie' or 'to share', depending on the tone. And so the study of intonation crosses into what would usually be considered the territory of semantics, which is the study of meaning, or perhaps grammar (and in fact linguists in the tradition of M. A. K. Halliday would argue that the distinction between semantics and grammar is a false one). Indeed, phonology is considered separately from phonetics, the study of the articulation of sounds, partly in order to cater for this kind of phenomenon; and phonology, unlike phonetics, has often been considered to be part of grammar, even though it is usually grouped with phonetics for the sake of convenience.

Fuzziness along the boundaries of how terms are defined is something which affects linguistics as much as any other academic field, and possibly more than most, as it is still a relatively young discipline. Ferdinand de Saussure's *Cours de Linguistique Générale*, compiled from lecture notes by his students after his death and generally regarded as the foundation stone of the modern discipline, was published in 1916. Even the very notion of what linguistics is, or what it should consist of, has often been a matter of disagreement (see Harris 2003). Apart from anything else, there is a particularly visible fault line separating 'theoretical' linguists, who tend to view language as an abstract system, and those for whom language is always and inevitably embedded in a social and cultural context (Hall 2005).

Rather than discuss at great length the possible ways of conceiving of the scope and subdivisions of linguistics, we have opted in this part of the chapter to provide very basic descriptions of what we regard as being the three core areas of the linguistic system: semantics, in which we include for good measure some mention of pragmatics; morphosyntax; and phonetics and phonology. Not everyone will agree with this way of dividing the territory up, but in the context of this book and its particular purpose, it seems to us coherent.

6.2 The study of language meaning: Semantics (and some pragmatics)

Semantics is the study of language meaning; but this apparently simple definition conceals enormous complexity. In essence, semantics refers to the relation between what Saussure identified as the 'signifier' (the form taken by a particular sign) and the 'signified' (what is meant by this sign). One way of approaching this relation, at the level of word meaning, is to use what is called componential analysis: in this way it can be shown explicitly what characteristics are denoted by a particular word. *Bull*, for example, would be [+bovine, +male, +adult], while *cow* might be [+bovine, +female, +adult] or perhaps [+bovine, -male, +adult]. *Calf* would comprise the components

[+bovine, -adult, +/-male]. Componential analysis is a handy enough tool for thinking through what we actually mean by a word, but it is only effective at a fairly limited level. The difference between *cow* and *calf* is straightforward, but how might you go about describing a more nuanced difference – say, between *understand* and *comprehend*? In addition, as the male/female component above suggests, simply to declare that a word comprises certain components is to make an individual, subjective judgement, and perhaps an ideologized one. Should, 'male' be the default, neutral position? More broadly, is it really the case that everyone thinks in the same way, or has the same mental map, as is implied here?

Other semantic tools allow us to describe and define the relationships between one sign and another: *hyacinth* is a hyponym of *flower*; *single* and *unmarried* are synonyms, and are antonyms of *married*. *Young* and *new* are both antonyms of *old*, but they are not themselves synonymous. And so on. There are other ways of analysing words, too, and beyond the level of individual words, meaning at sentence or utterance level might be analysed in any number of ways, or from any number of different perspectives. One influential theory, for example, is that of the speech act (Austin 1962), associated first with the philosopher J. L. Austin, and developed later by J. R. Searle. Here the emphasis is placed not on the relationship between words, but on the intention that lies behind the words, and the effect that the utterance has on the speaker. To say 'is it me, or is it hot in here?' is not merely a question or an observation: the *illocutionary force* of the utterance – that is, its intended objective rather than its surface form – is to request permission to open a window, or to invite an offer to open a window on the part of someone listening (and see the brief discussion of pragmatics below).

Now of course, you and I might not agree on what is meant by an utterance, or one of us might not be playing by the rules. As Coulthard and Johnson (2007: 201) suggest with reference to courtroom cross-examination, there are contexts in which Gricean 'rules' of communication (see Chapter 7) are subverted if not completely flouted (see text box). While most signs may seem to be fixed (we know, or are pretty sure we know, what is meant by *hat* or *house*, at least in our own culture), in fact when we communicate with another person, we take a gamble that that person will 'know what we mean'. Across cultures, this is obviously trickier still. If you ask a Mexican and an Inuit to draw a hat or a house, they will probably draw quite different things. More than this surface difference, though, they might well have different conceptions of what a hat actually is. For one, something used to help keep the head cool; for the other, something used to help keep the head warm. Generalized stereotypes exist, though, and can sometimes be surprising: Mexican or Peruvian Christmas cards often have snowmen on them, though their recipients may never have experienced snow directly, just as British ones have reindeer on them, though we may never have seen a reindeer.

A man approaches a house where a small boy is sitting on the steps. 'Is your mother at home, sonny?' he asks. 'Yes', says the boy. The man knocks on the door. No answer. 'Are you sure she's at home?' he asks. 'Oh, yes', replies the boy. The man knocks again, and again, and still gets no answer. Exasperated, he turns to the boy: 'I thought you said your mother was at home'. 'She is', answers the boy. 'But this isn't our house'.

Jokes, like this one from Les Dawson, quite often turn upon the infringement of one or more of the maxims incorporated in Grice's Co-operative Principle (Grice 1989: 368–72): Quality (truthfulness), Quantity (informativeness), Relation (relevance) and Manner (clarity). (See following chapter). The boy is, of course, telling the truth, but the man, being a rational listener, is misled by the boy's failure to volunteer a crucial piece of information, thereby disregarding the principle of Quantity.

It is necessary, then, to differentiate between *meaning* and *interpretation*; partly because there is a question of control – do you as the speaker/writer have ownership over the meaning of what you say, or do I as the listener/reader have the freedom to interpret? Both obviously could be the case, but the choices a speaker makes usually imply an attempt to constrain possible meanings: that is, you intend to mean a certain thing, and you intend me to understand it as it is meant. Where this breaks down, confusion or even conflict can ensue ('I didn't mean it like that!'). These kinds of communicative events were looked at in some detail by Kress and Hodge (1979). In some specific contexts and genres, ambiguity or opacity might actually be sought and valued. Poets, among others, might wish to de-constrain, or 'set free', possible meanings and interpretations of words; and comedy often plays with double meaning, or what is called in French 'double understanding' – *double entendre*.

Here, where interpretation as well as intended meaning must be taken into account, is where semantics shades into pragmatics. Or to put it another way, 'as soon as reference to speaker and addressee becomes vital to an analysis, that analysis properly belongs to pragmatics' (Atkinson et al. 1982: 216). Pragmatics, then, is the study of meaning that cannot be predicted from straightforward linguistic knowledge. It follows that it is, therefore, notoriously culture-bound (and remember what we said in Chapter 3 about how groups of speakers speak 'to each other', as it were, understanding their own terms among themselves).

Consider how much cultural knowledge of the world you would need, and in particular of the British, English-speaking part of it, in order to understand the following exchange, taking place in a busy office first thing in the morning:

Example 6.1

A: (*Sharply*) Isn't Jennifer in yet?
B: (*Sighing*) Tiddles is ill again.

What kind of position might Speaker A hold? What about Speaker B? Who or what is meant by the lexical item *Jennifer*? What is the relation of Jennifer to A and B? What does *in* mean here? In where, or what? Why is the tone of voice important? What does B's sigh suggest? Who or what is meant by *Tiddles*? How is *Tiddles* as a name different from *Jennifer*? Why is this important to the meaning of the exchange? How does *again* help us understand the underlying meaning of the exchange? We could go on. Understanding a language means not only understanding its structure, its grammar and lexis, but understanding how it is used in its social context: this, at its most basic, is what the groundbreaking American linguist Dell Hymes meant by 'communicative competence' (Hymes 1972), as opposed to the focus on purely linguistic competence, associated with Chomsky, that had previously characterized much linguistics.

In fact, semantics/pragmatics is almost infinite in its scope and complexity, and to study the relationship between language and everything that we use language to talk about is clearly as much a province of philosophy as it is of linguistics. What is more, language does not exist only to express meaning or to convey information. As Halliday has pointed out repeatedly, language is also the tool we use to structure and understand the world:

> Language is not a domain of human knowledge (except in the special context of linguistics, where it becomes an object of scientific study); language is the essential condition of knowing, the process by which experience becomes knowledge. (Halliday 1993: 94)

Learning one's mother tongue, then, is not just a process of learning which labels, or signs, to attach to things.

> A child learning a language is at the same time learning other things through language – building up a picture of the reality that is around him and inside him. In this process, which is also a social process, the construal of reality

> is inseparable from the construal of the semantic system in which the reality is encoded. (Halliday 1978: 2)

Semantics might therefore be considered an overarching aspect of meaning-making: meaning-making in the sense of trying to get a meaning across to another person, but also in the sense of making the world around us meaningful. Benjamin Lee Whorf in the 1930s, developing a position first advanced by Edward Sapir, famously claimed that this constructing of the world through language inevitably meant that speakers of different languages saw reality in different ways: this so-called linguistic determinism was the essence of what came to be known as the Sapir–Whorf Hypothesis. While the Sapir–Whorf Hypothesis still offers us an intriguing account of the relationship between language and the world, few linguists now think that thought is determined in such a black-and-white way by the language one happens to speak. Halliday, again, argues that although different languages express meaning in different ways – they have 'different semantic systems' – this does not mean that the speakers of those languages perceive things differently, simply that they focus on things differently: 'They pay attention to different characteristics . . . and so build up a rather different framework for the systematisation of experience' (1978: 198). Hence as we saw in the last chapter, equivalence gaps often occur, where what is specified in one language is not specified in another.

6.3 The study of language form: morphosyntax, or grammar

In Molière's *Le Bourgeois Gentilhomme* (1671), Monsieur Jourdain is delighted to be informed by his philosophy tutor that his everyday utterances, as they are not poetry, are in fact prose. 'Good heavens!' he exclaims: 'For more than forty years I have been speaking prose without knowing it!' There is something of this in popular conceptions of grammar, a word which is weighed down with associations of good and bad, correct and incorrect, 'proper' language and sloppy or debased language. It has, for many, an anxiety-inducing whiff of the schoolroom about it. Did they but know it, though, pretty much everyone has been speaking 'grammar' for most of their lives. For linguists, as we saw in Chapter 2, grammar is not an arcane and abstract set of rules to be learned by heart ('Don't end a sentence with a preposition'; 'The infinitive must not be split'): it is the key to all human language, standard and non-standard alike. It could be thought of as the elemental glue which holds the pieces of language together, if this were not so static a metaphor. Actually, it is more like a galvanizing force, bringing the inert matter of intrinsically meaningless sounds and sound combinations to life: think of the lightning crackling around the roof of the watchtower-laboratory in Universal's 1931 film *Frankenstein*. Grammar is above all creative, or as linguists say, generative: with grammar, an infinite number of utterances can be produced out of a limited number of sounds.

So what does grammar consist of? Descriptive linguists often prefer to use the term *morphosyntax* instead of the everyday term grammar, as it combines the twin aspects which make up a grammatical system. First there is morphology, which is simply word formation, or how the parts of a word fit together. The building block is the *morpheme* or the 'minimal unit of meaning or grammatical function' (in Yule 2006: 63). Morphemes can be free, that is, able to stand alone, or bound, in which case they have to be attached to another morpheme. So the English word *undelivered* consists of the free morpheme *deliver* and the bound morphemes *un-* and *-ed*. There are lexical and functional classes of morphemes, derivational and inflectional; Yule (2006) offers a clear and accessible introduction. Then there is syntax, or the rules governing how words are then formed into clauses or sentences. The name of Syntagma Square in central Athens celebrates the Constitution of the Greek Republic. Syntax, then, governs how a sentence is *constituted*, or how its constituent parts are put together to create meaningful utterances. As we saw in Chapter 5, different languages constitute themselves in different ways. Some languages have elaborate morphology and some, like Chinese, little or no morphology to speak of at all; correspondingly, the syntactic rules of some languages demand very strict word order, while those of others are quite relaxed. But all languages have grammar, and so do all the dialects and varieties of those languages: a language with 'no' grammar, as people sometimes describe creoles (e.g. Jamaican Patois), like a dialect with 'incorrect' grammar, is a contradiction in terms.

Correctness being a less useful concept than well-formedness (see Chapter 2), variation in morphosyntax, for our purposes, is chiefly interesting for what it *does*, or what it means in a social sense; the grammar of a language is not primarily a set of rules to be followed, but a conceptual resource that allows us to characterize and analyse variation in the shape and form of words and sentences. When you look objectively at language use (and for this kind of exercise linguists sometimes use what is called a *corpus*, plural *corpora*, a large collection of samples of natural language), you begin to see for example that the grammar of spoken English is often actually *different* from that of the written standard. Take the example of *there's*:

> The whole area of plural and singular forms is problematised by real evidence from spoken corpora. For example, the form *There's* is used

standardly in spoken English irrespective of whether the following subject is singular or plural.

- There's two directions you can take her
- There's a cafe up there to the right

(Carter 1999: 157)

To return to our poster data from Chapter 2, we have:

Example 6.2

'Helping Participations'; 'Promoting Students' Right'

In morphosyntactic terms, we would say that what is happening here is the singularizing of plurals and the pluralization of terms that in standard English would be singular. If we were to encounter it with sufficient regularity, we might venture to suggest that it is a tendency in South Asian English (see Kerswill et al. 2007). The logging of such variation is hence one of the ways in which linguists are able to differentiate one dialect or variety from another. A distinctive syntactic variation present in, among other varieties, African-American Vernacular English (or AAVE; black American English) is what is technically known as the deleted copula, or absence in particular circumstances of some form of 'to be':

Example 6.3

'I'm positive he dead' (from the film *Django Unchained*)

Where the verb 'to be' is present in AAVE, though, it does not always work in the same way as it does in standard English:

Example 6.4

'He be talking up a baby storm' (Twitter user describing her child learning to talk)

The observer of British language use with an ear or eye for syntactic variation will also no doubt have come across some distinctive use of *tense*, not by ethnically or regionally defined groups of speakers, but by groups sharing a profession (again, recall our discussion of 'belonging' in Chapter 3). There is what might be called the historian's present tense, which has spread vigorously in recent years to become almost the default mode for academic historians in the media hoping, perhaps, thereby to lend a sense of immediacy to their subject:

Example 6.5

> When Henry V takes the throne, one of his first actions is a very important reburial of that deposed king Richard II in Westminster Abbey. In other words Henry is almost I think recognising the seriousness of that and saying, 'OK, let's move on'. . . . He does sense the mood of the time, but I also think he brings something to it, that one of his instinctive skills as a politician is that he is a nation-builder, so he picks up on these things that are around, but not only brings them forward, but fashions them into something, and that's one of his superb intuitive skills. (*In Our Time*, BBC Radio 4, 16 September 2004)

Perhaps more immediately engaging, to some at least, is what we will call the footballer's present perfect tense. In this variation, the footballer's post-match TV interview uses not, as might be expected, the preterite or simple past tense for an event which is over and in the past, but the present perfect, rather as if he were watching a video recording of the game and imagining himself still in it. This is Shola Ameobi describing a goal for Newcastle United:

Example 6.6

> Obviously the angle wasn't great, but I've caught it and it's hit the back of the net before Brad Friedel's even dived. . . . It's obviously come at a good time for us, when we were chasing the equaliser. (*Sky Sports*, 16 October 2011)

This is also a common tense style in more basilectal (i.e. further away from the standard) London speech when a narrative is being recounted. (Overheard in an east London pub: 'So I've said to him, you're having a laugh! And he's turned round and he's said, no, I ain't') It is tempting to speculate – it is of course impossible to say with any assurance – that it is through the route of footballers from London going to play at clubs elsewhere in England that this syntactic quirk has spread.

This sort of observational analysis is what is facilitated by the tools associated with the study of morphosyntax – and, more essentially, why we do linguistics! We can do something similar, too, working primarily with only morphology, by which we analyse words into their component parts. Take the example of the English comparative. As we all know, the basic rule for forming the comparative is to add the bound morpheme *-er* to a word, or *-r* to its stem if it already ends in *-e*. So we get *smooth – smoother*; *simple – simpler* and so on. There are then various rules governing changes such as the spelling rule about reduplication of consonants, as in *red – redder*, and the use of the free morpheme *more* instead of *-er* to modify longer words in order to make them less ungainly and difficult to say, as in *patronising – more patronising*. All of these rules you learned at school or acquired over the years, along with some very well-known exceptions to the rules, such as *good – better*. So how can we account for the utterances in Example 6.7?

Example 6.7

> 'The soufflé needs to be much more sweeter.' (*Masterchef*, BBC TV)
>
> 'Policing needs to be much more firmer.' (Caller to BBC Radio 5 Live)
>
> 'I'm much more better than I have been. . . . Before it was much more worser.' (Sportsman interviewed on BBC Radio 5 Live on the subject of his illness)
>
> 'The sea is a lot more calmer tonight.' (Man interviewed on BBC Radio 4)

This is not a recent phenomenon, indicative of a sudden slide in standards, whatever people might think. Ian Dury's fine line about an amorous girl called Gina, 'a seasoned-up hyena could not have been more obscener' (from the song 'Billericay Dickie') dates from 1977; but note George, the carter's, judgement on some beer in Charles Dickens's *The Old Curiosity Shop* (1840–41): 'It's more flatterer than it might be,' George returned, 'but it an't so bad for all that'.[1] In fact, it's not even a purely English phenomenon: in Spanish you can hear *más mejor* ('more better') – a usage abhorred by purists every bit as much as its English counterpart.

Of course, what we are primarily interested in is not the morphosyntactic forms themselves, but what the forms signify. It is likely that these forms have arisen due to the universal drive towards linguistic expressiveness and the attendant feeling on the part of the speaker that the comparative form on its own lacks sufficient emphasis. This produces what Deutscher (2005: 99) calls 'inflationary weakening of meaning'; and the common addition of *a lot* or *much* as in *much more better* also suggests that this might be the case. It was via a similar process, as Deutscher shows, that the (originally standard) French *je ne sais* eventually became (the currently standard) *je ne sais pas* (2005: 98–9). These usages have been hovering just beyond standardness for a very long time, and may eventually make it, as it were. But because they are – for now at least – non-standard, they tend to be associated with lower social status and to attract the opprobrium of those for whom 'good' language necessarily means standard language.

6.4 The sounds of language

There are essentially two ways of talking about the sounds of language. On the one hand is the physiological description of sound production, *phonetics*, and on the other is the description of how the sound system works in a given language, *phonology*. We take each in turn.

6.4.1 Phonetics

Phonetics is concerned with the physical properties of speech sounds. Its primary function is to enable us to describe the production of sounds, or articulation. There are also areas of the field concerned with the perception of speech sounds by the listener (auditory phonetics) and the properties of speech sounds (acoustic phonetics). We are not going to concern ourselves with these here, nor attempt to list all the technical terms or all the sounds and symbols contained in the International Phonetic Alphabet (IPA). An accessible introductory course such as Roach (1991), or the relevant chapters of Yule (2006) will serve your purpose if you want to explore the area in a little more detail. But let's at least illustrate the principle by which speech sounds are described, by looking at consonants.

Consonant sounds are identified and described in a tripartite fashion: Is the sound voiced or voiceless? What is the place of articulation? What is the manner of articulation? Voiced versus voiceless is very straightforward: when you produce the sound, do your vocal cords vibrate? If yes, it's a voiced sound (like the /d/ sound in *dame*); if not, it's voiceless (like the /t/ sound in *take*). All whispering, therefore, is voiceless. Place of articulation refers to the place in the mouth where the sound is produced. If it is made by putting your two lips together, then it's a bilabial, as in /p/ and /b/. If it is made by lip and teeth, it's a labiodental, as in /f/ and /v/. If it is made by putting the tongue against the alveolar ridge – the ridge behind the top teeth – it's an alveolar, like /d/. Then there is dental, palatal, velar and so on: some languages have uvular and pharyngeal sounds, too. Manner of articulation describes the *kind* of sound it is: for example a plosive, also known as a stop (when you stop the airflow for a brief fraction of a second, as in /k/ or /t/), or a fricative (when you obstruct the airflow to create friction, as in /z/ or /v/); there are then other kinds such as affricate, nasal and approximant. You can see the various parts of the speech apparatus in Figure 6.1:

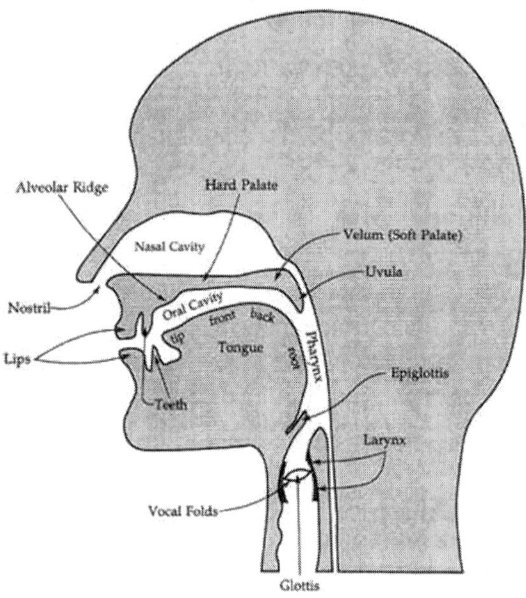

FIGURE 6.1 *Diagram of speech apparatus.*

Armed with these principles, we can set about describing in a basic way the various consonant sounds, each of which is allocated a symbol in the IPA. Let's take the consonant sound which begins the English word *thing*. First, it doesn't have any voicing. (If it did, it would instead be the sound at the beginning of the word *these*). It is produced by putting the tongue against the teeth, so it is a dental. And the airflow is obstructed slightly to create friction, rather than stopped, so it is a fricative. So we have:

*th*ing = /θ/ = voiceless dental fricative
*th*ese = /ð/ = voiced dental fricative

To give one more example, let's take the sound at the beginning of the word *pike*. It's voiceless (if it were voiced, the word would be *bike*); it's produced by putting the lips together, and the air is stopped for a fraction of a second, then released. So we have:

*p*ike = /p/ = voiceless bilabial plosive
*b*ike = /b/ = voiced bilabial plosive

Figure 6.2 is a chart of voice, place and manner of articulation which covers what Roach (1991) considers to be the phonemic consonant sounds of standard (received) British English pronunciation. If you look at the charts for other languages, or other dialects of English, you may find some consonants are different and there may be fewer or more than are shown here.

Manner of Articulation \ Place of Articulation	Bilabial		Labio-dental		Dental		Alveolar		Palato-alveolar		Palatal		Velar		Glottal	
Plosive	p	b					t	d			k	g				
Fricative			f	v	θ	ð	s	z	ʃ	ʒ					h	
Affricate									tʃ	dʒ						
Nasal		m						n						ŋ		
Lateral																
Approxi-mant		w								r		j				
	Voiceless								Voiced							

FIGURE 6.2 *Place and manner of articulation chart for English RP.*

Vowels, meanwhile, are identified and described by where they originate in the mouth (front, centre or back), and by degree of openness or closeness (see Roach 1991: 10–25). Using this basic method, every sound known in every recorded language in the world can be, and has been, identified, described and given a number and a symbol to represent it. This means that even if you cannot speak a particular language, if you have a good grasp of the IPA you can read out a phonetic transcription of an utterance in that language and be fairly confident of being understood by a native speaker – though of course you won't understand what it is that you have just said.

You might by now be thinking that this has little to do with *language* – it's more like physiology. This is so: your dentist, for example, might well have had to study some phonetics, while clinicians and technicians working in areas like speech therapy and prosthetic dentistry certainly have. Phonetics is purely physical, or physiological, and concerned only with sounds: what marries sounds to meaning, and hence takes us back towards the realm of grammar, is phonology.

6.4.2 *Phonology*

Where phonetics is physical, phonology is essentially abstract. It is often described as being concerned with the sound system of a particular language, rather than the actual sounds of language themselves. The fundamental building block of phonology is the phoneme, which is the smallest segment of sound in a language that can be used to distinguish meaning, or more specifically, which can be used to distinguish between two different words. Phonology is concerned with how these phonemes are organized and distributed within a particular language or language variety; in other words, with how they relate to each other. Phonemes are not, then, actual sounds as such: they are an abstract concept, of which real speech sounds are the phonetic realization. It is conventional in linguistics to show actual, precise phonetic realizations within square brackets, like this [ ], while phonemes are shown within slashes like this / /, as you will have noticed above. For any language you can make a phonemic inventory – that is, the list of sounds in that language which can be used to distinguish meaning. This is generally the first task undertaken by field linguists who are attempting to record and classify a 'new' (to them) language or to develop a writing system for a language that doesn't yet have one. The number of phonemes in the list can vary quite dramatically from language to language: the New Guinean language Rotokas has 11, while !Xu (spoken in southern Africa), has 141 (Crystal 1987). English has about 40, depending on what dialect of English you are looking at.

Like much of what is called structural linguistics, phonology depends on the notion of meaningful contrast; so a phoneme is identified and defined in terms of how it contrasts with other phonemes. That is to say: it is important to know not just what a sound is, but what it is *not*. This is why it is so difficult to acquire a native-like accent if you learn a foreign language as an adult. When you are learning your mother tongue as an infant, your brain quickly (actually *astonishingly* quickly) works out what are the meaningful contrasts in the language or languages that surround you. If you grow up as an English speaker, you learn to distinguish between the phonemes /v/ and /w/, because the contrast between the two sounds is capable of producing a difference in meaning (as in *vest* and *west* or *weird* and *veered*: a pair of words like this, or like *pike* and *bike* above, is known as a minimal pair). If you grow up speaking a language like Hindi or Turkish, to you [v] and [w] are simply allophones of the same phoneme; that is to say, they are just different ways of realizing the same phoneme (which is why we put them between square brackets rather than the slashes that indicate a phoneme proper), and replacing one with the other will not produce a change in meaning. So your brain learns to disregard the difference and concentrate on the things that are important in that language. In Hindi, for example, unlike in English, it is vital to distinguish between unaspirated /k/ and aspirated /k^h/, which are two different phonemes, capable of making a difference in meaning. In later life, the English teacher at your school in India or Turkey will insist that in English it is equally vital to distinguish between /v/ and /w/, and if you are a dutiful pupil you will try to do so. But it is horribly difficult to overcome what is literally the habit of a lifetime: a small voice in your subconscious is telling you that the difference doesn't *really* matter. Indeed, you might not even be able to hear it (and for that matter, nor might your teacher, if she is not a native English speaker). The word or sound that gives you away or marks you out as a non-native speaker is called a shibboleth, from the story in the Old Testament (see text box).[2]

As we pointed out in Chapter 5, the errors that people make in a second or foreign language often tell you something about their first language. This is just as true of phonology as it is of grammar. Hence the United Nations interpreter who heard a delegate say what sounded like 'and now I want to put the water tanks': it turned out to be 'and now I want to put the vote of thanks'.[3] Presumably in the delegate's mother tongue, neither /v/ and /w/ nor /t/ and /θ/ constituted contrasting phonemes. Regardless of all the years he had spent learning and speaking English, regardless of the importance of getting your English right in such a high-prestige context, still there was the little voice in his head reassuring him that /t/ and /θ/ were, if not exactly the same, just two ways of pronouncing what is basically the same sound. Tanks, thanks: how much difference can it really make?

Phonetics and phonology, like morphosyntax, constitute a vital resource for the noticer of language. Once you are able to describe and classify precisely the speech you hear, you can go on to analyse its features in terms of their social or communicative content. We might note, for example, that for younger, inner-city London speakers, [d] is becoming an acceptable allophonic variant of the phoneme /ð/. (Remember 'Dat is sick, man' from Chapter 1; and a card on a wreath of flowers left in a London street in memory of a teenager murdered there in a gang fight read: 'RIP brudda'). We can say that the place of articulation in the mouth has moved back one place, as it were, and the manner of articulation has changed, so a voiced dental fricative has become a voiced alveolar plosive.

Moving on from the mechanics of phonetics and phonology, because we know that this is a common feature in African-Caribbean English, we might venture a sociolinguistic hypothesis that the sound originally shifted because of the perceived prestige of 'black' speech in school playgrounds, and that its prominence now is an example of the embedding of the urban mixed ethnic code, or Multicultural London English (Rampton 2010; Cheshire et al. 2008). We might hazard a similar hypothesis about the process of monophthongization which renders *like* as /la:k/ as opposed to /laik/, and *right* as /ra:t/ instead of /rait/, and which can be heard with increasing frequency among young London speakers (see Kerswill et al. 2007; Cheshire et al. 2008 for very detailed surveys of these kinds of sound shifts). In other words, we need phonetics to describe what is happening, but phonology to systematize what is happening, and insights from social semiotics and sociolinguistics to explain the communicative value of the change in pronunciation and its importance from a societal perspective.

Shibboleth: or, how linguistics might save your life

Depending on your own language's phonemic inventory, there will be certain sounds that you find difficult to make, or even to hear, in other languages. We have a biblical example from some 4,000 years ago.

> *And the Gileadites took the passages of Jordan before the Ephraimites: and it was so, that when those Ephraimites which were escaped said, Let me go over; that the men of Gilead said unto him, Art thou an Ephraimite? If he said, Nay; Then said they unto him, Say now Shibboleth: and he said Sibboleth: for he could not frame to pronounce it right. Then they took him, and slew him at the passages of Jordan: and there fell at that time of the Ephraimites forty and two thousand.* (Judges xii: 4–6)

This is a splendid example of how deeply embedded the phonology of your native language is. All a fleeing Ephraimite had to do to save his life was perceive and reproduce the segment /ʃ/, the *sh-* sound at the beginning of the word *shibboleth*. But 42,000 of them said /s/, we are told, and died. Had they known about place and manner of articulation, phonemes and allophones, might they have lived?

6.5 Conclusion

In this chapter we have tried to introduce and illustrate some of the concerns of the core areas of linguistics, while skirting round the purely theoretical and emphasizing those aspects which are perhaps of most immediate relevance to the would-be linguistic ethnographer. As we commented at the outset, there is considerable argument about what linguistics might be said to consist of; boundaries are fuzzy and border skirmishes are not infrequent. This said, it is without doubt the case that all the disparate realms, principalities, enclaves and satrapies of linguistics in some sense need each other. The interconnectedness of all linguistic inquiry is nicely summed up in this statement by a leading expert in language typology and a practising field linguist:

> The discipline [of linguistics] is witnessing an intertwining of approaches to the study of language that have been evolving, often as independent

> strands, for well over a century. Major progress has been made in all traditional domains: phonetics, phonology, morphology, syntax, semantics, and discourse. The importance of understanding how linguistic categories and structures emerge over time, how children acquire them, and how social and cultural uses shape them, are now widely recognized. More is being learned every day about how language is utilized by speakers for social and cultural purposes. Technological and analytic advances have opened up possibilities for discoveries unimaginable at the outset, from fine acoustic analysis to the manipulation of corpora. Theories are becoming ever stronger, more detailed, and more sophisticated as we learn more about what occurs in typologically diverse languages. It is becoming increasingly clear that no aspect of language can be understood in isolation. (Mithun 2010: iii)

Why is this aspect of linguistics so important? The central tools and concepts that are used in linguistic description, and which we have introduced very briefly here, enable us to understand what language consists of at its very heart: how sounds are made and organized, how words and sentences fit together, how meaning is made. These principles operate across languages, free (at least in theory) of cultural and personal bias, enabling us to see the wholeness and unity which underlie the surface diversity of human language and communication. The central core of descriptive linguistics can be used to describe all languages and all varieties of language. A bilabial plosive, after all, is a bilabial plosive anywhere on earth and whatever language you happen to be speaking, and while the semantics and pragmatics of, say, politeness obviously vary from one culture and language to another, the *principle* of politeness exists in all languages, and the tools of linguistics give us the necessary terms to be able to discuss it. Descriptive linguistics therefore acts as a springboard, a set of technical concepts with which we can describe precisely what our language data consists of, before we proceed to social analysis and interpretation. As we commented in the introduction, not everybody enjoys the technical side of linguistics, but that is at least partly because its *relevance* is not always made clear to students. There is of course a great deal more to linguistics than the 'traditional' core – but that core is irreplaceable, and the noticer of language who spends some time becoming acquainted with it will find their efforts amply repaid.

In the next chapter we explain the general approach that we use in this book when analysing language and other textual data; that is, discourse analysis. We provide an overview of this approach before moving onto a more detailed account of the specific framework, social semiotics, within which we work. The combination of these two chapters (Chapters 6 and 7) provides the basis from which we can analyse and discuss the different examples provided in the three chapters that follow, demonstrating how linguistic knowledge and the tools it provides can offer insights into communicative activity from both the textual and social perspective.

Suggested reading

Jackson, H., and Stockwell, P. (2010), *An Introduction to the Nature and Functions of Language,* 2nd edn. London: Continuum.

Aimed at beginners in undergraduate linguistics, this book not only offers a comprehensive guide to the key concepts and theories in linguistics, but helps the student to gain expertise in analysing texts and discourses. It also provides study questions, summaries of each chapter and a glossary of terms.

Winkler, E. (2012), *Understanding Language: A Basic Course in Linguistics*. London: Bloomsbury.

Clear, comprehensive and entertainingly written, with lots of examples and a useful accompanying website.

Yule, G. (2006), *The Study of Language*, 3rd edn. Cambridge: Cambridge University Press.

Short, to the point and admirably clear, this basic introduction deserves its classic status.

7

A framework for analysis

7.1 Introduction

In the previous chapter, we introduced the basic descriptive tools that linguistics provides and in so doing showed how they can be used to illuminate different aspects of verbal communication. In this chapter we focus on the analytical approach that we use in this book, that is, discourse analysis, and explain its usefulness in drawing inferences about communicative activity. Of course, as we have already pointed out, it is difficult to separate the analytical frameworks from the descriptive tools and the purpose of this chapter is, essentially, to name and explain the approach, to disentangle the meanings attributed to the word *discourse* and to show how the approach can incorporate the analysis of non-verbal communicative modes.

7.2 Discourse analysis

Discourse analysis is the overarching approach to analysing communicative practices and communicative production in contemporary linguistics. It enables us to explore how we communicate, how we make our meanings and how those meanings are negotiated in the course of communicative activity; it allows us to 'read' below the surface. With discourse analysis we can focus on specific aspects of communicative activity so that we can say something about it that might be useful in exploring a given phenomenon. In Chapter 1, for instance, we used discourse analysis to examine different linguistic (and non-linguistic) phenomena that puzzled us and which we wanted to better understand, and in Chapters 3 and 4 we used it to explore communication across different domains and between people from different language and cultural backgrounds. Simply put, discourse analysis does exactly 'what it says on the tin'. It is what we do when we analyse communicative activity, when we use the evidence provided by texts to explore what is going on. From there we can begin to say other things about that communicative activity which can feed into debates in areas of human interest and concern as we have already shown.

It is worth pointing out that many discourse studies draw on additional research tools to provide further insights into the phenomena under investigation. Interviews with participants in a particular conversation or with the writer of a series of text messages, for instance, can offer the researcher new perspectives. Even passers-by of texts like the graffiti in Chapter 1, could be interviewed for comment. Language corpora, such as the British National Corpus of Spoken English referred to in Chapter 3, can also be used to shed light on aspects of the discourse under investigation. For instance, a researcher might want to know if the expression *innit*, as discussed in Chapter 1, is more widely used than commonly thought, and in what contexts. However, whatever further research tools one might use, if a phenomenological approach is used, as in the case of this book, discourse analysis is the most likely starting point.

7.3 Defining discourse

Before going further, it is necessary to clarify the term *discourse* itself because it has, like many terms of reference, acquired different interpretations and different uses over time. It needs to be distinguished, first of all, from language fragments such as isolated sentences or phrases which are generally analysed from the perspective of naming the different parts of speech, as in parsing. For example, the sentence 'She broke the round window.' can be described as follows,

She	Pronoun (personal)
broke	Verb (transitive)
the	Article (definite)
round	Adjective (attributive)
window	Noun (common)

or describing its syntactic structure.

She	Subject
broke	Verb (simple past)
the round window	(direct) Object

In these cases, the analysis is concerned with linguistic systems (language as a system of structures) and not with meaning (language as a system of meanings). Analysing language in this way is, of course, useful in its own right and apart from its fundamental importance in understanding the structural relationship between linguistic elements it can also be used to develop metalinguistic knowledge. In other words, it helps us to be able to talk about language explicitly by using the relevant terms of reference such as those we discussed in Chapter 6.

What makes discourse different to a language fragment such as the one above is that it refers to authentic stretches of language, real utterances in real communicative activity, obtained either by chance or by design (see e.g. Brown and Yule 1983). In this book, most of the discourse we refer to has been found through our own active observations, using a linguistic ethnography approach. However, it is also possible to obtain language data by design through establishing or seeking out a particular context where language samples can be collected. This kind of research is common where, for example, information about performance is sought, as for example in a school classroom, or when a particular question leads a researcher to want to explore certain social norms, such as, say, gender differences in text messaging. In research it is often the case that we encounter a phenomenon by chance and then go on to investigate it further by design. We analyse discourse because we want to say something about social interaction, about communicative practice and about meaning and interpretation.

However, there is sometimes a problem with how the term discourse can itself be understood. On the one hand is the linguistic interpretation associated with, for instance, pragmatics (e.g. Brown and Yule 1983), where discourse is taken to mean 'language-in-use', the utterances themselves as linguistic entities. On the other hand is the ideological use of the term associated with social relations such as status, power and identity, and although this sense of the term is associated with philosophy and sociology, notably Foucault (e.g. 1972), it has come to be linked inextricably to theories of communication connected with, for instance, social semiotics, social literacies and sociolinguistics (e.g. Hodge and Kress 1988; Gee 1996; Blommaert 2005), where discourse is viewed from both the linguistic and non-linguistic perspectives.

To illustrate the distinction between these two meanings, let's take the example of a universally understood genre, a joke, and its very well-known sub-genre, a national one-upmanship joke:

> An Englishman, an Irishman and a Scotsman were taking part in a survey about tea-drinking habits.
> 'I always stir my tea with my left hand,' said the Englishman.
> 'I always stir my tea with my right hand,' said the Scotsman.
> 'How about you?' the Irishman was asked.
> 'Oh me?' said the Irishman, 'I always use a spoon.'[1]

Now we can analyse this joke from the perspective of the textual resources used – the words, the way in which they are organized (cohesiveness), the grammatical structures and so on. That would be looking at it from a 'language in use' sense of discourse. However, we can also analyse it from the perspective of the social-cultural and ideological meanings of the joke. These kinds of joke can be more or less offensive; in this case offence is unlikely to be taken by any Englishman or Scot, though there are versions which could lead to dissent. The roles themselves can easily be redistributed to shift the national position or replaced with other nationalities (Peruvian, Chilean, Argentinian), different regional identities (Yorkshireman, Lancastrian, Northumbrian) or workplace threesomes (plumber, electrician, plasterer). In each case, there is an ideological meaning which is social-cultural and to do with identity, attitudes and sometimes, power.

It is this understanding of discourse that lets us know, for example, which newspapers support which political view. If, in the United Kingdom, you call someone a Guardian reader or a Daily Mail reader, what are you saying about them? Are you just stating a fact or are you implying something about their point of view, their personality, their social position? Are you criticizing them, disassociating yourself from them, teasing them? It all depends on your own point of view and on the social-cultural context of the moment.

What is of particular interest to linguists who, like us, adopt a social semiotic approach to discourse analysis, however, is not just the way in which ideological views are presented with the actual content of an utterance but how that content is articulated with the semiotic or textual (verbal, visual, gestural) resources that have been chosen for the purpose of a given communicative event. In other words, how do the elements that are involved in the production of a text work to produce particular kinds of meanings? To avoid some of the confusions surrounding the concept of discourse per se, we use the term *text* to refer to the communication in its material or represented form and the term *discourse* to refer to the sociocultural, or ideological, meaning. (See below for further clarification). Figure 7.1 overviews the different elements that a social semiotic approach to discourse analysis might take account of.

This approach to discourse analysis encapsulates both branches of discourse – the linguistic (or textual) and the ideological (or the social-cultural relations) as outlined above. It is the approach which we consider to be most useful for exploring the language phenomena that this book is concerned with. To help understand the approach we now clarify the three basic concepts represented in Figure 7.1: *context*, *text* and *semiotic resources*, concepts we have already come across in earlier chapters but which we now explain in more detail.

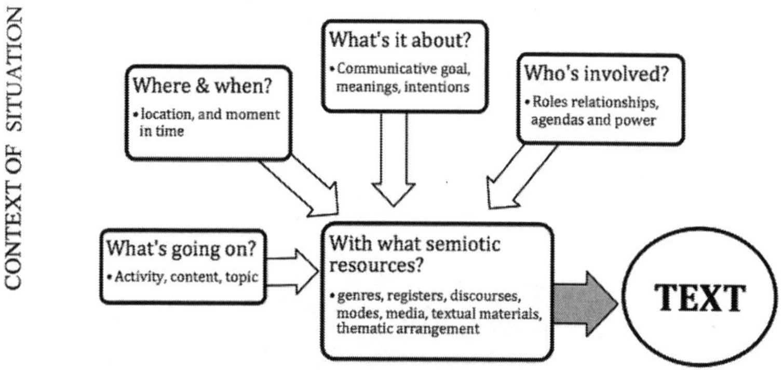

FIGURE 7.1 *A social semiotic framework for analysis of texts.*

7.4 Key concepts

7.4.1 Context

Some time ago, the glasses company, Specsavers, ran a newspaper and billboard advertisement which used the following semiotic resources: a photograph of a ball boy's torso and a photograph of a football. The ball boy image has a cross against it and the football has a tick (see Figure 7.2). In order to understand the intended meaning of the advertisement one would have to be familiar with the context in which it was designed. Without that contextual knowledge, even though the ad might work as a puzzle, the whole sense of it would be missed.

The term, context, refers to the circumstances in which any communication occurs. In Chapter 1, for example, the discussion about the graffiti involved not only the text itself but its location, its purpose, its intended audience, etcetera. Context refers to the *where*, the *why*, the *between whom* and even the *when*. Knowledge of context is fundamental to how we understand a text as we have already seen in Part I, although that does not mean that the same *experience* of the context is shared by everyone involved in a given textual interaction. For instance, a policeman and a detainee may share the context but their experience of it is likely to be very different. The spatial context, for instance, for the policeman is his place of work, whereas for the detainee, it is a place of detention. The activities that take place will also be experienced very differently. For the policeman an interview may be understood as a means of gaining information, whereas for the detainee it may involve giving away as little information as possible. In fact, who we are, our pasts, our cultures, our experiences, our identities, everything that we know comes into play when considering our experience of a given context, as has been discussed by, among others, Blommaert (2005), Pavlenko (2008). In fact, to a greater or lesser degree, no two people experience a communicative event (or any event, come to that) in the same way, although, of course, the whole purpose of communication is to be understood!

FIGURE 7.2 *Specsavers advertisement poster.*

This is something that the linguist Grice (1989) focused on in what he called 'the co-operative principle' and developed in what are known as Grice's Maxims (see also Chapter 6). These are, in a simplified form,

1. Quality – Speak the truth, be sincere
2. Quantity – Say neither more nor less than is necessary for the purpose at hand

3 Relation – Be relevant

4 Manner – Be clear, avoid obscurity

In other words, Grice argued that in communicative interaction our aim is to make our meaning as understandable as possible, otherwise there would be no point in communicating in the first place. Taking these maxims into account, then, when we see such an advertisement as the Specsavers one, we assume that it is intended to be meaningful, even if we don't immediately or exactly know what that meaning is. That is to say, upon being confronted with a text, we always first and foremost look for meaning in it.

The Specsavers advertisement itself relies upon a very specific piece of contextual knowledge which is highly localized within a particular community at a particular point in time. If you don't get its meaning it is because, as we discussed in Chapter 3, you are not a member of the community in which it works. So, to put you out of your misery (if you don't understand the Specsavers advertisement), it relies on two contextual understandings. The first is the long-standing video advertising campaign that the company has developed which involves showing humorous situations based on mistaken identity due to people's failure to wear glasses ('Should have gone to Specsavers', being the catchphrase). For example, an elderly shepherd shears his sheepdog, having mistaken her for one of the sheep, or a young woman passionately embraces a complete stranger, mistaking him for her boyfriend, who stands by bemused. The second essential contextual element concerns an infamous incident at an English Premier League football match in which a player was seen to kick a ball boy who, allegedly, held onto the ball too long in the final moments of the match. With this contextual knowledge, the ad becomes meaningful, witty and effective, albeit with a limited lifespan as, unlike the other ads in the campaign, it requires very specific contextual knowledge about the incident. Of course, if you were unfamiliar with the game of football, you would also need to know something else very important: that the point of the game is to kick the ball, not to kick a person!

If we think of context in this way, we can begin to understand how important it is to take account of it when analysing and discussing communicative activity and textual production. In fact, all communicative activity involves making choices based on what is required by the context. There is a constant interaction between the social, as encapsulated in context, and the material, the semiotic resources we use in textual production (see English 2011). These two combined dimensions are always at play in communicative activity.

1 紅磡	1分
2 紅磡	5分

If you can't read a particular script, and see a sign written in it while in a foreign country, you might try to make it meaningful by using contextual as well as co-textual clues. Try it with this sketched version of a sign seen in Hong Kong.

Unless you know at least some written Chinese, you will not be able to understand the writing on this sign. If you have never seen Chinese characters before, you may not even know that it is writing. What is familiar are the numbers, 1, 2 and 5. These offer some potential way into what the sign says: perhaps it is a list or an indication of how many things there are. By now you will be aware that the images next to the numbers are probably words. This is down to your knowledge of how communication works. If you look a bit more closely at the words as represented by the characters, you will notice that what is next to number 1 is identical to what is next to number 2, and the same goes for numbers 1 and 5 on the right of the sign.

Now if I tell you that you are on the platform of the Hong Kong metro system you will realize that this is a sign indicating train arrivals – particularly if you are familiar with other metro systems around the world. You might wonder if the left-hand 1 and 2 refer to platforms, but then what about the right-hand numbers 1 and 5? Using your contextual knowledge, alongside your experiential knowledge of other metro systems, you can probably infer that the sign is showing when the next trains are due and that each of the trains is going to the same destination. You can probably also infer that the character to the right of the right-hand numbers probably means 'minutes', as in 1 minute and 5 minutes rather than seconds or hours. As a language-aware person, you might also realize that there doesn't seem to be any difference between the two 'minutes' characters even though, in English, 1 minute is singular and 5 minutes is plural. After all this, what you won't, unfortunately, know is where exactly the train is going!

Luckily, as this was in Hong Kong, the electronic timetable sign switched between Chinese and English at regular intervals, as is shown here.

1 Hung Hom	1 min
2 Hung Hom	5 min

7.4.2 Text

In Chapter 1 we discussed the concept of text, but want to include it again here as it is a key concept in the analytical repertoire. In our earlier discussion, we extended the conventional meaning of the word to include all forms of meaningful representation articulated in some evidential/representational way. We pointed out that for something to be considered a text it had to have substance, cohesion and meaningfulness. If we are to analyse a text (or a textual interaction such as a conversation) then we have to consider its situatedness (contextual), its social function (interpersonal), its purpose (meaning potential) and its material nature (textuality) (Halliday and Hasan e.g. 1989).

As we also discussed, the text is the object of our analysis and comprises what we might consider to be a complete utterance. It could be a single word, uttered in a particular way, such as 'Help!', or a single image, like on a school student's exercise book, which transcends its depicted meaning, or a lengthy written contract, or an unapologetic announcement about train delays. As Kress (2010: 147) has explained,

> [t]he text . . . is recognised – from the maker's as much as from the viewer's/ hearer's/reader's perspective – by a sense of its 'completeness' in meaning . . . – it 'makes sense' by itself, in its appropriate social environment.

To understand this is to understand how linguistics helps us to focus on and then analyse *pieces* of language in seeking to explain communicative phenomena.

A key concept in understanding a text is what Halliday, drawing on the social anthropologists Malinowsky (1923) and Firth (1950), calls 'the situation' or rather 'the context of situation'. This refers to those aspects of communicative activity which are not textual (i.e. not the semiotic resources, either verbal or non-verbal). These include aspects such as the particular location, the expectations of the participants, cultural knowledge and experience as we have discussed above. It is the interaction between the material semiotic resources and the context that allows meanings to be made. '[T]he relation between text and context is a dialectical one: the text creates the context as much as the context creates the text. "Meaning" arises from the friction between the two' (Halliday 1989: 47). The relationship between the text and the context is fundamental in showing how communicative activity works, and can be better understood by considering communicative activity to involve three interrelated elements: the situation, (what is going on, where, when) in which the communicative event takes place, corresponding to Halliday's 'field', the participants (the people taking part), as in Halliday's 'tenor' and the semiotic resources (how the communication is produced) similar to Halliday's mode. These combine to produce a text as Figure 7.1, shows.

In Figure 7.1 the context of situation (where, when, what's going on, what's it about and who with) is not only what gives rise to the text that is produced but influences how it is produced. If you're outside on a busy street you may have to talk more loudly. If the person you are communicating with is on the other side of the street, you would probably use gestures rather than words. The same applies to the participants, not only who they are as individuals as such but what they bring with them in terms of their experience, expectations, interest, relationships with one another (intimacy, authority, etc.). By considering these categories together, we can move towards an understanding of communication as a complex of textual practices (see e.g. Kress 2010; English 2011) in the course of social (communicative) interaction.

7.4.3 Semiotic resources

Semiotic resources are the elements we bring together in producing our texts. They can be divided into two basic categories, resources which both reflect and promote the social meanings of a text (contextual resources) and resources which provide the substance or materiality that is the text itself (material resources). In Chapter 1 we discussed how this might work with the example of being lost in a foreign city. The important thing to say here is that these resources are called semiotic because they all affect or contribute to how a text means (or can mean) and they are chosen specifically in order to produce those meanings.

The first group (*contextual resources*) includes:

> *Genre* – what kind of text it is. Everyday interactions can be seen as genres. For example a job interview or a service encounter in a shop can be categorized as genres because they are framed within particular social contexts, involve particular social relationships, seek to achieve particular goals and have culturally anticipated conversational (or textual) moves (e.g. Hasan 1989a,b). Based on our experience and the norms of interaction we know, pretty much, what kind of communication we will engage in when we go for a job interview or when we ask for something in a shop and we know, more or less how things will proceed. The category of genre also applies to cultural products such as poems, novels, essays or plays. As with the everyday genres, we have expectations of what a poem will be like in contrast to, say, a short story; and within these genre categories are sub-genres, as in sonnet versus haiku. Genres develop out of social and creative activity and they develop because they are the best way to do what they do. Genres allow us (or force us) to shape our meanings in particular ways (e.g. English 2011). A good example of this is a Twitter tweet which, with its character limitation, is a genre that pushes us to produce our meanings differently compared to how we might produce them were we to choose an alternative genre such as an email.

Discourse – the ideological meanings and community affiliations a text promotes often considered in terms of identity, power relations and agency (e.g. Ivanic 1998; Fairclough 2001; Blommaert 2005). We have already discussed this category in some detail in Chapter 3 in relation to the notion of community and we have exemplified the ideological aspect in our discussion above. Essentially, discourses are used to reflect and promote particular identities and community belonging. If we take the example of a sexist remark, in making it a speaker may be asserting a masculine, macho identity so as to show (or claim) membership of a community of other like-minded people. However, someone may equally use that same remark because they belong to a generation or culture where such comments are considered unproblematic. In this case the speaker may be unaware of the ideological message that their remark promotes but it nevertheless identifies the speaker as a member of a particular age-related or cultural community.

Register – what the relationship is between participants. In Chapter 1 we discussed this category in relation to what we called register transgressions in the case of the recorded message and the email requesting a reference. It concerns the ways in which we adapt our utterances to reflect and promote particular interpersonal relations. It might involve hedging strategies to mitigate asking a favour ('You couldn't give me a lift to the station, could you?') or it might involve strategies for creating a distance between speakers by choosing impersonal forms ('All passengers are required to have a valid ticket for their journey'). Register can also be understood in the sense of degree of formality in that we adjust how we say (or write) something according to things like the status of our addressee, as we discuss in Chapter 5. (How well do we know them? Are they senior or junior to us, or are we expected to consider them to be so? How authoritative do we want to be?).

The second group (*material resources*) includes:

Mode – the manner of communication. Put simply, mode refers to whether a text is spoken, written, signed, gestured, drawn and so on. Of course it is possible that several modes interact simultaneously, in which case we can say that a text is multimodal. The term mode is also used (Kress and van Leeuwen 2001) to include what we are calling *textual materials* (see below). For them, and it is possible to see why, resources such as a particular colour or a particular grammatical choice affect the meaning of an utterance. Using *may* instead of *will*, or pink instead of blue modalizes the 'thing' that is being represented. However, for the purposes of clarity, we reserve *mode* for the manner of the utterance and *textual materials* for the representational elements that the different modes draw on (see English 2011).

Media – the equipment used in textual production. Following Kress and van Leeuwen (2001) equipment refers to things like vocal cords, hands and fingers, keyboard and digital marks on a screen, eyebrows; anything, in fact, that we use physically in communicating.

Textual materials – what a text consists of. As previously mentioned, these are the elements that combine to represent our meanings. They include grammatical structures, items of vocabulary, tone of voice, colour of ink, etc. Textual materials are, essentially, what we use, hear, see, experience when engaged in communicative interaction.

Thematic arrangement – how a text is organized. This category includes things like sentence structure (as opposed to grammar) where we might decide to highlight one aspect over another by its position in a sentence. It can refer to spatial and physical arrangement and sequence of images, words, gestures and so on.

An important thing to bear in mind in relation to this approach to communicative analysis is that all the categories contribute to meaning and all affect the others. They act in a kind of symbiotic relationship where choosing one pathway leads to a chain reaction of other semiotic choices. Sometimes the initial pathway doesn't work for us in producing our meaning so we have to choose a different way. This often happens when trying to explain something (as in the case of writing this paragraph!). You start from a particular point only to find that it doesn't let you put across the idea you wish to communicate. So you either tinker with a word here and there or you cut your losses and begin again from a different starting point which may be grammatical, lexical or thematic.

We realize that many of these concepts overlap and may appear overly detailed. However, it is only by separating out the different aspects of communicative activity and analysing them separately and in relation to each other that we can better understand the layers of meaning, both social and textual, that are involved in any communicative event. The approach to discourse analysis that we have described here is at the heart of the kind of linguistics we are interested in. It is the fundamental analytical resource in unpacking communication and, by making the implicit explicit, it can offer real benefits not only to linguists and other language specialists, but also to a wide variety of professional and general 'real life' domains as we discuss in Part III of this book.

7.5 Conclusion

This brief overview of a long-established approach to the study of language has sought to clarify, along with Chapter 6, the analytical resources that are of fundamental use to linguists interested in real communication; the communication that people engage in every day, everywhere in the world. We recognize that not all linguists adopt this approach to discourse analysis but for us it has proved the most useful and usable strategy. In the next three chapters we use these resources to analyse examples of textual production from a range of contexts and genres and using different communicative modes. In this way, we show how a linguistics lens can offer us new and sometimes unexpected perspectives on what is generally taken-for-granted, day-to-day communicative interaction. This, after all, is why we do linguistics.

Suggested reading

Gee, J. P. (2010), *An Introduction to Discourse Analysis,* 3rd edn. New York: Routledge.

Clear, entertaining and accessible, this book introduces the tools of discourse analysis and shows how they can be used to describe and explain communicative phenomena from a social and cultural perspective.

Kress, G. (2010), *Multimodality: A Social Semiotic Approach to Contemporary Communication.* London: Routledge.

Written by one of the most influential scholars in the field, this book shows how social semiotics can help us to capture the complexities of communication in all its multimodal glory. Though theoretically challenging in parts, it is an important and engaging book with real-world, familiar and personal examples to explain and exemplify the concepts developed and used.

Paltridge, B. (2012), *Discourse Analysis: an Introduction,* 2nd edn, London: Bloomsbury.

A helpful systematically arranged book that uses examples from a wide range of texts to examine different approaches in discourse analysis including pragmatics, multimodal analysis, corpus linguistics and critical discourse analysis.

8

Speaking and spokenness

8.1 Introduction: What do we mean by *speaking*?

We open this chapter with a task partly because we want you to jump in at the deep end and partly because we believe that *doing* is the best way to understand. So, look at Example 8.1 below and decide where you might place it on a speaking–writing continuum. In other words, do you think this is more like writing or more like speaking? How easy is it to decide and what factors come into play when considering this example? We will be discussing this example in the last part of this chapter, but we wanted to raise the question of spokenness and writtenness right from the outset.

Example 8.1

Time	From	Message
21:31:32	ILE	wth havnt u dun da plan omg
21:32:29	CB	but we arent doin socio cw
21:32:55	ILE	yer we are she gave us da pre-plan
21:33:07	CB	no we rnt
21:33:15	ILE	yer we are
21:33:19	ILE	shit jo
21:33:39	CB	no we rnt
21:33:51	ILE	yes we are
21:34:57	CB	no we rnt
21:34:17	ILE	jo we are
21:34:26	CB	not
21:34:39	ILE	lol no ur rite were not muahaha
21:34:58	CB	lol

The reason we started the chapter in this way is because we want to explore what we mean by speaking and spokenness; that is the qualities or features of spoken communication. In the process of our discussion of spokenness, we also consider writtenness in revealing how these modes differ in their production and the semiotic resources available to them. As with previous chapters, we build our discussion around examples of different communicative phenomena to find out, using our linguistics lens, what they can tell us.

8.2 Representing spoken communication

When writing about spoken communication, one of the problems that need to be addressed is how to represent it visually, on the page or on the screen, both for the purposes of demonstration and for analysis and exemplification. For modes such as writing or other visual texts, representation is not a problem for the analyst as the text itself is a 'representation'. For speech, however, we need to find ways of representing not only the words and sequence, but also the sounds and the gestures, gaze, clicking fingers and other physical modes of meaning making (see e.g. Domingo 2014). Of course, using multimedia resources, it would be possible to provide an audio recording of the communicative event, or, even better, a video recording. In the first case, listeners would be enabled to experience the sounds of the conversation and notice how meanings are produced both verbally and audially. In a video we would be able to see the additional resources of gesture, facial expression or proximity that would further combine to produce the meanings the participants are making. However, in a book that is written down and printed on paper, we have to rely on a written representation of that conversation.

Let's look at this using a fragment of conversation between two people. Like our other examples, this is a genuine conversation, spontaneously audio recorded by one of us for just such a purpose as this. We have given the participants the pseudonyms John and Mike. The question we are going to consider is how we can most usefully present the conversation and what our aims might be in so doing.

8.2.1 Literary representations

We are all familiar with how novelists represent speech in their stories, identifying who is speaking, showing that something is to be read as speech by the use of some kind of punctuation, usually double quotation marks (". . ."). Example 8.2 illustrates this in representing the recorded speech referred to above.

Example 8.2 (Represented as Received Pronunciation – RP)

"Well anyway, so I'll sort that out. What I'll do is I'll grout the floor today, then you can see the colour that it dries to" said/suggested John.
"Right, yeah, ok" said Mike/Mike agreed.
"But if you want me to do just one patch, I'll do one patch. But I think it'll be alright if I do the lot." said John/John added.

Here the novelist wants to include dialogue as part of a narrative so as to authenticate the interactions between the characters. Dialogue enables a different kind of understanding compared to prose. It allows the conversational effect of a to-ing and fro-ing of utterances in the attempt to arrive at some kind of shared understanding, agreement or resolution (see e.g. Kress 1994; English 2011). However, because the speech is embedded in a larger prose piece, the writer needs to indicate this by using various typographical techniques such as line spacing and double quotation marks. In addition to this, the writer needs to explain who is saying what and what's more, how the speakers are saying it. Hence we tend to find novelists attributing the different utterances to the different participants by using verbs such as 'agree' or 'argue', or 'ask' and so on, rather than a simple 'say'. In fact, novelists often go further than this in the conveyance of particular interpersonal interactions by combining these attributive verbs with adverbial expressions. For instance, instead of, *"Right, yeah, ok" Mike agreed*, we could have *"Right, yeah, ok" Mike agreed reluctantly*, thereby substantially changing the interpersonal impact.

A further aspect of Example 8.2 is that we have no idea of how the conversation sounds, the tone of voice of the pronunciation of the participants. We can imagine the sound to a greater or lesser extent depending on how much background information there is regarding the individual participants. For instance, are they both RP speakers or do they have regional accents? What is the tone of the conversation? Is it light or heavy? These and other aspects cannot be deduced from the conversation as it is represented in writing, but only through the inclusion of additional information.

To give a clue as to the sound of this conversation, when we played it to a group of non-native speakers, most of them experienced problems in understanding parts of it and some couldn't understand it at all. This was partly because the topic and some of the key vocabulary was unfamiliar to them but largely because one of the speakers has a strong regional accent. This last is something that novelists sometimes attempt to reflect using a mix of punctuation and irregular spelling to represent regional and/or, in the case of English at least, class accent. Example 8.3 shows how this might be done.

*Example 8.3 (Attempting to reflect non-*RP*)*

"Well anyway, so I'll sor' tha' ou'. Wot I'll do is I'll grout the floor today, then you can see the colour tha' i' dries to" said/suggested John.
"Right, yeah, ok" said Mike/Mike agreed.
"Bu' if you want me to do jus' one patch, I'll do one patch. But I fink it'll be alrigh' if I do the lot." said John/John added.

These two examples show some of the ways that writers attempt to get around the problem of representing speech in writing. In fact, fictional speech must be viewed as something quite different from authentic speech. In fiction the whole piece is a construct, and fictional speech is an approximation of real speech, sitting inside the author's context, imported in the service of the author's narrative. The characters do not speak on their own behalf, but on behalf of the author (see e.g. Volosinov 1986; Bakhtin 1986). This is not to say that fictional dialogue is ineffectual or second rate. On the contrary, it is a highly developed literary form which enables writers to let their characters reveal themselves. Speech in a novel offers a far more dynamic representation than if the conversation were reported indirectly as in Example 8.4, which makes for a very dull read.

Example 8.4 (Represented as reported speech)

John agreed to sort out the problem and suggested that he would do the floor grouting that day so that Mike could see what colour it dried to. Mike was happy with this suggestion. Nevertheless, John offered to do only just one patch if Mike wanted, though he thought that it would be alright if he did the lot.

8.2.2 Linguistics representations

From a linguistics perspective, however, we have different reasons for representing speech as 'writing'. We might, for instance, be interested in analysing how the speech actually sounds in which case we draw on resources made available by phonetics and transcribe it phonemically (see Chapter 6) as in Example 8.5. If you know what sounds the characters refer to by being familiar with or having access to a chart showing the place of articulation (as provided in Chapter 6), or knowing where and how in the mouth a particular vowel is produced, you will be able to hear how the conversation sounds and even produce the sounds yourself. This is how voice coaches train actors to speak with different accents. The diacritics are used to show the tonal movement of the voice (intonation) too.

Example 8.5 (Phonemic transcription using intonation direction arrows)

John: / weʊ enɪwaɪ səʊ aʊ sɒʔ θæʔ æʊʔ wɔʔ aʊ du: ɪz græʊʔ θə flɔ: tədaɪ ðen yʊ: kən/

Mike: /raɪʔ/

John: /si: ðə kʊlə ɪʔ drai:z tu:/

Mike: /ye əʊkeɪ/

John: / buʔ ɪf yə wɔŋ mɪ tə du: dʒʊs wəm pætʃ aʊ du: wəm pɑtʃ bʊʔ aɪ fɪŋk ɪʔl bi: ɔraɪʔ ɪf aɪ du: ðə lɔʔ /

Representing speech in this way can be immensely useful in a number of different analytical fields. For example, it enables us to talk about phonological variation or change within a particular language such as how people adjust their accent (or pronunciation) according to who they are talking to or the circumstances in which they are talking. In everyday parlance, this is known as 'putting on an accent' and has traditionally been used to refer to someone who tries to sound posh.

In Britain, where notions of class are deeply intertwined with accent, much is made of this in numerous comedy series (e.g. the BBC's *Keeping up Appearances*). More recently a study (Boorman et al. 2013) undertaken as part of a third year linguistics module at Manchester University, which showed how David and Victoria Beckham[1] had adjusted their accents 'up', hit the news and led to a string of articles and TV discussions including on the BBC's *Newsnight*.[2] However, a trend that is now more noticeable, at least in England, is the reverse of this, whereby people with upper-class accents are tending towards a more working-class or proletarian accent. The classic trend is towards what is known as Estuary English (Rosewarne 1984) which is an identified hybrid accent associated with the Thames Estuary (around Essex and Kent) and which we can hear being adopted by many politicians whose normal accent might be considered too 'posh'. Typical of Estuary English is the 'glottal stop' which generally replaces final /t/ sound as in 'got' [gɔʔ]. Try listening out for this when you next hear a British politician talking in interview, particularly male, privately educated politicians who fear that they lack the 'common touch'. You can also hear it among younger members of the British royal family.

In Example 8.5, the phonemic transcription indicates that John has a particular regional accent, north London – specifically Camden – though morphosyntactically he uses standard English, at least in this exchange. We know about his specific accent because, in fact, we know John personally and that he was born and brought up in that area. However, if we didn't know him we would still be able to offer a fair guess at the general region (London and Estuary) from some of the features of pronunciation that the transcription reveals: the frequent use of the glottal stop or the pronunciation of 'way' in his 'anyway' using the diphthong /ai/ rather than the RP diphthong /ei/. Also his front-of-mouth pronunciation of the word 'do' as /du::/ as opposed to the RP /du:/ is typical of north London. Mike uses the glottal stop with the word 'right' in his first contribution, but when he later says 'OK', he uses the RP /ei/ and not the /ai/ used by John. This suggests that he may tend towards RP as, in English, it is often in the vowels that accent is audible. However, as he says so little, we would be unwise to infer too much. Of course, listening to an audio representation would help with regard to the 'sounds' of the conversation and a video would be even better as it would supply evidence of other semiotic resources such as gesture, gaze, facial expression, posture or even a physical object like a colour chart which combine to produce meaning. But best of all would be actually being there in the moment, party to and participant in the conversation.

There are many other ways in which phonetic/phonemic transcription can be helpful, including in language learning and teaching to help with producing new vocabulary (as in dictionaries), in forensic linguistics in identifying suspects for instance, where they come from or whether they are who they say they are (see Coulthard and Johnson 2007). It can be used as the basis for recording languages that do not have a writing system or, indeed, to develop a writing system for such a language. In fact this kind of transcription is an invaluable resource across a wide range of fields within the broad area of linguistics.

However, phonetic transcriptions as in Example 8.5 do not lend themselves easily to the kind of analysis that focuses on the *social* aspects of a conversation. They are not very user-friendly and they are rarely used for the kinds of analysis that this book is concerned with. For this we tend to draw on conventions developed for conversation analysis (e.g. Jefferson 2004) which is closely associated with the study of pragmatics (see Chapters 6 and 7)

Transcribed from audio recordings, this form of representation is essentially a way of representing, in writing, how a conversation moves between the participants. Unlike the literary representations we showed in Examples 8.2–8.4, it is not an invented construct, nor is it mediated by authorial decisions as to how it should be understood (e.g. He argued – vs. – he said). Unlike the phonetic transcription in Example 8.5, a conversation analysis approach to transcription is concerned more with conversational interaction than with the sounds alone, although it is important to point out that how we sound also contributes to our conversational meanings. A conversation analysis transcription is helpful in enabling us to refer to different aspects of a conversation which aspects are to be referred to will depend on the interest of the person doing the analysis. It may be, for instance, that she wants to explore a specific feature of speech such as 'turn-taking', linking this, perhaps, to how the participants position themselves in relation to each other, for instance girls' and boys' contributions in the classroom (e.g. Baxter 2002). Alternatively, the analytical focus could be on the communicative success or failure from the perspective of cultural norms and practices, for instance as discussed in Chapter 3 or in a forensic linguistics analysis, as we discuss in Chapter 14.

Let's now take a final look at the conversation between John and Mike, but this time using a conversation analysis transcription and analysing it from its interactional perspective.

Example 8.6 (Conversation Analysis Transcription)

Key: (.) micro pause, (..) longer pause; : lengthened sound; . falling tone; └ overlapping

John	Well anyway. (.) so I'll sort that out. (..) What I'll do is I'll grout the
	floor toda::y then you can └
Mike	Right. └
John	see the colour it dries to.
Mike	Yeah OK. └
John	But if you want me to do just one patch I'll do one patch. (...)
	but I think it'll be alright if I do the lot.

Home recording, 24 August 2008

As will already have been noticed in this part of the conversation it is John who does most of the talking whereas Mike's contributions are minimal. From a conversation analysis perspective, we can say that John is 'holding the floor' because his conversational turns are longer and more propositional. If we were simply to consider the length of turns, we would say that John is in control here with Mike acting as a kind of foil to John's propositions. In fact, Mike's contributions can be understood in two ways. In line 3 his 'right', which overlaps rather than interrupts John's flow, could be seen as what is called back-channelling; that is when we make a sound such as 'mmm' or say a word like 'yeah' or 'right' to show that we are both listening and involved. This is something that occurs in most, though not all, languages (e.g. Australian Aboriginal languages are often characterized by spells of 'comfortable silence', as noted by Eades (2000: 167)) and in some more obviously than others. For instance, if you listen to Japanese people talking together you will hear the word 'Hai', which is an important signal that you are both listening and engaged, generally used with greater frequency than an English person would use 'mmm' or 'yeah'. Back-channelling, then, is a way of maintaining interpersonal cohesiveness; oiling the wheels of a communicative interaction. Without it we feel uncertain about whether the others involved in the conversation are interested, if they are awake or, in the case of telephone conversations, even still there!

So far we have explained that a phonemic analysis can show us what a conversation sounds like while a conversation analysis can show us how it moves between the participants. What we move on to now is what we can learn about the social meaning(s) of the conversation, by considering it from a social semiotic perspective using the by now familiar discourse analysis approach that we explained in the previous chapter (for convenience, we use the conversation analysis transcription in Figure 8.6 as our point of reference). In this approach we consider what is said between whom, why and with what semiotic resources and in so doing we can understand Mike's contributions as revealing something more than 'simple' back-channelling.

From a common-sense perspective, there is no difficulty in understanding that John is organizing the work schedule and the work schedule involves two activities: something that we don't know about, but that will be sorted out by John and something that we can know, that is the grouting[3] that he will do that day. Mike's own minimal contributions involve two expressions of agreement with what John proposes. However, from the same common-sense perspective, we can also realize that despite John's control of the conversation, it is Mike who will make the ultimate decision about whether or not the schedule will go according to John's plan. The relationship between the participants could be said to be unequal, at least in terms of the events proposed, if not in the expertise of the participants. The question is, how do we know that? And the answer lies in the textual resources used.

From the use of the personal pronouns, 'I'll grout the floor', 'you can see', it is clear that it is not Mike who will be doing the work (the grouting) but John. John is checking with Mike to see whether his proposal meets with approval. This is further confirmed by John's anticipation of a possible objection (line 6) even despite Mike's 'Yeah, OK' which John overlaps. His use of 'if you want me to. . . . I'll do it' clearly positions Mike as the one who makes the final decisions. Nevertheless, John also has his own authority, that of his professional knowledge and expertise, which is expressed in the final remark (line 7).

Why is this conversational extract worth analysing, you might be asking yourself? First of all, it offers the chance to explore different ways of *representing and analysing* spoken communication. More importantly, though it shows that even the most mundane examples of speech and dialogue can teach us about language, social relations, regional identity, linguistic behaviours; in fact it can tell us anything we want to know about communication provided we know how to look for it. This is part of being a good linguist and a good *noticer of language*.

In the next part of this chapter we look at the material characteristics of speaking, in other words, spokenness, examining it particularly from the perspective of how we make our meanings orally. In the process of this discussion we inevitably have to consider 'writtenness', since by placing the two modes in juxtaposition it is easier to see their distinctive configurations.

8.3 Spokenness and writtenness

The first thing to make clear is that although both speaking and writing concern verbal communication, they are quite different modes of communicative activity and offer very different ways of producing meaning. The activity of writing (rather than transcribing) is not simply an act of representing speech in written form, nor is speaking an oral version of writing. This may seem too obvious to need pointing out. But given that many popular opinions on language, particularly in relation to notions of correctness and standards, are based on written rather than spoken language, we feel it a point worth making (see also Chapter 12). The two modes are, in fact, qualitatively distinct in character and afford qualitatively different ways of understanding, representing and reflecting the world, although Biber (1988) has suggested that there is as much variation between different genres within the modes as between them, and we must therefore be cautious in suggesting a purely binary comparison.

Although we talk about speaking and writing as being essentially verbal modes of communication, both of them incorporate other communicative modes in their production. Speaking, as already mentioned, usually involves other, non-verbal modes such as gestures (nudges, clicking fingers), facial expressions (raised eyebrows, screw-face) and even the way we are sitting (hunched up) or standing (leaning away), each of which contributes to the intended (and sometimes unintended) meaning. Writing incorporates modes of colour or size, for instance, in offering meanings beyond the verbal, a theme we develop in the next chapter. Some of these non-verbal modes become systematized; punctuation in writing, intonation in speech, and some become culturally conventionalized such as gestures, like shrugging shoulders, or the use of colour such as red for teachers' corrections or, in Thai, for the speech of ghosts. In the present discussion, however, we focus specifically on the verbal elements and on the ways in which these affect and are affected by the interactions that each entails.

8.3.1 *Interactional characteristics*

When we speak we also listen and, if in the same physical space, watch, and when we write we also read. Every time we read, even when we read what we ourselves have written, we engage in an interpretative process which is, essentially, one of making (or remaking) the meaning of the text that has been produced. This is a largely silent, internal process also characterized by reflection. In spoken interactions a similar process takes place, but this time it is usually vocal, external and immediate. This is a key difference between writing and speaking. Speaking is a co-production involving negotiation of meaning between the participants, who are present. Writing, by contrast, relying on the writer to cater for the absent reader's interpretative needs, tends to be more explicit and self-contained. Let's look at this in a little more detail.

Speaking has what we might call communicative immediacy: it is of the moment. The 'other' is present and usually visible so participants can adapt and modify their meanings in response to each other's feedback. For example, if you notice that your co-speaker is looking puzzled or bored, you can adjust or adapt what you are saying or even say something completely different. For example, in the conversational transcript (Example 8.6) above we can infer an instance of this in lines 5–7 where John offers an alternative suggestion to the one he has just made (But if you want me to do just one patch I'll do one patch) which overlaps Mike's verbal agreement (Yeah, OK). The question we might ask is why does John offer this alternative when Mike has apparently agreed to the original one? Without being there, or having a video recording, it is difficult to say for sure, but there are certain possibilities. Perhaps Mike's verbal agreement (*Yeah OK*) may have been accompanied by a facial expression, a grimace maybe, or it might have been said with a questioning tone. Either of these would have communicated that he was not entirely happy with the first proposition and hence prompted John's alternative offering. Alternatively, it could be that John is simply thinking aloud and working through the possibilities himself. As observers of language, we cannot provide a precise answer to this question, particularly if we weren't actually there, but we can speculate. After all, the purpose of a linguistic ethnography approach is not to provide answers but to propose possibilities and offer insights into the texts we are considering.

This to-ing and fro-ing between participants in the flow of conversation, making and remaking meanings, means that saying something may appear less tightly structured than writing something and a 'complete' meaning may take longer to achieve because it is based on negotiation rather than presentation, as is the case in writing. Halliday (1989) describes this looseness as 'clause intricacy' which is further characterized by what he calls 'lexical sparsity'. This contrasts with what he calls the 'clause complexity' and 'lexical density' that characterizes written communication. This distinction can easily be felt by listening to a written text being read out loud. Unless it has been specifically written to be told, such texts can appear to an audience as heavy-going and even impenetrable, precisely because of the complexity of its organization and its lexical density. We have been to many a conference where presenters have simply read out their papers, making no modifications to mitigate the writtenness of the text. Such 'talks' are always hard to follow and can result, as we ourselves have noted, in sending some members of an audience to sleep or to catch up on their emails or Facebook posts!

8.3.2 Representational characteristics

However, it is not necessary to sit in an auditorium to identify differences between speaking and writing. The distinctions can easily be confirmed by transcribing examples of spoken discourse and analysing them from the perspective of the semiotic resources that are used in their production; that is, from their *material* perspective. Such texts can appear, in written form, as long winded, circuitous and fragmented but, when spoken and listened to, they come across as perfectly coherent, well organized and even polished. Example 8.7, which is a short extract transcribed from a university lecture on natural ecosystems, illustrates this point.

Example 8.7

> **Key:** (.) micro pause; (..) longer pause; (…) extended pause; . falling tone
>
> Now what I've (.) what I want you to imagine at the start (.) is a core community. (…) what I want us to imagine is a core community. (..) eventually. (.) and I'm going to talk about everything in relation to this core community. (…) that will be in a moment. (...) the key divisions. (.) er (.) the (.) the (..) of this formation. (..) um (.) of this classification. begins as follows.

On our showing a longer section of the transcribed talk to the academic concerned, he was appalled at what he thought must have been an incoherent disaster. In fact, it had been a highly successful lecture which drew on all the resources afforded by speaking and which had been much appreciated by the students who had attended. What makes this a successful spoken text is its quality of spokenness. For instance, features of what is known as *addressivity* whereby the speaker speaks directly to the audience using the personal pronouns 'you' ('what I want you to imagine') and, more inclusively, 'us' ('what I want us to imagine'). There is an example of a different kind of addressivity ('and that will be in a moment') which, like the promissory statement ('I'm going to talk about'), signals the arrangement of his talk and is designed to help the audience prepare themselves for what is to come. The speaker also uses repetition, a particularly common resource in lectures, which helps ensure the audience has got the main point. For example, the term of reference being introduced, 'core community', is mentioned three times and the directive ('I want you to imagine') is also repeated. We find examples of what we call *repair*, also typical of spoken communication, whereby we start off along one linguistic track only to realize it is not the most apt choice for what you want to say. There are two instances of this here: 'now what I've' is repaired into 'what I want' and later on 'er the the' is repaired to 'of this'. There are pauses in this extract which give the audience time to absorb the point or which give the speaker time to think how to say the next thing. Equally there are two instances of *fillers* (er, um) which are also associated with thinking time, perhaps to choose or find the right word or structure. Overall, despite the seeming hesitancy and repetitiveness, this is a powerful and confident example of the lecture genre.

If we now compare the above example with the following (Example 8.8) which is an extract from a written article by the same person, we can see how differently he arranges his ideas and the different choices he makes in clause relationship. In this case there is frequent clause embedding; that is a clause within a clause, unlike in Example 8.7 where clauses are chained in an additive way. In other words, the spoken version chains a series of stand-alone (or independent) clauses, clauses that make sense by themselves, whereas in the written example there is a combination of independent and dependent, or subordinate, clauses. In fact, Example 8.8 contains eight distinct clauses, only one of which, shown in bold, is an independent clause, and together these make up the single sentence that this example comprises.

Example 8.8

> **These distinctive formations**, the canopies of which are dominated by six leaf-shedding members of the Dipterocarpaceae, **have been much neglected by ecologists**, although they often comprise the most important single formation over much of the region, and play a significant role both in the ecology of the area's distinctive forest wildlife and in the economy of many local peoples.

Another feature which characterizes writtenness, particularly in formal writing such as this, is nominalization. This is when we put together self-contained units of nouns and adjectives known as 'noun-phrases', to use as the subject or object of a clause (e.g. the area's distinctive forest wildlife). Verbs are often turned into adjectives (e.g. leaf-shedding members instead of members which shed leaves) to facilitate the process of nominalization. It is this that leads to some of the lexical density that Halliday refers to and partly to the organizational complexity. Nominalization avoids the need for lots of simple clauses and fewer verbs and promotes instead the embeddedness and indirectness of clause complexity. In the written example (59 words) there are only four verbs (are dominated; have been neglected; comprise; play). This contrasts markedly with the spoken example (60 words) which has eight verbs (want; to imagine; want; to imagine; am going to talk; will be; begins; follows) in what is essentially the same number of words.

Addressivity, as we discussed it above, is also missing in Example 8.8, something which is often absent in academic and even more so in some other formal genres such as legal contracts. This is not to say that the writer is not addressing a reader, but rather than the addressivity is disguised. One way of achieving this is by the use of the passive form of the verb (*It has been done* instead of *Someone has done it*). In Example 8.7 there is not a single instance of the passive out of the eight verbs used, whereas in 8.8 two out of the four verbs are in the passive form (have been neglected by; are dominated by). This use of the passive enables the writer to foreground the recipients, or objects, of the neglect (These distinctive formations) and the domination (the canopy) rather than those who are doing the neglecting and dominating. In this way the author can maintain the theme of the sentence (distinctive formations) which would not otherwise be possible without the aid of the passive.

8.3.3 Explicitness vs implicitness

Spokenness and writtenness can also be distinguished by the degree of verbal explicitness that is required to ensure, or at least, facilitate understanding. As already mentioned, we need a higher degree of verbal explicitness in writing than in speaking to cater for the lack of instant feedback that would be provided if we were talking with someone. Kress (1994: 23) points out: 'Spoken texts may leave information implicit because the speaker knows what the hearer knows and because he can assess as he speaks whether he has been correct in his assessment.' Furthermore, the environmental context is available for speakers to share and refer to non-verbally. An example of this is where a person might say 'Did you see that?', referring (and perhaps pointing) to something that can be clearly seen by all those present. Such verbal (though not communicative) vagueness would be an entirely unsuccessful strategy to use in writing as the reader would not know what 'that' referred to. The flexibility that spoken communication allows in the range of semiotic resources available makes it semiotically more complex than writing though perhaps less verbally explicit as the following example illustrates.

Howard (2008) used data that he collected in the street to analyse the genre of asking for directions. His aim was to problematize the routinized examples that English language teaching course books use by showing that in real-world encounters the genre looks and sounds very different to what is typically presented. Example 8.9 illustrates what really happens on the ground, by showing how speakers draw on numerous other semiotic resources in addition to the verbal in meaning making.

Example 8.9

Key: (.) micro pause, (..) longer pause, : lengthened sound, . falling tone, └overlapping, . . . back-channelling

The two speakers giving the directions to the researcher, <S1>, are an elderly local couple who appeared to be out for an evening stroll. Whilst <S2> was the first to answer <S3> took over and <S2> was left to point out the way using his hands.

<S1> Excuse me, do you know how to get to Victoria Park from here?

<S2> That's it straight across there straight (..) across there see the gates?

<S2> └That's Victoria Park over there dear look

(<S1> Ah)

└see that (<S1> Yeap) see that car there

└<S1> Yeap

└look there's a car go up (..) down

there see the gates (<S1> Yeap) that's the park

<S2> └By the car

<S1> Ok thank you very much

Howard (2008: 67)

If we were to present this example written down as a piece of continuous prose, it would appear fragmented, ungrammatical and even incoherent. That is if you are judging it as a piece of writing. As we have already pointed out, people often mistakenly base their assumptions on what constitutes 'good grammar' and correctness on writing, assuming, as Kress has pointed out, that 'speech is also organized by the sentence as its basic linguistic unit' with everything spelt out. However, a live conversation does not work like that. As this example shows quite clearly, a conversation is a 'multimodal ensemble' (Domingo et al. 2014) comprising a mix of both verbal and non-verbal semiotic resources and relying on the contextual resources that are available to the physically present participants. Furthermore, because we are familiar with the genre of asking directions, even without being there, unable to see 'the gates' or 'that car', we can nevertheless have a pretty good idea of what is going on. We know that there will be pointing to accompany 'over there dear look' or 'see that car there'. We know that there will be glances back and forth to each other and in the direction of the identified points of reference (the gates, the car) and we know that there will be an arm and hand gesture to communicate 'straight across'. We know all this because we have done it ourselves. Representing it using the tools of conversation analysis, Howard manages to give us a flavour of the experience, but if we were writing it as part of a novel, we would have to add descriptions of the context in order to make verbally explicit what, in the live event, are non-verbally explicit co-textual and contextual meanings.

8.4 Speechlike writing

For the final part of this chapter, we want to present some examples of texts which use the qualities of speech despite their being produced with writing. In the first example, taken from a political campaign email, the issue concerns register (see Chapters 1 and 7). In the second example, a series of instant messages (MSN) between two teenagers, we show that despite their written realization, they are, in fact, an authentic live conversation. The question we want to ask is what is it that makes each of the examples speechlike and why have the writers (they are definitely written texts) written them in the way they have?

8.4.1 Political campaigning

Example 8.10 is an extract from an email received around the time of the candidate elections for members of the European parliament (names have been changed for purposes of anonymity). The email is from an existing member of the British parliament asking for support for her preferred candidate, giving several reasons why. Example 8.10, which is produced using the genre of a conventional (paper-based) letter with its classic greeting (Dear) and semi-formal closing (With best wishes), is a fragment taken from the email. What stands out, though, despite the conventional use of salutations, is the way in which the text shifts between discourse styles. Of particular interest here is the section we have underlined. It looks (or sounds) speechlike. It uses colloquial expression, it has strong addressivity and the writer draws on the kind of spoken contextualization we described above. However, when we look more closely we can see that despite the attempt to appear like speech, the grammar used is actually more typical of written communication.

Example 8.10

> Dear Friend,
>
> Please join me in voting for Susan Small #1 as London Xparty candidate for MEP.
>
> *It's as simple as that, really. Out of six good candidates – not to mention innumerable emails, text messages, and doubtless more to come – Susan sticks out to me*
>
> With best wishes,
> Dorothy Dobbs MP

Focusing on the section we have italicised, at first sight it appears to be very loosely written. The first sentence, consisting of a free-standing clause, ('It's as simple as that, really.') acquires its quality of spokenness from the way in which it references back to the initial request to vote for Susan Small by using the referent 'that' and by adding the modifier 'really' to add a personal voice to the comment. It is just the kind of thing we might say when giving advice or encouragement to someone. The second sentence comprises two parts, presented as if in unequal relationship to each other. There is the main clause, 'out of six good candidates Susan sticks out to me', which carries the desired message and the comment, 'not to mention innumerable emails, text messages, and doubtless more to come', which is placed, using comma-like dashes, in subordinate relationship to the main clause. Reading it quickly, you might not pay attention to the detail of how the sentence is structured but if you thought about it, you might think there was something a bit odd about how the two parts were juxtapositioned. Because it has been presented in writing, as a sentence, we expect there to be a logical relationship between the different parts; the bits in the subordinated part referring in some way to the bits in the main part. The problem with this sentence, though, is that this does not happen. In fact, using the logic of sentence structure, the implication is that the 'innumerable emails' and 'text messages' are the same sorts of things as the 'six good candidates', which clearly they are not. In other words the writer has suggested that both sets of things are in the same semantic category (see Chapter 6). It is this which gives the sentence its awkward quality and which might cause a reader to take pause.

So what is going on here? Our suggestion is that the writer, in seeking to promote a sense of camaraderie, borrowed the kind of clause intricacy that we discussed earlier, the chaining of clauses that typifies spoken texts, while using the morphosyntax, or clause complexity, of writtenness. In the attempt to sound chatty, the writer forgot to pay attention to coherence, and in so doing undermined the natural-like, authentic tone it tried to achieve. Ultimately, the email produces what we might call a 'faux' spokenness which, instead of achieving the camaraderie it seeks, can serve to irritate precisely because of its false note. This is something that speech-writers and public relations personnel would be wise to bear in mind when producing material for politicians and other public officials.

8.4.2 Instant messaging

The next example (Example 8.11) is the series of instant messages (MSN) between two teenagers of around 16 or 17 years old that we used at the beginning of this chapter. As you will see from the times noted against each of the messages, the series was produced over a period of just under three and a half minutes. Unlike the email above, which borrowed the discourse of a conversation, this example is a genuine conversation. But instead of using speech, it uses writing.

Example 8.11

Time	From	Message
21:31:32	ILE	wth havnt u dun da plan omg
21:32:29	CB	but we arent doin socio cw
21:32:55	ILE	yer we are she gave us da pre-plan
21:33:07	CB	no we rnt
21:33:15	ILE	yer we are
21:33:19	ILE	shit jo
21:33:39	CB	no we rnt
21:33:51	ILE	yes we are
21:34:57	CB	no we rnt
21:34:17	ILE	jo we are
21:34:26	CB	not
21:34:39	ILE	lol no ur rite were not muahaha
21:34:58	CB	lol

Our aim here is not to comment particularly on digital writing as such (for this see e.g. Crystal 2008) but rather on the conversational nature of the correspondence itself. We can call it correspondence because it is definitely writing but, unlike writing, which lacks the immediacy of speech, the exchanges in this example typify those of the kind of quick-fire banter that usually only occurs with face-to-face talk. Each comment is a response to a prior comment as the participants negotiate towards the conclusion (21:34:39) and the conversation flows as a co-production between the two participants. As they are not physically co-present, they make use of the semiotic resources that texting affords such as the ubiquitous 'lol' to denote laughing or joking or 'omg' to denote a kind of mock shock horror, both of which were conventionalized in the early days of text messaging in order to reduce the message size. 'Lol' and 'omg' (laugh out loud, oh my god) have their essential meanings but they also denote membership of a certain generational community, one that is young or young adult[4] (see Chapter 3). Those outside that community, typically those in the public sphere, who use these same expressions on Twitter produce the same kind of false note as the email in Example 8.10. Trying to adopt discourses that don't 'belong' to you invariably fails to convince.

Analysing a sequence of messages such as Example 8.11 raises interesting questions about the nature of spokenness, writtenness and digitalness. What mode of communication do we consider messaging, texting, Whatsapp or online chat to be? Where, for instance, do they fit on the writing–speaking continuum? For example, research (Lenhart et al. 2008) has found that teenagers themselves tend not to consider these kinds of interaction as writing at all. These and other questions will be further considered in Chapter 9. The point here is – is this speaking, writing or something else altogether?

8.5 Conclusion

In this chapter, we have explored speaking and spokenness from the perspectives of representation, its textual quality and its distinctiveness in relation to writing. Our aim has been to show how linguistic representations of spoken texts can inform us about such issues as language variation, shifts in pronunciation or social relationships between speakers. We have drawn attention to ways in which we make use of the very different sets of semiotic resources available to each mode (verbal, non-verbal and contextual) and how these can sometimes be borrowed across modes to good or bad effect. In the process we have also raised questions about taken-for-granted understandings of the status of speaking and writing, particularly in connection with notions of correctness and standards. In the next chapter we focus explicitly on writing and other visual modes – because of course communication is not just a matter of words.

Suggested reading

Carter, R. and McCarthy, M. (1997), *Exploring Spoken English.* Cambridge: Cambridge University Press.

This very accessible book is particularly useful on two accounts. First it presents a range of naturally occurring conversation samples and comments on them in detail. Secondly, and more importantly, it demonstrates how spoken grammar works and how it must therefore be considered as distinct from written grammar and equally valid.

Coupland, J. (ed.) (2000), *Small Talk.* Harlow: Longman.

This edited collection, which uses authentic conversation examples such as talking about the weather, gossip at the dinner table or chit-chat in the workplace, demonstrates how a discourse analysis approach allows us to represent, describe and, using the insights from pragmatics or social semiotics, for instance, shed light taken-for-granted talk in everyday speech.

Liddicoat, A. (2011), *An Introduction to Conversationa Analysis,* 2nd edn. London: Continuum.

A practical book which guides readers through the processes and practices of actually doing conversation analysis. For those interested in analysing conversational flow, this is a very useful book.

Sindoni, M. G. (2013), *Spoken and Written Discourse in Online Interactions: A Multimodal Approach.* Abingdon: Routledge.

This book uses the context of online interactions to discuss how speech and writing both act and interact in our everyday communications. The author explores how these conventional modes are being re-shaped by the semiotic resources made available by digital media and how these, in turn, both shape and are shaped by the social interactions that take place online.

9

Writing and writtenness

9.1 Introduction

In the previous chapter we used the theme of speaking and spokenness to discuss not only issues to do with spoken communication but also, necessarily, issues that concern writing. This is because it is helpful to juxtapose in order to make visible things which might otherwise be overlooked. In this chapter we develop the theme of writing and writtenness in relation to concepts of literacy. We also want to show that writing is an inherently reflective activity not only because it requires a particular kind of thinking in the process of production, the kind that is based on pause and consideration of how best to 'put' things, but also because writing is a *technology* (Ong 1982), which involves the use of tools for its realization. This means that writing is almost never, if ever, spontaneous in the way speaking or gesturing can be. In order to write we need implements such as a pen or a keyboard and a surface on which to write and this need alone means a kind of separation from the thought to the act. Even when we write using a finger, we need something additional to make our marks visible, such as the steam on a car window.

In keeping with our view that communication is essentially a multimodal activity, the examples we use in this chapter reflect this view in that they are 'multimodal ensembles, designed so that each mode has a specific task and function' (Kress 2010: 28). Our examples, then involve other visual modes used in conjunction with the verbal dimension whether it be pictorial, diagrammatic or an intrinsic part of how the verbal is represented (font style, colour, etc.).

We have organized the chapter around a series of case studies with which we explore themes such as what writing is for and what it means to be literate by analysing examples of the kind of literacy activities we engage in every day.

9.2 Learning to make use of writing

Our first case concerns what is often called 'early writing' activity and consists of two examples of literacy activity produced by my (Fiona's) son.[1] Each was done at a different age and each exemplifies a development in understanding about what writing can be for. The first is an instance of what we might call 'public writing', a kind of writing often assumed to be the territory of the professional or the expert. The second is an example of 'private writing', which, in this instance, is used in a highly functional way. Each of these examples is a multimodal ensemble involving both image and writing in a complex of meaning making. Of course, when I first saw these texts my responses were entirely spontaneous and appropriate to the genres they represent. It was only on revisiting them that I adopted a linguistic focus, analysing them as exemplars of different kinds of literacy activity.

9.2.1 *Public writing*

The first example (Figure 9.1) is a Mother's Day card[2] produced when my son was around the age of 4 or so. In designing this card, he chose both writing and drawing to produce the particular message he wanted to give.

FIGURE 9.1 *Mother's day card.*

The main impact of the card comes from the image of two people hugging; one large and one small; one with the arm coming down and over and the other with the arm coming up and under. The smaller figure is looking up at the larger one while the larger one, with a big grin, looks sideways-on either at the viewer or down at the other figure. The single word *you* is carefully placed at the top, more or less overarching the two figures. There are some faint vertically placed marks down the left hand side of the card, which is drawn on a page of white paper. It is not possible to decipher them, but they may reflect the ways in which other cards he may have seen use writing both vertically down the side of an image as well as horizontally.

The question that we want to tease out here, though, is how this card can be interpreted as a text. What message is intended and how do the different modes of writing and drawing interact in producing the message?

At first sight, there is nothing particularly unusual about the card with its different represented elements. Children often mix image and words when making products of this nature and indeed, apart from my delighted, maternal response to the card, it did not strike me as being particularly unusual. When I first received it, I understood the drawing as showing me, the larger figure, hugging my son, my arms stretching down and (protectively?) over him, his arms reaching up and the word *you* to be referring outwards to me (this is for you). However, I was wrong. When my son, aged then about 15, saw it pinned onto my office wall, he explained it for me as follows. 'That's you there, mum' pointing to the diminutive figure on the left, 'see, you're wearing your glasses and jeans. And that's me (pointing to the larger figure) with the tracksuit bottoms I always wore'. It was this event that made me look again and *notice* how my son had designed his message. My long-standing misinterpretation had been caused by my failure to read the card as a *text* but view it instead as a picture, taking my son's use of size as a visual representation (me as bigger than him) rather than a metaphorical one in which size represents agency. In so doing, I had missed all the, now obvious, clues to the card's intended meaning.

If we now look at this example as a text, as we did with the graffiti in Chapter 1, we can work to understand how the different elements cohere to produce the message intended. There are similarities between the two in that they each comprise a single written word used in conjunction with pictorial representation. However, unlike the graffiti, where the status of the word *pay* and its grammatical function as an imperative were both anchored by the other textual elements (the pointing finger and the parking meter), here the status and function of the word *you* is less obvious. So what is it doing here? One answer is that my son simply wanted to include some writing as display; in other words, showing that he can produce letters to make a word. However, we do not think so because the choice of the word *you* does not seem to be random. If you are going to have a single word on a Mother's Day card, the word *mum*, a noun which intrinsically identifies or names itself, might have been a more likely candidate and would certainly more closely reflect the commercially produced Mother's Day card genre. The choice of *you* suggests something else is intended, something that is linked to the specific context of the specific mother and the specific meaning of the whole ensemble. It says, for instance, *you* not *she*. It also communicates a strong sense of addressivity (I'm 'talking' to *you*). But, because it is a pronoun, a 'grammatical' word which has a relational and referential role, we look for some kind of syntactic interaction with the other textual elements. Its status as a pronoun makes it either subject or object of a verb or, in this instance, the verb-like representation of the depicted action of hugging. The word *you*, then can now be understood as a verbal representation of the card's visual grammar (see Kress and van Leuwen 1996) referring to and reinforcing the meaning of the drawn figures. The status of the word depends on how the figures themselves are identified and hence the direction of the hug. In my mistaken understanding, the *you* would be the subject; that is, 'You (mum) are hugging me.' (son)'. By contrast, when *you* has the role of object, the message, 'I (son) am hugging you (mum)', offers a much more poignant meaning. In fact by analysing the interplay between the context, the purpose and the participants on the one hand and the choice of semiotic resources, on the other, as we discussed in Chapter 7, produces precisely the kind of message that Mother's Day cards are supposed to do; love coming from the child rather than the other way round. In designing and producing his card, my son had clearly understood this and I had clearly not!

9.2.2 *Private writing*

Our second example (Figure 9.2) was produced a few years later at around the age of 7 or so. It is similar to Figure 9.1 in that it combines writing with image, but it is quite different in its communicative purpose.

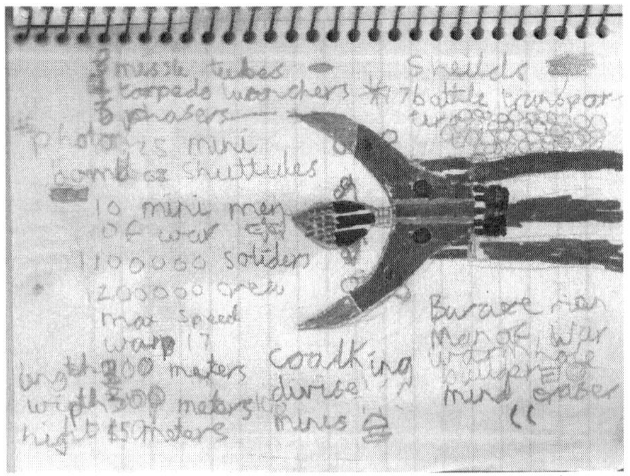

FIGURE 9.2 *Child's notebook page.*

This example, which is a page from a notebook, is a piece of private writing intended for personal use only. It is what we might call a 'service' text, rather like the notes we make when planning a more formal (public) one such as a job application or a book chapter. It is not meant to be read by others like the previous example, but was produced instead to serve a particular purpose of the producer's own. This is very different to the earlier example with its outward-looking interaction – from me to you. Here the interaction is inward, from me to me.

Unlike the Mother's Day card, the textual elements are not intended to cohere as a grammar, but instead are juxtaposed in a relationship by which the image offers a diagrammatic re-presentation of what is expressed verbally in writing. At first sight, I thought the image was of a person, one of the fantasy soldiers that my son used to play with at the time. However, I now see it as representing a battle craft along with an inventory of things that the craft contains. It says in writing, 'here are all these things' (the world told) and 'here is what it looks like when everything is in place' (the world shown). In other words, the two modes (writing and drawing) complement each other and in so doing contribute jointly to producing a visual representation which shows thinking in progress and a record of what has been thought. As such it can be seen as representing a very different stage in the child's writing development: one in which the child understands the value of writing (and drawing) as an aid to thinking. It shows reflexivity.

9.2.3 Genre awareness

A further point that can be understood from these two examples is the degree to which my son had developed genre awareness and the understanding of what resources are used in both of the textual genres he produced. It is unlikely that anyone had sat down with him and told him what to say or do with either text, but it is undoubtedly the case that he had encountered other examples of each of these genres. His design of the Mother's Day card shows his familiarity with the 'special occasion' card genre and his understanding that such cards are supposed to reflect the meanings of the special occasion at hand. His choice of semiotic resources are not random but specifically selected precisely because it is a Mother's Day card and not, for instance, a birthday or Christmas card. He has learned how to *represent* feeling as well as enact it, having recontextualized the act of hugging from the physical to the visual.

The second example, what we are calling the service text, is similarly informed by other textual productions that the child has come into contact with. For example, the juxtaposition of words and images in complementary relationship is typical of the many information books, such as the Dorling Kindersley Series, popular with young readers and definitely much loved by my son.

In both examples (Figures 9.1 and 9.2) the relationship between the different elements, the modes and the different textual materials they draw on, respectively, is one of co-production. The words do not 'anchor' the image in the way that Barthes (1977: 40) argues captions seek to 'anchor' photographs in a newspaper. Instead the words and images combine in complementary relationship to produce, as Kress has said 'the world told' and 'the world shown' (2003: 1) in a single multimodal text. Each mode, writing and drawing, affords different ways of representing things. Following Kress (e.g. 2010), explaining something in writing involves naming things, for instance, whereas drawing involves knowing their topology.

The two examples used in our first case study show a developing awareness that writing can do things in ways that differ from the more immediate mode of speaking. Writing allows us to produce lasting texts, ones that we can pass on to others, go back to and enjoy, as in the card, or ones that we can use as a point of reference, perhaps even modify, as in the notebook page. Realizations like these lie behind what we mean by *literacy*, a problematic term which is often misrepresented in public discourse, but one which is still used and useful and which we move onto unpack.

9.3 Being literate

If we were to ask you how often you use literacy or engage in literacy activity in the course of a day, you may respond by saying something like, 'Oh well, I don't have much time to read' or 'I'm not really very good at writing'. On the other hand, you might say that you spend hours every day in front of the computer, writing books or articles or sending emails and posting Facebook messages. It all very much depends on how you view literacy and writing. As we saw in Chapter 8, the majority of teenagers in the study by Lenhart et al. (2008) did not think of texting or messaging as writing. This is not surprising, as a substantial body of research shows (e.g. Barton et al. 2000; Street 2001; Barton and Papen 2010; Lillis 2013). The everyday literacy practices we all engage in are often overlooked as being instances of reading and writing. One way of finding out how often we engage in literacy is to keep track of every instance in the course of a single day as is shown in Ivanic et al. (2009). This would be quite a substantial task if you did it rigorously as you would find yourself having to include instances ranging from reading the label on the shampoo bottle in the shower, glancing at the headlines on the newspaper belonging to the person sitting next to you on the bus, scribbling down a name and phone number, through to more obvious activities such as making notes during a work-based meeting, writing an essay or reading a novel. Such an exercise helps us to realize how much of our lives are bound up in literacy activity.

As we showed in the previous chapter, writing is not simply a case of representing speech by using orthographic marks (graphemes) linked, to a greater or lesser degree, to the phonemic system of a given language. Just think about when you write things yourself. You may know what you want to say, in your head so to speak, but when it comes to putting that thought into writing, it is never a process of direct transfer from thought to written words and sentences. The act of writing gives a new shape to the idea in your mind – it realizes it as writing. Equally, if you have been involved in a particular conversation and you want to record it in a diary, the process of writing affects the way in which you can represent that conversation. This is because writing is a highly reflexive activity. Unlike speaking, where thoughts, once uttered, cannot be withdrawn leaving no trace, in writing we can take the time to think about how we are going to present our thoughts, read what we have written and revise it if we are not satisfied. As Barthes (1977) points out:

> Speech is irreversible: a word cannot be retracted, except precisely by saying that one retracts it. To cross out is here to add: if I want to erase what I have just said, I cannot do it without showing the eraser itself (I must say:'or rather. . .' 'I expressed myself badly. . .'); paradoxically it is ephemeral speech which is indelible, not monumental writing. All that one can do in the case of a spoken utterance is to tack on another utterance.'(190)

Of course, there are occasions when we use writing to record real speech (as opposed to fictional speech), for example during official events such as in a court of law or parliament. In these cases, the aim is to have a written record of exactly what is said (verbatim), although the transcribed words themselves do not provide the whole meaning as we discussed in the previous chapter. This can be seen in the same light as an audio or video recording of such events which 'collects' what is uttered without any attempt to filter it. Such writing is neither analytical nor reflective and if it were, it would not achieve what it is meant to achieve; that is a record of what was uttered. By contrast, note-taking, which can also be understood as a way of recording what someone is saying, is a very different kind of record-keeping to those described above. Note-taking involves selection because there is insufficient time to record every word that is said. Moreover, because of the constraints of timing, alternatives need to be found to represent the kinds of semantic information that writing affords with its specific syntactic resources for foregrounding ideas or indicating relationship between ideas. As Figure 9.3, which is a page of notes taken during a university seminar, shows, we tend to use other, usually non-verbal, resources instead.

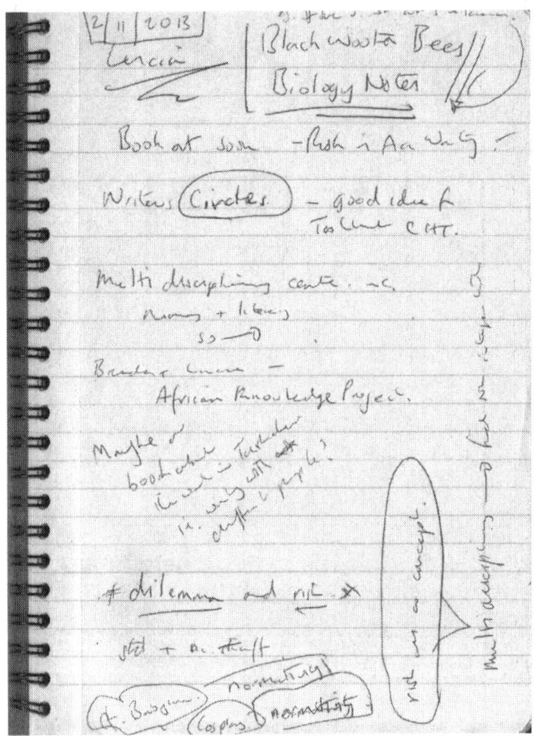

FIGURE 9.3 *Lecture notes.*

The kind of literacy demonstrated in this example, as with the previous two examples, is a much more complex understanding than that of coding and decoding. In each example, the writers demonstrate not only the ability to code, but also the ability to analyse and reflect. Being literate entails more than the possession of a set of autonomous skills (see Street e.g. 2001) which allow us to produce and interpret the different (ortho)graphic arrangements used in a given language. Being literate means first, that we know that writing is a resource for producing and communicating meanings, secondly, that we can use it ourselves to produce our own meanings and thirdly that we can interpret others' meanings. Being able to recite the alphabet means that someone can imitate and memorize a sequence of sounds, and being able to copy the written alphabet means that they can replicate a visual shape. They don't, though, mean that someone is literate. However, if someone understands that those visual shapes and phonetic sounds are resources that can be used to produce and understand meanings (semiotic resources), then we move into the realm of literacy, as the examples from Fiona's son show. They are meaningful and interpretable and have identifiable purpose. They were produced to act on and in the world and as such are instances of literacy as *social practice* (e.g. Street 1984; Bazerman 1988; Barton 2007; Kress 2010), something we *do*, not something we have.

If you think of the European alphabet how many letters do you think of? The English alphabet has 26 letters, along with French and German, but not all languages use the same number. Spanish has 27 letters (it used to have 29 until 2010!), Swedish has 29, Polish and Russian have 33, while the Italian alphabet has only 21 letters. Does this mean that Polish is a very difficult language to write or that Italian is very simple? Essentially, transcriptions were established at different times in the history of different languages using different criteria for decisions about what sounds (or phonemes) it is relevant to represent symbolically. The fact, for instance, that in English orthography we have only five vowel letters (a e i o u) even though, phonologically, we have at least 14 vowel sounds, and 22 if we include diphthongs, means that the alphabet could be considered inadequate. However, to include all the vowels as letters would produce its own problems. An alphabet of getting on for 50 letters would begin to defeat the purpose of having an alphabet in the first place! By contrast, Spanish has five phonological vowels which are matched by its five alphabetic vowels. Spelling in Spanish is, therefore, easier than spelling in English, though that does not mean that *writing* in Spanish is easier. Spelling in English is difficult because the basis on which the spelling was established was not solely dependent on pronunciation. This is one reason why an overreliance on phonics for teaching reading in English is problematic.

This then brings us onto the issue of whether the term literacy and literate can be extended to other communicative modes, as in 'digital literacy' or 'visual literacy'. According to the Oxford English Dictionary (2001) the term 'literate' is defined as on the one hand 'able to read and write', and on the other hand 'having or showing education or knowledge, typically in a specified area: *we need people who are politically and economically literate*'.

As we have already pointed out, the terms 'literacy' and 'literate' are problematic when it comes to how to use them and what they effectively mean. As Kress argues, in his discussion of multimodality, 'The term "literacy" whatever the prefix (e-, media -, mobile –, computer -, visual -, emotional -)

becomes ever more vague the further it is extended' (2010: 102). Nevertheless, for the purposes of our discussion, and because we are not trying to invent the world in this book, the term has a useful role to play. For us, *literacy* and *being literate* concern active participation in visual textual activity and practices, in other words the creative production of visual texts and the interpretative engagement with such texts. Like Kress, we recognize the need for new concepts to capture the different affordances of multimodal communication. Like Barton et al. (2000) and Street (2001), we view literacy activity as situated and occuring in all sorts of places and in many different ways. The examples we analysed above are three such instances. In the next section we offer more examples of literacy activity with our Case Study Two which looks at examples of informal literacy activity between friends.

9.4 Literacy between friends

Our previous case study looked at a child learning that he could do things with writing and drawing. In the first instance it was communicating feelings as well as participating in the culturally understood practice of Mother's Day and its associated genre, the Mother's Day card. In the second instance, it was that the visual representation of an idea and a design could serve as both a design activity and a record of that design through representing the idea schematically, using an image, and verbally by naming different components of the idea. In this case study we look at literacy interaction between friends; specifically we look at two examples of correspondence from 'far away' places. Each uses a different genre: the first is a postcard and the second is a Facebook page. Our aim is to see what the communicative opportunities of each genre enable the correspondents to do with what resources and how this affects the communicative impact. Both of the texts are what might be considered public in that they are available to a wider audience than the one that is specifically being addressed. A postcard is not usually placed in an envelope, for instance, and is therefore available to be read by a wider audience than the specific addressee; the Facebook page is available to all Facebook friends and their friends too.

9.4.1 *Holiday postcard*

In their discussion about 'ordinary writing' with particular reference to Edwardian postcards, Gillen and Hall (2010: 169) point out that during this time almost 1 billion postcards were being sent each year in Britain alone. At that time, the holiday postcard, which represents the majority of postcards sent today, was only one of several different postcard genres. Gillen and Hall go on to explain that the phenomenon of sending postcards was, at the time, symptomatic of what was viewed by the contemporary publication, *The Girl's Realm Annual*, as being 'a period peopled by a hurried generation that has not got many minutes to spare for writing letters' (cited in Gillen and Hall 2010: 171). They also cite an article from the *Manchester Weekly Times* of 1890 which anticipated that the postcard would enable one to 'write one's thoughts in pencil as soon as it occurs, and dispatch it through the first messenger of the first receiving box one comes across' (2010: 170). Today, such a description conjures up the image of the avid Twitter user as he dashes off a tweet the moment a thought, no matter whether it is interesting or relevant or even profound, comes to his mind. Gillen and Hall also point out that postcard sending was a case of ordinary people corresponding about all sorts of things using what was at that time a very cheap postal service which involved several collections and deliveries a day. Then, it was possible to send a postcard in the morning and to have it delivered within the same day. Nowadays, a postcard usually takes 2 or 3 days, and a holiday postcard, typically sent from abroad, takes even longer with postcards sometimes arriving after the sender has already returned from their trip! So if the postcard in the early twentieth century was intended as a means of instant (or near instant) messaging, what is the purpose of the postcard today? Another thing to note about a postcard is that it is a multimodal ensemble, similar in many ways to the digital domains that Domingo et al. (2014) discuss when considering online writing.

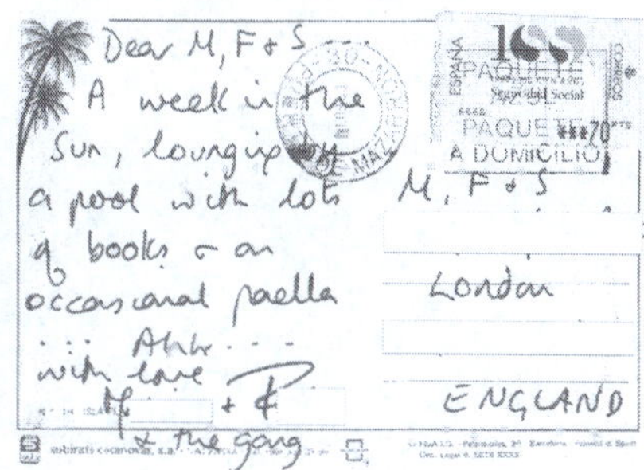

FIGURES 9.4a AND b *Holiday postcard*

The postcard in Figure 9.4, from which the names and address have been hidden for reasons of anonymity, is immediately recognizable as a holiday postcard. Most readers will be familiar with the genre, having sent postcards yourselves and having received them from others. The practice of sending them has an almost ritualistic quality about it, involving finding the shop to buy them from, choosing the 'right' pictures, deciding who to send them to and hence what to write on them and, finally, searching for stamps and where to post them. In fact, they can become something of a holiday duty, even chore.

The photographic image on our example is typical of the holiday postcard depicting as it does a beach scene. It may be the actual beach that the people who sent it were visiting, but it could equally be a generic beach somewhere in the region. There is a title written on the picture side (Isla Plana) and then the location 'Costa Cálida' so we know that it is 'abroad' and roughly where abroad. However, because this is a photograph taken by an unknown photographer, the meanings are borrowed meanings and the scene depicted could equally be one of relaxing times on the beach or one of two strangers happening to be on the beach at the same time, or even a couple in the middle of an argument. We can make up any story about this photograph that we choose, but we will never know what it actually shows. The point is that it doesn't matter what is going on. What matters is what it represents (*'aren't we lucky here with the blue sky and the sea/mountains/historic town/exotic location')* not what is depicted (the actual spot, the actual experience). This, as we will see later, contrasts with the kinds of holiday images possible when using digital media. Of course, in our reproduction of the postcard, we are using only grey-scale colours which means that a key aspect of the meaning is lost. In the original colour version,[3] the sky is a clear blue and the sea blue changing to turquoise as the water approaches the beach. In colour you can see the warmth whereas in grey, we have to imagine it.

Turning now to the other side of the postcard, the theme of holiday and sun is reinforced by the two palm trees positioned to frame the written message suggestive of the way they might appear on the actual beach where the senders might actually be, writing the postcard itself. And even though there is no evidence of any palm trees in the photograph on the other side, this is not important. The palm trees, almost peeping over the top of the written message, create a writing environment which affords a 'having a nice time' narrative and to write a 'bad time' story in such an environment would be at odds with the design. Finally, and noting in passing the other indicators of 'abroadness' such as the stamp and the postmark, which we might study on receipt of the postcard to see exactly where our friends are and perhaps even how long it took for the card to arrive, we come to the written message itself.

It is worth pointing out that postcards are one of the few remaining written genres where handwriting still retains its dominance and although it is possible to download a digital postcard and write your own message on it in type font or a pseudo-script font, there may not be any internet access or even a wish to use it in the holiday context. On our postcard we can see that there appear to be two 'hands', that of the actual message writer and that of a second person who filled in the last part of the address. Only handwriting allows visible traces of a writer's identity, a personal character that digital fonts deny. The postcard is addressed to M, F & S and the greeting also refers to them as M, F & S even though the senders have used full versions of their own names alongside '& the gang' in the unedited[4] postcard. What this tells us is that the correspondents are likely to be close friends, so names are assumed to be understood. It is not necessary to fully name the recipients, and postcards frequently omit a named greeting as here, but it is important for the senders to name themselves. If they had actually signed themselves M & P only, there would have been a degree of ambiguity about who had sent the postcard, unless, of course, the recipients were completely familiar with the handwriting.

As for the written part of the message, it is succinct in its information, as postcards must inevitably be because of the limited space, but warm in its interpersonal meaning. Note that it does not contain a single fully-formed verb structure. The action is embedded in the naming of the activity, a kind of inventory of experience. It is a highly nominalized piece of writing, typical, not of spokenness but of writtenness, as we saw in the previous chapter. It describes, not at all what is going on in the photograph on the other side, but rather what is going on for the senders themselves. The photograph signifies holiday in a warm seaside location in general, the written message tells us the kind of holiday the senders are actually having (It's only for a week; there's a pool so they are probably swimming in it; they've got lots of books to read; they're eating nice Spanish food.) These details tell us something about the senders and what they like doing which may, of course, be very different to the things that other people like doing; the people shown in the postcard for instance. Note that there is no reference to the sea or the beach. Perhaps this is because the photograph says that for them. Even the handwriting, which gives the impression of casual ease, replicates the light tone of the written message, while the use of the onomatopoeic '. . . Ahh. . .' articulates the pleasure of the experience. It is a classic example of the genre.

Finally, what happens when the postcard drops through the letterbox of the addressees? Which side do they look at first, the picture or the writing and how might that influence their reading of it? Holiday postcards can appear as a kind of smug commiseration to the poor people 'back home'. However, they can also be a reminder of friendship, a momentary sharing and a welcome change from the abundance of junk mail that increasingly arrives through the post in these days of minimal letter writing.

The next example, what we are calling the 'holiday Facebook post', shows how the opportunities offered by digital media in general and the Facebook platform in particular, afford different communicative possibilities and different perceptions of holiday messages.

9.4.2 Holiday Facebook post

According to the World Bank, reported in the *Washington Post* (June 2012),[5] there were due to be 1 billion registered Facebook users worldwide by the beginning of 2013. Based on these figures, if we assume that every registered user visits Facebook once a week and posts, say, ten messages of one kind or another (wall post, share, like, comment, photograph, YouTube video) that means that at the very least 10 billion messages a week are being sent although the number is likely to be much higher than that. This phenomenon, along with Twitter and other social networking sites, is nothing new when we consider the postcard phenomenon during the first 10 years of the twentieth century, reported in Gillen and Hall's study referred to above. It seems that, as human beings, we like to communicate experience and far from writing diminishing, as predicted by certain moral panickers towards the end of the last century, more writing is done by more people than ever before in the history of the world. As we have noted, people do not always consider themselves to be writing when they are texting or posting on Facebook even though the terms (texting, posting) used to denote the act of producing these messages derive from writing activity. We suggest the same applies to reading which, for many people, involves the reading of books or other published written materials and not scrolling through a Facebook homepage or doing a Google search. What we are particularly interested in here, though, is what digital media lets us do and with what semiotic resources using the approach that we used in our postcard example.

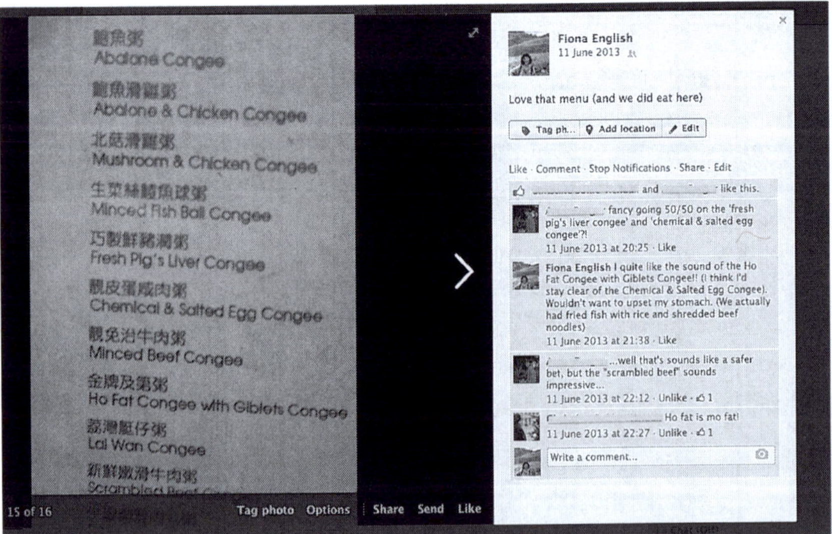

FIGURE 9.5 *Facebook screenshot.*

Most readers will be familiar with the genre that the screenshot in Figure 9.5 shows, just as you will have been familiar with the postcard genre in our previous example. What we want to discuss here is how the affordances of each provide different communicative opportunities. The postcard offered the senders the chance to signify 'being on holiday' by using both the stock photographic image provided on one side of the card and the designated space on the other side personalize the experience. The direction of such messages is essentially one way, from the sender to the receiver, and although the reader of that postcard re-imagines the information based on what they know about the sender and the place where they have gone, the interaction between the parties is remote and delayed. This reflects our discussion about writtenness in the previous chapter. The Facebook post, however, is different in two main regards even though it comprises essentially the same textual modes – a photograph on one side of the screen and writing on the other. The first difference is that the photograph was taken by the holidaymaker herself rather than by an unknown professional photographer. The second is that the writing part allows for, or rather invites, interaction and develops into a conversation between the sender and her 'recipients'. These differences make this a very different kind of holiday communication to the postcard despite the elements that they share.

In this particular Facebook correspondence, I (Fiona) had posted a series of photographs taken while abroad, each representing something I had found interesting or, in the case of the image above, quirky and amusing. Unlike the postcard, these photographs are representations of personally experienced phenomena rather than the generalized postcard photograph. In other words, the image, including its own verbal elements, provides a personal message just as much as the verbal conversation that gets going alongside. In fact, in this case we could say that the image is what I wanted to share while the initial written message ('Love that menu (and we did eat here)') acts to authenticate both the menu that is shown (it is a real menu) and the menu that is experienced (I had a meal at this restaurant).

In contrast to the postcard above with its inventory of the kind of experiences that would be familiar and therefore understood by the readers, this message offers an unfamiliar experience, or at least one that is assumed to be unfamiliar. The message itself can be even more succinct than that of the postcard because it refers directly to the image. It names the image (menu) but it does not describe it as, say, a caption might do. Instead it offers what we can call a framing comment which tells readers how I want them to understand the image and which, it could be argued, says more about me than it does about the photograph itself. When I write, 'Love that menu' what exactly do I mean? Do I mean that I love the food it offers? The truth of the statement can be better understood in conjunction with the added-on, parenthesized comment, '(and we did eat here)', where the use of 'and' and 'did' combine to suggest the meaning of 'despite the menu we ate here'. In fact, I am not commenting on my love of the food, but rather on my love of the menu with its translated names of the dishes. This was, of course, the motivation for photographing the menu in the first place. Posting it on Facebook is because I thought my friends might also enjoy the translated names and because, perhaps, it denotes not only where I am but the kind of experience I am actually having. This, I hope, might appear exciting or even daring, thereby indicating that I'm the kind of person who's willing to go to off-the-beaten-track places.

The resultant correspondence is just the kind of interaction that I had hoped for with this post. The comments show that some of my like-minded friends understood why I had taken and posted the photograph. However, it is perfectly possible that others who viewed this posting may have taken it at face value, not recognizing the intended irony because they do not belong to the particular community, as discussed in Chapter 3, for whom I envisaged the joke. The point, though, is not the content of the correspondence and whether it is jokey or serious, but the way in which that content becomes transformed by the interventions made by my friends. Unlike the postcard with its overview of the holiday, the Facebook post allows a more specific representation offering a *view* rather than an account, sharing an experience rather than describing one.

Both these examples of literacy activity show how different media and the different opportunities they provide for affect the kinds of messages we can produce and the literacy practices that they give rise to. The holiday postcard invites no direct interactional response from its readers apart from, perhaps, when the participants get together at some later date. The holiday Facebook post, by contrast, invites interaction, using the 'like' button, making a comment or even 'sharing' with other friends. In fact, if there were no follow-up at all, the poster would be disappointed as it could be read as a judgement on the degree of interest the post is considered to elicit. A Facebook post is, therefore, a more challenging thing to write than a postcard. This is a theme we return to in the next chapter when talking about identity and power in different communicative settings. In the final section of this chapter, however, we consider the case of literacy-like communication in contexts where writing may not be the most effective mode of communication.

9.5 Literacy in diversity

Blommaert (2010: 1) opens his book with the assertion 'Sociolinguistically, the world has not become a village' as a challenge to the now somewhat hackneyed metaphor of the global village. He goes on to argue that the world is a much more complex and, indeed, complicated place than the culturally homogenous village of the imagination would lead one to suppose. One aspect of this complication concerns writing and written communication across what are educationally, culturally, linguistically, socially and politically diverse communities, whether across the globe or within villages themselves. How can communication which depends on writing for its distribution be effectively achieved across the globe when not everyone shares the same language or uses the same script for writing, or can write and read at all? In our first example, using the case of Pakistan, we look at how a society accommodates diversity in levels of literacy in the context of a general election. Our second example concerns the reading of images in the context of linguistic diversity.

9.5.1 *Reading symbols*

We first came across the image shown in Figure 9.6 on a Facebook entry of one of our students. It intrigued us not because of its visual design, nor for its use of the numeral '4' standing in for the word 'for', a borrowing from text messaging that has become ubiquitous in the public domain. What attracted our attention was the omission of the article (*a* or *the*) before the noun 'bat', an example of linguistic variation (or deviation) that we discussed in Chapters 2 and 5; and, of course, the rather intriguing invitation to vote for (a) bat.

FIGURE 9.6 *Pakistan 2012 election campaign poster.*

We recognized the linguistic phenomenon as characteristic of South Asian English and we began to have an inkling of what the invitation was about once we remembered that it was election time in Pakistan and that one of the candidates was Imran Khan, former captain of the Pakistan national cricket team. We confirmed this by carrying out a simple Google search of the phrase which revealed that the slogan, 'vote4bat', made appearances in many different genres: posters, tee-shirts, graffiti, leaflets, sometimes using the phrase by itself and, more often, accompanied by an image as in our example. However, the question that remained was why did it say 'vote4bat' and not 'vote for Imran Khan'? The answer lay, as we discovered on further investigation, in the way in which Pakistan designs its ballot papers.

In Pakistan, according to UNESCO, only just over half (55%) of the adult population was defined as literate in 2009. Of course, as we have suggested above, what is meant by literate is imprecise, but these statistics indicate that there might be difficulties of electoral access for a large number of people. Added to this is the fact that, Pakistan is a multilingual country and despite the establishment of Urdu as the national language, there may be large numbers of the population who do not actually speak it, let alone read it. In order to respond to this linguistic complexity, the Electoral Commission of Pakistan, like many other countries, including India and Egypt, allocates symbols to the different parties from an official list of 227 images, some of which can be seen in Figure 9.7.

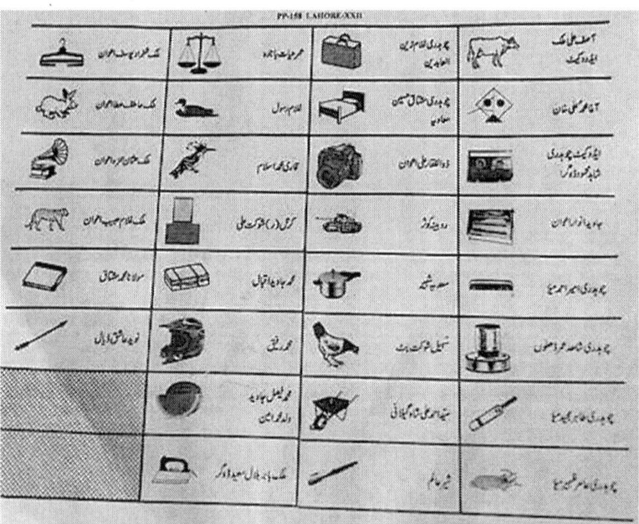

FIGURE 9.7 *Chart of party symbols used for the 2012 Pakistan election.*

The different parties apply for the symbol they favour and where there is competition for a particular symbol, a draw is held. Some parties rank their preferences so that if they fail to get their first choice, the second or third may be available. As Figure 9.7 shows, the range of symbols is very wide and, to those of us unfamiliar with such a system, includes a bizarre range of items.

Some have obvious references to other meanings; for instance the scales for justice, the arrow for truth, the tiger for strength or fierceness or the book denoting learning and knowledge and, in Pakistan, religion. However, most of the others are more obscure. What does the coat hanger denote, or the toothbrush? And how would a party respond to being allocated one of those?

In fact, despite the supposed arbitrary allocation of the symbols, parties rush to get the ones that they consider most desirable, which, according to a leading Pakistan newspaper, *Dawn*,[6] are 'the sun' or 'the book'. This suggests, as is to be expected, that the symbols are not, nor ever could be, arbitrary – as the allocation of the cricket bat to Imran Khan's party, Tehreek-e-Insaf (Pakistan Movement for Justice), confirms. It is also worth noting, of course, that cricket in Pakistan is more than just a sport, it is a national passion.

At the time of the actual ballot, the papers appear without any written information to state which party is which. They show only the symbolic image. This explains why our campaign poster in Figure 9.6 proclaims 'vote4bat' and is accompanied by an image of a cricket bat, rather than 'vote4Khan' or 'vote4 Tehreek-e-Insaf'. It is not just that the bat has an association with Imran Khan's career as a cricketer (although it is an important reminder to the electorate); it is the fact that voters will actually be voting, as in putting their cross or fingerprint, next to a picture of (a) bat.

9.5.1 *Reading without words*

Global corporations also make use of communicative modes other than writing in order to deal with the linguistic diversity of their markets. So, just as the ballot papers discussed above use images as a universal means of catering for the whole population in Pakistan, many multinational corporations opt for figurative rather than verbal communication, particularly where things need to be explained for safety reasons, for instance. The Swedish furniture corporation, IKEA, is a good example of one such company because many, if not most, of its products need to be assembled at home and instructions need to be provided. Since IKEA's customers are unlikely to be skilled joiners or plumbers and are located worldwide, speaking a myriad of different languages, these instructions need to cater for all. Figure 9.8, which is a page from one of their instruction booklets, shows the solution that they have come up with. The question is, without any verbal explanation how do we know this is a set of instructions and how do we know how to read them?

As anyone who has had to assemble a piece of furniture at home knows, you need to develop a kind of home-assembly instructions literacy in order to work with this kind of text. However, if we were to show this page to someone who had never encountered such a text they might read it very differently to those of us who have worked with such genres before. On the one hand, the comic-strip layout and cartoon drawings suggest a storyline, but on the other hand, the inventory of items might sit oddly in juxtaposition with the narrative. Following Grice's co-operative principles discussed in Chapters 6 and 7, the uninitiated would seek the assumed meaningfulness and might ponder along the following lines.

FIGURE 9.8 *Page from an IKEA instruction booklet.*

In the first drawing a man (he has a man-like rather than a woman-like shape) is smiling happily, but what is he smiling about? He appears to be saying something as denoted by the speech bubble, but what he is saying is not words but an image of a screwdriver pointing down towards the shape of a screw head. (Of course, to understand this much we need to know that a speech bubble indicates that someone is speaking and we need to recognize the meaning implied by the arrangement of the items inside the bubble.) But what exactly is he saying? Is he saying that he's got a screwdriver, or is he asking for one, or telling us we need one? And what's going on in the next strip? Is it the same person and if so why has his mood suddenly changed? He looks puzzled and there's a thought bubble with a question mark (always assuming that we know what a question mark is) so he wants to know about something, something about the box that's open beside him. Maybe that's why the next picture shows him making a phone call. He's phoning to ask about the box and they must be giving him the information he needs because he's smiling again. But why have they drawn those screws in the bottom half of the page? We could go on, but will stop here, since the point has, we feel, been made. The point is that we don't need to be familiar with the genre to make up a meaningful narrative using the semiotic resources provided, but we do need to be familiar with it to understand the intended meanings or at least the kinds of meanings intended.

Treating this page of instructions in this way is not entirely fair, though, because much of the ambiguity would disappear if we were actually in the process of assembling the item and had the different components to hand. And this is the point of this text – it is designed to be used only within a certain, very specific context. What is more, familiarity with the genre means that each time we come across a similar set of instructions, whether from IKEA or another company, we are already primed on how to read them.

This kind of literacy is similar to that developed while playing digital games (see Gee 2007 or Cutting 2011). In that context, certain meanings become associated with certain game elements and once a player is familiar with these associations in one digital game she can recognize them in others. A good example of this is the typical association of water with recovery whereby, as a player's strength diminishes through being injured in a fight, for instance, they have the opportunity to replenish their energy by visiting a watery place such as a waterfall or a stream or fountain. Games may not all use the same semiotic resources for the same purposes, but once a player is familiar, or develops games literacy, she can more easily recognize the alternatives.

9.6 Conclusion

This chapter has used three case studies to explore different kinds of literacy practice and in so doing consider what is the nature of literacy itself. We have used our examples to demonstrate how writing, along with other modes of visual representation, can work either separately or together to produce meanings. We also wanted to show that literacy is not just something we get when we go to school, as is often thought, but it is something we are always in the process of developing as we encounter new forms of literacy practice – think of academic literacy (essay writing, journal articles, etc.) or Tweeting or blogging – using particular kinds of knowledge in particular kinds of ways. In the next chapter, we look more closely at how textual design, that is the choice of semiotic resources as in lexis, syntax, colour, shape, tone of voice, etc., can promote particular versions of reality. In other words, we look at ways in which we shape our communication to produce the message that best suits our purpose, whatever it may be.

Suggested reading

Barton, D. (2007), *An Introduction to the Ecology of Written Language,* 2nd edn. Oxford: Blackwell.

A now classic discussion on literacy which opens our eyes up to how it can and should be conceived and hence understood.

Barton, D. and Papen, U. (eds) (2010), *The Anthropology of Writing. Understanding Textually Mediated Worlds.* London: Continuum

A wide-ranging collection which analyses writing in such diverse contexts as cattle farms in France, health centres in Britain or fieldwork notes in Mali, exemplifies not only the texts themselves but also the practices and the experiences associated with them.

Blommaert, J. (2008), *Grassroots Literacy: Writing, Identity and Voice in Central Africa.* London: Routledge.

This excellent book, which is an ethnographic study of two sets of handwritten documents, explores and analyses not only how the documents are produced in terms of language or other semiotic resources, but what the texts tell us about the writers themselves and how they are located within the wider context of globalization.

Lillis, T. (2013), *The Sociolinguistics of Writing.* Edinburgh: Edinburgh University Press.

This book lifts the study of writing out of the ghetto of schooling and skills and places it firmly in the social domain as an object of sociolinguistic inquiry in its own right. Using examples from different writing contexts, it provides a thought-provoking account of different issues and approaches not only to the study of writing per se but also to sociolinguistics more generally.

10

Choosing our words

10.1 Introduction

Over the last two chapters we have discussed how we can analyse communicative interactions using the frames of reference and framework that we proposed in Chapters 6 and 7. However, although we inevitably touched on it, we didn't specifically focus on the ways in which we shape our communications according to how we want them to be understood. Of course, all communication involves shaping meaning, but what we are interested in here is how the semiotic choices we make promote a particular view. In Chapter 1 we used the example of mistaken register in an email to illustrate how social relations can be encoded in the linguistic choices we make. In this chapter we develop this theme in exploring how we consciously, and sometimes very carefully, choose our words (or tone of voice, gesture, colour, etc.) to promote a particular 'version of reality' as Kress and Hodge (1979: 16) have put it.

10.2 Naming as a semiotic resource

An example of what we mean when we talk about choosing our words is how we choose to name something. For instance, a particular bugbear of ours, and we are not alone in this, is the way in which people who use public transport in London and beyond have mysteriously been transformed from being *passengers* to being *customers*. However, if we use our linguistics lens, we can see that this terminological shift is neither mysterious nor accidental but rather a very conscious decision by those responsible for public transport to change how we see ourselves as users of the service. As a *passenger*, I am someone who is travelling from A to B in some form of transport but one which I am not actually driving myself. Someone else is doing that on my behalf. The term *passenger* is, therefore, specific to this kind of activity and its metaphoric use (e.g. She's one of life's passengers) emphasizes the relaxed, even passive quality of the meaning. However, once I become a *customer* these meanings disappear. The travelling aspect is removed and the experience becomes commodified like any other purchasable item and I, the erstwhile passenger, am now made into a consumer of the commodity. This substantively changes not only my sense of identity but that of the transport providers themselves. The relationship between us becomes more transactional: no longer service-like, acting on behalf of the users, but business-like, acting on behalf of themselves. A change such as this is not just a word change, but a *category* change. *Customers* fall into a different semantic category to *passengers* and swapping one for the other is, we argue, an ideological choice rather than a lexical one, designed to alter both the conceptual and the actual relationship between the participants. This is something that was picked up in the recent student demonstrations in England protesting against the raising of university fees, as can be seen in Figure 10.1. The students who produced their placard were intuitively aware of the importance of category and somewhere, in the offices of Transport for London, someone understood it too.

FIGURE 10.1[1] *Placards during a 2010 national student demonstration in London.*

One way of spotting other examples of category choice is to notice how the same event is named in different media outlets. For example, in British reporting of recent conflicts around the world, the terms *insurrection* and *insurgents*, with their negative spin, are used when people are fighting against a favoured government while *uprising* and *rebels*, which offer a more positive impression, when they are against a disfavoured one. In fact, category choice is one of the most argued-over territories when it comes to how we present our world view (think 'political correctness'). It has been discussed by many linguists over the years (e.g. Bolinger 1980; Cameron 1995; Fairclough 2001) but is not confined to academic debate. The following extract, from a BBC report[2] on a survey conducted with disabled listeners about the terms of reference to disability that they most disliked, is one such example.

> [I]t was interesting to see that disabled people had voted 'special' as fifth most offensive. 'Special service', 'special school' and 'special needs' are phrases used in an attempt to be positive about disability. But in the same way women don't like being elevated to 'lady', disabled people find it patronising to be lifted to the status of special. It differentiates them from normal, but in a saccharine manner. Disabled people are different, but not better or more important. Besides, putting them on a pedestal does not appear to be shifting attitudes or solving the appalling disability unemployment situation. Clearly, language in this field is a hotch-potch of confusion. (Rose 2004)

What we are talking about here, then, is communication at the level of discourses as defined in Chapter 7. In our example of passenger versus customer, we need to understand the contextual circumstances in which the change from one to the other has taken place. In our example, it is that of the marketization of what are considered to be essentially public services and the growing sense of unease that this has created among many sectors of the British population. For visitors to the country who are unaware of these contextual factors, whether they are called a customer or a passenger may well be irrelevant. But for the locals it is quite a different matter. They *notice* the change because they know the context and are therefore sensitive to the layers of meaning this category change represents, what Kress (2010: 113) calls, the 'layering of discourses'.

Same category – semantic shift

For many people, having middle-class values is clearly something to be admired while for others it denotes hypocrisy, pretentiousness and double standards, as in the following headline taken from the *Times Higher Education* weekly journal in July 2011:

> Widening Access: are we imposing middle-class values on everyone?

The juxtapositioning of 'impose' and 'middle-class values' is a clear example of the phrase being ascribed a negative value. How does such a semantic shift happen? Can you think of any others?

10.3 Mode as a semiotic resource

As we have just seen, category choice is a powerful way of promoting an ideological (world-view) stance. However, it is not the only way we choose our words but how we use them. For example, how much time do you spend carefully composing a witty Facebook entry on your wall or making an apposite comment against someone else's posting? These essentially public spaces force us to think about how we are presenting ourselves and how we want to be viewed by our different readers. One such example is how to think of the 'right' message to put in a workplace leaving card. If you simply sign your name, you might give out the message that you don't particularly care about the leaver or simply that you don't remember who the person actually is. However, if you sign your name at a jaunty angle and add a smiley face, the 'signature' can be understood as friendly, breezy and informal, much more fitting for the occasion. This kind of adjustment is also known as 'modalizing' (Hodge and Kress 1988: 123) and it is this process that we now consider.

Think about a teacher deciding to use a green pen instead of a red one to annotate students' work. Why would he make such a choice? How does it affect its social meaning? How might it be understood by the students?

We now look at three examples of communicative interaction and, using the social semiotic framework (Figure 7.1) explained in Chapter 7, we consider how they have been shaped to promote particular 'versions of reality', to re-use Kress and Hodge's (1979: 16) comment referred to above. Figure 10.2, which is a simplified version of Figure 7.1, sets out the basic approach which is to explore the interactions between the *material* (genres, textual materials, etc.) and the *social* (what's going on, where and why, who's involved and what their social relationship is, etc.).

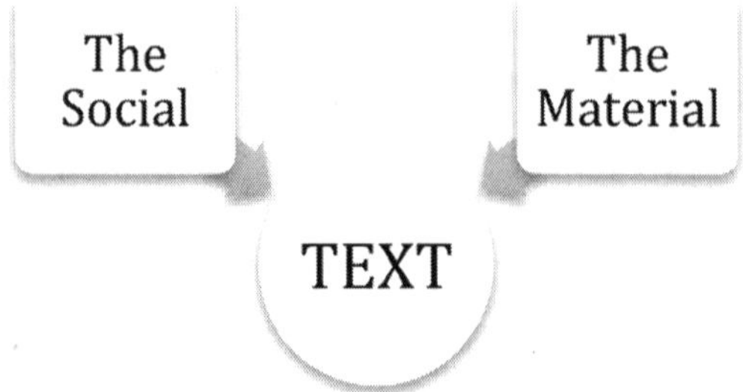

FIGURE 10.2 *Simplified analytical framework.*

All these factors interact in the process of textual production in every communicative activity, as we discussed in Chapter 7.

10.3.1 Power play – modalizing as mitigation

The first example is an exchange of two workplace emails.[3] In analysing this text we want to keep an open mind for as long as possible in our effort to understand what it can tell us, so rather than present the whole correspondence, we take them as they would have unfolded in the course of normal online interaction starting at the beginning with the first one.

Extract 10.1

> Subject: AB123 Module Log
> Date: 21/08/2010
> From: John Smith john.smith@urbanuniversity.ac.uk
> To: joe.bloggs@urbanuniversity.ac.uk, jim.brown@urbanuniversity.ac.uk
>
> Dear Joe and Jim,
>
> > Just a gentle reminder that we'll need a module log for AB123
> > Best
> > John

At first glance, this is a very straightforward communication from one colleague to another. We can tell this from the fact that they all share the same address. John addresses his colleagues by their first names and signs himself off using his own, suggesting a friendly and equal relationship between the participants. However, this tells us little about the status of the co-respondents as it is usual practice to use first names in British universities, even among colleagues of different institutional status, and to do otherwise would have been strange. It is, though, worth pointing out that choosing how to address someone can be a social minefield (see Chapter 14) and in certain contexts using someone's first name may come across as disrespectful or patronizing.[4]

Furthermore, once we know that this is a university setting and, if we are familiar with certain institutional terms of reference, such as *module*, we will know that the communication is about course documentation and regular institutional practice.

For most readers, this email would be interpreted as a directive from the writer, John, to the addressees, Joe and Jim, even though he does not specifically ask them to do anything. It is the kind of directive that seeks to disguise its authority by suggesting joint responsibility for a task which is intended to be undertaken by those who are directed. It is an example of workplace power relations in action. So, despite the absence of any obvious terms of request or demand, what is it about this message that makes us intuitively understand it in this way? The first clue lies in the stated fact that a document is needed, so we assume that somebody is expected to provide it. Who that somebody might be is not revealed and, on the face of it, responsibility could lie with any or all three of them or even with someone else altogether. In this sense, we know that some kind of action underlies this message. However, this does not explain why we identify it as a request and why we know that it is John who is doing the actual requesting and that he assumes he can do so. To tackle these questions we need to turn our attention to the linguistic resources John has drawn on in shaping his email. In other words, we need to explore how certain linguistic resources used in this correspondence encode the social rather than the literal (or propositional) meanings of the message. Here it is again.

Just a gentle reminder that we'll need a module log for AB123

As we have already suggested, despite its avoidance of the usual syntactic forms used in making a directive, the email fits into the 'directive' genre.

There are three linguistic clues to why we might understand the message as a directive rather than as a statement of fact and which point to the encoded social meanings that typify many communicative interactions where power relations are relevant (see also our mention of illocutionary force in Chapter 6). These are John's use of the expressions *just, gentle* and *we'll* which, despite adding little or nothing to the core, propositional meaning (This is a reminder. We need a module log.), fundamentally affects the way in which we receive and understand it. Let's now take each of these in turn, starting with the adjective *gentle*.

The first thing to say about this use of *gentle* in 'a gentle reminder' is that despite its pragmatic effect, a 'gentle reminder' sounds friendlier, for instance, than a plain 'reminder'; it provides evidence that it is undoubtedly a directive. By deciding what kind of reminder it is, John asserts his own authority over the correspondence. Not only has he initiated it, he also determines its status. In fact, the use of *gentle* here could be seen in the same light as *polite* in 'polite notice' and *kindly* in 'kindly fill and send' that we discussed in Chapter 1, not making the message less authoritative but rather making it more so. However, as we suggest later, this does not seem to be the intention in this email, nor does it answer the question of why John chose to *disguise* his meaning in this way. For this we have to wait a bit longer while we consider the other two linguistic clues.

The next clue, then is John's use of the 'downtoner'[5] *just*, an adverb which could be understood in one of two ways: either to mitigate the force of the reminder (it's only) or to serve as an intensifier disguising annoyance. After all this is a task *reminder* and not a task initiator! The final element worth noting is John's use of the distancing future form *will* in 'we'll need' as opposed to the immediacy of the present 'we need' which would have been the more authoritative choice. The same can be said for his decision to use *we* instead of *I*, whereby the latter would have emphasized his ownership of the task rather than any active involvement. This could suggest that John, while seeking to position himself as the person in authority by initiating the directive, also attempts to mitigate his role by choosing these modalizing resources. Let's now see what response John's email received and consider what it adds to our discussion.

Extract 10.2

From: Joe Bloggs joe bloggs@urbanuniversity
Date: 25/08/2010
To: John
cc: Jim

Yes indeed!

This response is unlikely to reflect a misunderstanding of John's directive. The brevity of the reply along with the exclamation mark all point to it being a rejection of not only the directive itself but also the authority that John Smith's original email claims. In fact, it goes some way to explaining why John modalized his request so heavily and suggests that his use of *just* and *gentle* and *we'll* may well have been a kind of linguistic self-protection!

Ultimately, what this example shows is how modalizing can be used to both promote and mitigate authority and power. However, what it also shows is that choosing our words does not always produce the outcome we seek.

We modalize in many different ways. For instance, we can say 'I hate you!' but smiling meanwhile and speaking with a soft tone so as to communicate the opposite meaning, here using the resources of non-verbal modes (facial expression and tone of voice) to adjust the meaning of the spoken words. Or we can use grammatical forms to mitigate the affect of a potentially uncomfortable message as in the use of the past tense instead of the simple present in '*I wanted to ask*' in the request 'I wanted to ask if you could lend me £50'. In this case the simple past form of the verb *wanted*, instead of the simple present form *want*, which would be more suited to the actual time frame, somehow indicates reticence, awkwardness or even self-effacement.

Why this is so is not entirely clear but it could be connected to the way we use the past in reporting something that has previously been said. The use of the past tense indicates a kind of second-hand telling, telling something that does not originate with the person doing the telling. For example, Mary might say to Anne 'I really hate getting up early!' and Anne might go on to *report* this to Sally as in 'Mary told me that she *hated* getting up early.' Using the past here does not mean that Mary no longer hates getting up early, but rather that the original telling of it is now in the past. What's more, reporting speech in this way creates a kind of distance between the reporter and the thing she is reporting on. Following on from this, we suggest that the pastness of *I wanted*, in 'I wanted to ask' serves to distance the act of asking, and hence the asker, from the act of getting. Here the distinction in time (past for a present act) could be being used as a metaphor for the distinction in terms of power between the two participants. Either way, it is clear that in English the past tense can have a modalizing function as well as a temporal one.

What do the following examples tell you about the relationship between the participants?

- Can you lend me fifty quid?
- Lend me fifty pounds, would you?

What additional semiotic resources (e.g. tone of voice, facial expression) might be used here so as to mitigate the request?

What about:

- Lend us a fiver.

Why 'us' when it is referring only to one person (me) and what's the effect of the use of 'fiver' instead of five pounds?

Whose interests are being served by each choice, the asker or the lender?

10.3.2 *New Times, changed attitudes – modalizing as ideology*

'Coffee Logo Stirs Racism Row' (*BBC News* headline, 1999).

Some years ago, after McCormick Foods took over the company that produced *Camp Coffee*, there was a decision to make changes to the label that had been on the product. This coffee-flavoured essence produced in Scotland since 1885, is said to have been introduced during colonial times in response to requests from the Gordon Highlanders, a British army regiment, for a coffee drink that could be brewed up easily (before the days of instant coffee) during military campaigns in India. The row referred to in the BBC headline was stirred up, not by the logo itself but by the message the scene depicted on the label (Figure 10.3) was thought to promote. McCormick Foods have not commented on their decision to redesign the label, but as can be seen, the new version (Figure 10.4) offers a very different narrative when compared to the old one.

FIGURES 10.3 AND 10.4 *Camp Coffee labels, past and present.*

When we have shown these to students, first the old then the new, they have tended to laugh out loud. The ideological shift is immediately obvious, achieved by means of adjusting the social relationship between the two depicted protagonists. The standing, tray-carrying *servant* becomes the seated, coffee-sharing *colleague*, another example of category change this time represented pictorially instead of verbally. However, although this is the most prominent difference between the two versions, it is not the only thing that has changed. The new version has a crisper feel than its older counterpart, partly resulting from the affordances of modern printing but also from the fact that there is less clutter on the newer label. The ceremonial sword at the soldier's feet in the original version has disappeared, although his headgear remains. The product name 'Camp' has been restyled in blue against a clean background, providing a top frame for the picture of the two men. The flag in which the motto sits now flutters from the tent top instead of sticking out stiffly. Both men are smiling contentedly. One of the most intriguing changes is one that is almost unnoticeable; that is a change in the skin colour of the Indian soldier. In the earlier version he is depicted with a darker skin tone than the British soldier; in the new version, both are represented with an identical light skin colouring.

What these differences mean is open to interpretation, but what is clear is that the designers realized that updating the relationship between the two men led to an updating of other elements in the picture. Perhaps a sword was too reminiscent of the colonial campaigning days. Maybe the newly fluttering flag reflects the less formal relationship between the two men. The stylized product name might be thought to evoke the mountain peaks of the Himalaya rather than the military camp suggested by the two tents in the original (notice that the new label has only one tent). The point is that the new design seeks to mitigate the anachronistic narrative of the original version by adjusting the existing elements (the military paraphernalia, the two military personnel, the flag, the tent(s), the motto 'Ready Aye Ready', the overall colour scheme). In this way it retains its provenance and reassures customers that it is the same old Camp Coffee that was produced for the British army in India during the late nineteenth century.

A question we might wish to ask ourselves is whether either version comes anywhere close to the 'truth', and if so, what kind of truth they represent. In the end, although both labels are fictions, each says something about the social attitudes of its own times.

Think about other companies that have made adjustments by modalizing their branding in this way. McDonald's hamburger group, for instance, have recently changed their own branded colour scheme of yellow on red to yellow on green in Europe and North America while in India it seems they are opting for a more muted colour scheme. What has motivated these changes? What version of the world (and themselves) are they seeking to promote?

10.3.3 *Point of View – Thematic modalizing (arrangement)*

Our third example is a fragment from the TV debate (*The Big Fight*) on national language policy in India referred to at the beginning of Chapter 4. It demonstrates that choice of thematic arrangement, how we organize our ideas, is a powerful resource in shaping our meanings. We offer two versions of the same conversational fragment and ask the following question. Which version offers the more sympathetic view of the political party it mentions, Version One or Version Two? (We have changed the name of the party to X Party, as it is irrelevant to the present discussion.)

Version One

The X Party of course being very much in the news on the language question, I understand now your party's apologizing for its actions in the house, but uh I'm not very sure whether you have changed your views on language one way or the other.

Version Two

The X Party of course being very much in the news on the language question, I'm not very sure whether you have changed your views on language one way or the other, but uh I understand now your party's apologizing for its actions in the house.

Although each version contains the same three main propositional elements,

- The X Party is very much in the news on the language question.
- The X Party is apologizing for its actions in the house.
- The presenter is not very sure whether the X Party has changed its views on language.

most competent speakers of English would unhesitatingly choose Version Two as offering a more sympathetic view of the party's behaviour.

So how do these two versions *mean* differently despite the use of identical words and grammatical structures? The answer lies in how the speaker has arranged the propositions. In Version One, the foregrounded point is the question of whether the party has changed its views on language, while in Version Two the speaker stresses the apology. The conjunction 'but', like other concessive connectors (e.g. however, nevertheless), tends to signal a speaker's or writer's preferred view, while what precedes the 'but' tends to be offered as a (reluctantly) conceded point. The following invented sentences further demonstrate how this works. In these examples, the speaker of the first version offers a more optimistic view than the second version by foregrounding 'still having time' rather than 'lateness'.

> It's late, but we've still got time to get there.
>
> – versus –
>
> We've still got time to get there, but it's late.

In spontaneous spoken communication, arrangement is likely to be additive whereby we shape our meanings as we go along. We may need to correct (or repair) something we have just said, or ensure that we have made the point we intended. We may respond to a puzzled facial expression observed from our audience or simply to a sense that our point is not getting across properly. In the above example (We've still got time to get there, but it's late), the 'but it's late' could have been added in response to a co-respondent having adopted a relaxed attitude – maybe settling back in a chair or deciding to have another cup of tea. By contrast, in writing, and other visual communicative modes, arrangement is a compositional choice. In other words, because of the reflective quality of writing, we make conscious decisions about how we arrange our ideas and whether that arrangement foregrounds the point we wish to make. For instance, it is significant whether we write:

> Politeness strategies vary not only across languages but also across different English-speaking cultures.
>
> – rather than –
>
> Politeness strategies vary not only across different English-speaking cultures but also across languages.

This is because the 'not only – but also' arrangement involves what is called in linguistics 'given' and 'new' information. In the first case what is given (i.e. assumed known) is that politeness strategies vary across languages (not only) and what is new (i.e. presented as new) is that they also vary across different English-speaking cultures (but also). In this way the writer can foreground the idea she wishes to promote. How we arrange our ideas, even at sentence level, can have a profound effect on how those ideas can and will be understood.

Arrangement as a modalizing resource is not, though, confined to verbal modes of communication. All modes involve arrangement, whether they are intended to be understood as text or not. The following photographic examples illustrate the salience of arrangement in what Kress and van Leeuwen (1996: 181) call the 'meaning of composition' (see also Berger 1972). Look at them for a few seconds and think about how they are different.

FIGURES 10.5 AND 10.6 *Lordship Recreation Park, Tottenham, London.*

Consider how your eyes travel across each picture, from left to right or vice versa. Or is it the angle of the line of the kerb marking out the pavement from the pathway that directs your gaze? Just by flipping a photograph horizontally like this it is possible to feel a kind of difference between them, even though it is hard to put your finger on exactly what that difference is. The positioning of the different items (the lampposts, the benches, the signpost, the people) all play their part in the overall composition. Reversing those items means they are viewed from opposite sides and this affects how the viewer experiences them. Without knowing the actual scene depicted or having previously seen the photograph in its correct orientation, it is impossible to tell which is the original and which is the reversed one. If you were asked to choose, your judgement might be influenced by particular factors such as whether you are more accustomed to reading left to right, as in English, or right to left, as in Arabic or Hebrew. If, however, we tell you that Figure 10.5 is the original version (and it really is), does that change the way you see Figure 10.6?

Essentially, as a non-specific photograph, it is neither here nor there which of the two versions shows the 'real' point of view. However if the intention is to record the exact scene, *Lordship Rec in the snow*, the point of view becomes relevant and semiotically significant because to change the orientation would be to change the 'truthfulness' of the photographic representation.

10.4 Conclusion

This chapter has focused on ways in which we seek to shape or manage our meanings by choosing particular semiotic resources. It sought to show the importance of paying attention to how meanings are composed to achieve specific outcomes that go beyond the literal. It also showed how contextual aspects such as interpersonal relationships, social attitudes or ideological agendas influence our compositional choices and how an understanding of this helps us become more active, more discerning and more effective communicators ourselves.

To finish off with, we want to refer to an online discussion hosted by a magazine called *The Vagenda*. It concerned a question posed by a male reader who had offered his seat on a London Tube to a woman who he described as older than his own mother. The response he received from the woman apparently confused him, not because she declined what he considered a generous offer but because of what she actually said to him. According to his report the exchange went like this:

> Young Man: Excuse me love, do you want to sit down?
> Woman: I am NOT your love! (said with an expression of disgust)

His discussion post attracted a good response from readers, all women, who all identified the reason for the outrage as being to do with context and appropriacy; 'love' was the wrong choice of word, used by the wrong person in the wrong situation. Here are a few extracts from the responses received. The first concerns the question of who might be able to use it to whom, linking it to region and age.

> Love was exclusively used by the women of my Lancastrian family for all people, all ages and all genders. I have never used it, because I am not my Mum or my grandmothers. However, living in the North I see it is used by all genders to all genders for all occasions. By older people for younger people, but that's all.

The next one, offered by the magazine itself, refers to the specific context of a service encounter,

> Allow me to give you a little GCSE Bitesize revision session over the appropriate use of the terms 'pet', 'love', 'chuck', etc.
>
> Unless uttered by close friends and family, these terms are only acceptable IN A SERVICE INDUSTRY CONTEXT, and only then
>
> - when there is sufficient badinage/friendliness to not render said pet term weird
> - when it is not a come on

- when it is being said by the person behind the bar, desk or till
- when the person saying the word is older than the person it is being said to, EXCEPT

subcategory a) - when it is being used sarcastically, like when a certain customer is being a complete cock to you.

While a third rejects it as ever being appropriate:

What?? Why are we even having this conversation? It's patronising! That's why she doesn't like it! End of discussion.

As we have seen throughout the book, despite the obvious fact that we are all expert users of language, regardless of what language it might be, we are not always expert observers of language. Choosing our words (or whatever semiotic resource we might use) is by no means a neutral activity. Communication is not simply a matter of output and input, but rather a co-production between participants co-existing in a given context whether it be face-to-face, as in speaking or remotely, as in writing and other visual modes. Whether you like being addressed as 'love' or not depends on who you are, where you come from and what you're doing at the time; and whether you are someone who can use the term depends on the same criteria. Sometimes we get it wrong, sometimes we misinterpret, but usually we manage to get there in the end! There is so much more to language than a set of structures, a lexicon of words and the physical means to articulate.

This chapter completes Part II of the book. In Part III we move onto the discussion of why we think linguistics is a worthwhile pursuit, not only as a field of study but also because of the very real contribution it can make to real-world issues.

Suggested reading

Fairclough, N. (2001), *Language and Power,* 2nd edn. Harlow: Longman

This now classic book, which was first published in 1989, established an approach to critical discourse analysis that has been widely used and built on. The systematic and highly detailed way of analysing discourse that it presents shows how different texts promote particular ideological perspectives.

Johnson, S. and Ensslin, A., (eds), (2007), *Language in the Media: Representations, Identities, Ideologies.* London: Continuum.

This edited collection is concerned with not only how media chooses and uses language to promote particular versions of reality, but also how it represents language issues and debates as we also discuss in Chapter 12. It is a rich source of highly relevant discussion.

Machin, D. and Mayr, A. (2012), *How to Do Critical Discourse Analysis: A Multimodal Introduction*. London: Sage.

This is an excellent introduction to critical discourse analysis which explains the theories, concepts and analytical practices associated with this approach in a highly accessible way. It complements the present chapter very well with its detailed and systematic approach and its updating of the area to incorporate theoretical and textual developments.

PART THREE

Why do linguistics?

Introduction to Part III

In the final part of the book we want to show why we think linguistics is an important and useful body of knowledge, not just for linguists themselves, but for everybody. We believe that linguistic knowledge can make a strong contribution to our understanding of the social world and to this end we have focused the final part of the book on making the case for the study of language as a fundamental part of the educative process and for linguistic knowledge being seen as an essential part of our general knowledge. We feel it is of particular importance at this point in history where the linguistic map is becoming more complex as the result of globalization and the ease of connectivity between people, either in person or via the internet. We are all by now familiar with the benefits this brings as well as with the degree of anxiety that surrounds these rapid changes. Knowledge of the kinds of things we have been discussing so far, we believe, can be helpful in mediating our path through this plethora of linguistic and social uncertainties.

We have organized Part III around a series of themes that allow us to demonstrate the practical contribution that linguistics can make to our understanding of communicative interactions and their social effects. Chapter 11, with its discussion of *translanguaging*, shows that many of our commonly held views about language, with concepts such as native speaker or bilingual, stem from an unnecessarily narrow understanding of how people use language. In Chapter 12 we consider how language-related issues are represented, or rather, misrepresented, in the media and in general public discourse, and how even a basic understanding of linguistics would prevent many of the moral outrages and misinformed decisions that these representations provoke. We move on, in Chapter 13, to ask why the study of language does not figure in the school curriculum and show how, if it did, some of the misunderstandings discussed in Chapter 12 might have been avoided. In Chapter 14, we discuss the contribution that linguistics can, and does, make to the workplace with particular reference to examples from service-oriented contexts such as GP practices, police stations and call centres. We conclude the book with a series of claims that we wish to make in arguing for the relevance of linguistics and the added value it brings to our general knowledge and understanding of how the social world works.

11

Translanguaging: When the mixed code is the code

11.1 Introduction

In Chapter 1 we looked at the idea of text as a piece of communicative practice which might incorporate different elements (speech, writing, facial expression, pictures, colour, gesture and so on) woven together in order to achieve a particular communicative effect. Later, in Chapter 3, we considered how identity and community are enacted and expressed through linguistic practice, and towards the end of Chapter 4, we began to think about how people in multilingual environments perceive and use the linguistic resources available to them. In this chapter we set out to bring these related themes together, looking at the idea of multiple language use as a communicative practice in itself. In order to do this we adopt a perspective informed by the general approach to language use represented under scholarly rubrics including, but not confined to, translanguaging (Lewis et al. 2012; García and Li 2014, García 2009; Creese and Blackledge 2010), translingual practice (Canagarajah 2013a) and polylingual languaging (Jørgensen 2008). The speakers who actually do it, of course, might call it something else, or call it nothing at all. 'Translanguaging' has come under attack, not least for being a singularly inelegant word (Edwards 2012: 43 accuses those who use it of having 'remarkably stannous ears'), but more substantively for being unnecessary and obfuscatory. Edwards's broadside against the entire concept (2012: 41–5) is a bracing read, and scores some palpable hits, but the usefulness of the notion, as far as our purposes here are concerned, lies less in its theoretical originality than in its implied shift of perspective. The principal aim of using the idea of translanguaging is to explore the potential of looking at languages not primarily as structural systems (though of course they are certainly that) but instead primarily as resources which can be combined, adapted, juxtaposed or subverted, as speakers use what they have to hand, linguistically speaking, in order to achieve their communicative ends. What we are doing in this chapter, then, is first *noticing* how people in multilingual contexts use language and languages, and secondly, attempting to account for this use in terms of identity, symbolic value and, above all, communicative effect.

11.2 From languages to language

We have used the notion of 'super-diversity' (Vertovec 2006, 2007),[1] and Blommaert (2008) suggests 'Multi-Everything', to capture something of the cultural flavour of twenty-first century London; Otsuji and Pennycook (2010) refer to identity-making through multiple language use as 'metrolingualism'. However, multilingualism itself of course has a long history in British society, and is not necessarily urban, either, as Canagarajah (2013a) reminds us.[2] So-called 'macaronic' poetry flourished in medieval England, where Latin was a familiar tongue alongside French and English (familiar whether you understood it a lot, a little or not at all). Sometimes this style of poetry consisted of little more than cod Latin endings to commonplace English words, used for comic or satirical effect. However, it was also used to heighten the emotional and stylistic impact of, for example, love poetry, as in the following extract from the elaborate, anonymous lyric written in around 1300 known as *De Amico ad Amicam*, or 'From a (male) friend to a (female) friend', where all three languages are used.

Example 11.1

Ma tres duce et tres amé,
Night and day for love of thee
Suspiro.

Soyez permanent et leal;
Love me so that I it fele,
Requiro.

In Chapter 4 we discussed how the notion of code-switching has been used in sociolinguistics to describe how speakers alternate or move between one language and another. The above is code-switching in the sense that there is variation from line to line (to most elegant effect), but we would suggest that it is not *merely* code-switching – or rather, that the term code-switching does not really capture its essence. The content, syntax, rhythm and rhyme, the very message of the poem, flow naturally from one language to the next, so that, as the literary scholar Elizabeth Archibald (2010) suggests, the effect is more that of a single linguistic system. Another medieval verse actually mingles codes within lines (a practice sometimes referred to as code-mixing, as opposed to switching), with the two languages, Latin and English, fully integrated both grammatically and stylistically, and both being essential to the meaning of the piece:

Example 11.2

Illa iuventus that is so nyse
Me deduxit into vayn devise;

Infirmus sum, I may not rise –
Terribilis mors conturbat me.

Archibald remarks of the poet John Skelton (c.1460–1529) that his writings so seamlessly fuse English, Latin and other languages that it is hard not to imagine that 'he himself thought and sometimes even spoke macaronically' (2010: 286). Indeed so, and this is of course a literary scholar's phrase. In traditional sociolinguistic parlance, we would say that Skelton and his contemporaries were doubtless habitual code-switchers and code-mixers; though the seamless quality is perhaps better evoked by Canagarajah's (2013a) term, code-meshing. (The faint hint of surprise or caution in Archibald's tone is worthy of note: we will have more to say in a little while about underlying monolingualist assumptions).

In essence, educated people like these writers lived in what was at least a trilingual society, or in Scotland and Wales, at least a quadrilingual one (see Crystal 2004: 121–39); moreover, literary activity was being carried on at various times also in Irish and Cornish (Canagarajah 2013a: 52–3). It would be natural to them to use all the linguistic resources available to them. Their writings are therefore 'texts' in the particular sense suggested in Chapter 1 and throughout Part II, of different strands woven together to create a new, other kind of communicative device which is whole and cohesive in itself. The cohesion derives from the fact that each element of the text depends upon the other elements for its interpretation (cf. Halliday and Hasan 1976), even though two or even three supposedly different and discrete languages are in play. In allowing such texts to be made, we might say that the affordances of multilingual societal contexts differ strikingly from those of monolingual ones. Archibald is hence probably right to claim (2010: 287) that 'we should read macaronic poetry not as an occasional *jeu d'esprit*, but rather as a reflection of the multilingual society of England in the later Middle Ages'. This applied to the ancient world, too. There is a documented history of code-switching, sometimes accompanied by changes of script, sometimes not, in Latin inscriptions and other texts. There were switches of course with Greek, but also with Gaulish, Etruscan, Oscan, Umbrian and Aramaic, among others (Adams 2003). There was code-switching in writing; inevitably there would have been code-switching in speech.

Now consider the following. It is an email message written by a German woman to her German husband: the couple have been living in the United Kingdom for over 30 years.

Example 11.3

> *Heute frueh war der carpet Mann da und hat alles ausgemessen. Hier ist sein estimate, das ich ganz reasonable finde. Bitte email es zu Ian. Die Teppiche sollen Ende der naechsten Woche gelegt werden. Es war difficult to persuade him. Nigel and I did our best and he promised. If OK gehe ich hin und gebe ihm 50% deposit mit Chq. I also pay today die Arbeiter direkt, zusammen £1100. House begins to look very nice, tidy and clean.*
>
> [The carpet man was here this morning, and has measured everything. Here is his estimate, which I find quite reasonable. Please email it to Ian. The carpets should be laid end of next week. It was difficult to persuade him. Nigel and I did our best and he promised. If OK I'll go ahead and give him 50% deposit with Chq. I also pay today the workers direct, together £1100. House begins to look very nice, tidy and clean.]

We can do some linguistic analysis on this, of course, noting some of the features which particularly stand out. There are some very clear code-switches involving individual words: *Hier ist sein* estimate, *das ich ganz* reasonable *finde.* The underlying syntax of this sentence is German, not English: note the characteristically German word order of the relative clause, with the verb at the end (a word-for-word rendering would be 'which I quite reasonable find'). The sentence beginning *Die Teppiche* ('the carpets') is entirely German, in both syntax and lexis. In the following sentence, though, what begins as German *Es war* ('it was') abruptly shifts into English. A later sentence does the opposite, beginning in English (*If OK*) but continuing in German, with the verb placed as the next (i.e. second) element in the sentence, conforming to the German syntactic pattern (word-for-word: *If OK, go I ahead*). So is the dominant or 'base' language German or English? Is *email* a 'real' code switch, or the use of an English loan word?[3] The German for 'cheque' is *Scheck*: notice here how the writer uses the English word (in abbreviation) but capitalizes the first letter, in the German style. *House begins* seems odd, as does *I also pay* – would a native English-speaker not be more likely to write *House is beginning* and *I'll also pay*? And *clean and tidy* rather than *tidy and clean*?

A straightforward linguistic analysis, it seems, will only get us so far. Gardner-Chloros (1995: 71), in identifying the 'fuzzy-edged' nature of code-switching, points out that 'even within what are generally accepted as code-switches, we are dealing with a number of overlapping phenomena whose individuality cannot be captured within traditional grammatical categories'. Moreover, what purely structural and lexical analysis cannot tell us is why the writer uses these particular switches and mixes, and why in these particular contexts. Many linguists attacked this problem in the 1980s and 1990s, from different angles or theoretical positions: among other things there are grammatical approaches to code-switching, psychological approaches, approaches based on social theory (see Milroy and Muysken 1995). But perhaps, as Gardner-Chloros (1995) herself in fact suggests, the problem lies in our conception of what 'a language' is: the socially constructed idea of languages as being separate and discrete is preventing us from fully appreciating the reality of how language is actually used. Perhaps even to ask why it happens is to assume, subconsciously, that it is monolingual practice that is, or should be the norm (see Woolard 2004).

The email in Example 11.3, then, is certainly an example of code-switching or code-meshing (and how!). But it is tempting to see it as something more than just a mixture of English and German, especially as the English does not always follow the normative standard, and the German is so thoroughly interpenetrated by the English. Rather than code-switching for effect, for ease of expression, or for structural reasons, it might be argued that this looks more akin to the so-called Spanglish of many American Latinos (see e.g. Montes-Alcalá 2009). 'Spanglish', though, has an empirical existence in the public mind in the United States, indexical of a fairly well-defined ethnocultural group and social identity (Morales 2002), even if not all linguists approve of the term or the discourse that is sometimes built around it (see Otheguy and Stern 2011). Our email appears, rather, to be simply the way of communicating that this particular couple have developed together over time, a creative process in which the resources of both English and German are used at will, remade and recast into something new. It is not, we might suggest, a mixed code in the sense of two things being used alternately; rather, the mixed code *is* the code, and this is the 'language' that they speak to each other; not a new language in the sense of having its own norms and rules (they might never use some of these particular structures again) but the creative interplay of two existing codes. If we could get inside their heads, we might even find that they do not think of themselves as using two languages: they are just using *language*, in the way that Jørgensen (2008) conceives of and describes as 'polylingual languaging'. This is perhaps also what Gardner-Chloros (1995: 70) was getting at when she observed that '[t]he use of the term code-switching implies a binary choice – that at any given moment speakers are either operating in one mode or in another, which is clearly distinguishable from the first. This is an over-simplification'.

Gardner-Chloros bases a good deal of her theory on observations from Alsace, where Alsatian (an Alemannic German dialect) and French have co-existed for centuries. Similar kinds of interaction, though, have been noticed and remarked upon in a number of traditionally multilingual communities. One of the major examples is India. A good deal is known about India because Indian intellectuals and academic researchers tend to publish in English, and many commentators on mixed language use in India focus, with some reason, on the use and significance of English there. However, as Canagarajah (2009: 5) notes, in fact the tradition of plurilingual communication in South Asia predates the period of British influence there, and is considered 'natural' to the ecology of the region by local linguists. Certainly the juxtaposition of English and Indian languages is noticeable, as in a roadside advertisement for a Christian dating website seen in Kerala: *Where lakhs of Christians come to get married!* (One lakh = 100,000).

Such intermingling illustrates the way in which English has made itself local in India, participating in established plurilingual practices in the way discussed by Pennycook (2010) among others. Canagarajah links the reality of plurilingualism explicitly to the theoretical concept of translanguaging (see e.g. García 2009; Creese and Blackledge 2010), and makes the crucial claim that in contexts such as India 'proficiency in languages is not conceptualized individually, with separate competencies developed for each language. The different languages constitute an integrated system' (Canagarajah 2009: 5). If this is indeed the case, then we might conceive of translingual practice (Canagarajah 2013a) as being in essence the natural behaviour of plurilinguals: people operating in a multilingual context, able and willing to draw with differing degrees of proficiency on some or all of the languages that they encounter, but treating the whole of their language resources as a single, integrated competence. They might consider monolingualism neither natural nor desirable. Indeed, they might even agree with such as Blommaert (2008) that in casual, unexamined, day-to-day communication (or what Heller [2007: 13], after Halliday, calls 'the messiness of actual usage') it is often actually very difficult, if not impossible, to draw reliably straight lines between one named, discrete language and another.

11.3 Translingual practice, identity and indexing

Just as this applies to linguistically diverse India, it is immediately obvious that it could equally well be applied to super-diverse urban arenas in the

'West'. Li Wei (2011: 1228) says of his Chinese-British subjects at a London university:

> Being multilingual, rather than monolingual, is an integral part of the young men's identity. But this multilinguality does not mean to know all the languages fully and separately. They want to be able to pick and mix amongst the languages they know at various levels. They want to do translanguaging.

Here, then, the implied formalism or systematicity that lurks in the phrase 'code-switching' falls away, and we have instead what Canagarajah calls 'not an identifiable code or a systematized variety [but] . . . a highly fluid and variable form of language practice' (2009: 7). The crucial word here is *practice.* Translanguaging is something that speakers do, not something that they learn at school, or read about, or theorize. This approach, it seems to us, is highly relevant in understanding what is happening in places like present-day London, Manchester, Los Angeles, Rotterdam, Hong Kong and other highly diverse cities. Hence, for example, the English spoken by young British-Bangladeshis in the London district of Tower Hamlets can be characterized not just as English with some Bengali and Sylheti borrowings, but as a mixed code of identity; such speakers sometimes refer to the way they speak as *mash-up,* as in the hybrid musical form. The borrowing is not formalized: it is random and spontaneous, with speakers collectively or individually constructing their own norms as languages bump up against each other (and see Cheshire et al. 2008; Rampton 2010; Block 2006). You would expect to find here a positive attitude to linguistic spontaneity and variation, an attitude of openness to the original and the unexpected, in the way that Khubchandani (1997) suggests for India; and you would not be disappointed. As our Bangladeshi student Rafi (he of the student union posters discussed in Chapter 2) told us about the way he and his friends spoke English among themselves: 'Presumably there are so many mistakes, and you're not aware. . . . But you say it in your own way, to other mates, that's fine. In your own style, that's the thing.'

The 'pick and mix' approach to code choice might of course involve a measure of projection or representation of the speaker's identity, in the sense of indexing the group or groups to which they feel they want to belong. Indeed, among multicultural Londoners, we would consider this element of projection of identity to be very much to the fore. Take this piece of speech, recorded in an east London café:

Example 11.4

> *Akhi, I was raased! I just couldn't get up.*

The speaker was a British Muslim, probably of Pakistani or Bangladeshi background, in his twenties, talking to a group of similar young men who were obviously all friends. *Akhi* is the Arabic for 'brother'. Arabic terms are often used between observant young Muslims in British cities, who might be from the same or different ethnolinguistic backgrounds but who share an interest in the learning and use of Arabic for religious reasons. Here *akhi* is also perhaps a calque[4] on the familiar inner-city term of address (what Rampton 2010: 11 calls a 'vernacular vocative') *bruv* or *bro,* (for brother, close friend). *Raased* or perhaps *rassed* is a Jamaican-derived term, here used evidently with the meaning of 'tired out, exhausted'. Rampton (e.g. 2006) has noted in some detail how ethnically 'black' words and pronunciations have steadily gained ground among the young in London over a period of years, as a reflection of the 'cool' perceived to be embedded in the fashions, speech and music of young black Londoners – though as Kerswill et al. (2007) show, London's diversity is such that there may be many potential sources for any particular language feature.

The language choices hence index a series of chosen or desired identities within the peer group and, we might suppose, within the wider society; the choice is in itself an 'act of identity' (Le Page and Tabouret-Keller 1985), and in this sense it carries echoes of our discussions in Chapters 1 and 3 of how community is enacted through language. In this case, the language might say, among other things: I am English (or perhaps British); a Muslim (and a serious, self-identifying one)[5]; young or youngish; from London; from the inner city rather than the comfortable suburbs. This 'sociolinguistic hybridization' (Blommaert 2008: 85) could of course be explained in traditional terms as code-switching, or the use of loan words, but explanations of this kind seem not to place sufficient emphasis on that element of desired hybridization as a coherent style of communication in its own right. Parts of London, and especially east London, constitute some of the most ethnically and linguistically mixed places on earth: these young men exist in a highly diverse environment, and wish to express complex, diverse personal and cultural identities (Block 2006; Harris 2006). As in Li Wei's group referred to above, they want to do translanguaging.

As noted above, US Hispanics have long been considered to have developed a hybrid code, popularly known as 'Spanglish', both expressive of and indexing their consciously mixed identity. I (Tim) was once talking in Spanish to a US-born Mexican-American man, César, in Los Angeles. I happened to ask if a friend of his, whom we had been talking about, had also been born in the States. He replied:

Example 11.5

No, man, he's mexicano de allá. Me, I'm mexicano de aquí.

[No, man, he's Mexican from there. Me, I'm Mexican from here].

There are various ways in which one could read this, but at one level it feels very much like an act of translingual identity-making. We had been talking in Spanish; he had presumably been happy to do so, and I knew from previous conversations with César that he was proud of his Mexican ancestry. We then move on to the ethnic ancestry of his friend, and at this point it would seem that he wants to differentiate himself from the friend. It becomes important to him to index a different facet of his identity, not the proud Mexican, but the proud Mexican-American, and he does this by shifting into a new discourse style, with new affordances (Blommaert 2008: 83 talks about 'a whole *repertoire* of personae' – and we discuss the notion of repertoire itself below). But it is not that the two codes are mixed, per se. Rather, as we suggested with the example of the German couple in the United Kingdom, the mixed code *is* the code. It reflects identity and it performs identity, while in terms of language competence, for US Latinos like César 'the different languages constitute an integrated competence' (Canagarajah 2009: 6).[6]

Strikingly, a corollary of this is that strict grammatical correctness is not always an indispensable criterion when language competence or, we might better say, communicative competence is conceptualized in this way (as is noted in Canagarajah's discussion of Indian plurilingualism, referred to in Chapter 4). The following fragment was recorded in a busy primary school classroom in Southall, west London. An Indian classroom assistant had been attempting to say something in Punjabi to a group of Punjabi-speaking children, but had found it increasingly difficult to make herself heard. Having asked them several times in Punjabi to quieten down, she finally came out with:

Example 11.6

Childrens, don't noise.

Perhaps if they had been older, the children would have ignored or mocked such usage. But in this case, the communicative strategy was successful, and the children stopped talking and listened. We might surmise that the use of an English utterance here, grammatically well-formed or not, indexes authority and the rules of the school, in a way that Punjabi (for these children the language of the intimate domain of the home) in this context cannot. The affordances of multilingualism, then, seen from the perspective of translanguaging, have the potential to be exploited even where linguistic competence in the language(s) is limited. Communicative competence is of course another matter. The speaker needs to have sufficient communicative awareness to know that a switch of this kind, in this context, will work; in another context it could very easily have been an embarrassing failure. In some multilingual contexts at least, then, speakers can choose to use the linguistic resources that they have, even if these are imperfectly controlled or their rules imperfectly assimilated (and see Chik 2010 for similar cases of Putonghua/ Cantonese/English mixing in Hong Kong pop music). This is language that does the job: language as communicative practice, rather than as a system of words and letters, neatly parcelled up and divided off from the systems of words and letters that constitute 'other' languages.

We can take this a step further. Where languages have been in contact with each other for a long period of time, where heavy intermixing of the codes has spread to most or even all domains of communicative activity, and where formal education is limited, speakers *might not even know* if or when they are employing the resources of multiple language systems. In a Paraguayan bar not far from the border with Brazil, I (Tim) once came across a group of local (in principle, Spanish-speaking) children gathered around a television watching *Operação Dragão* – that is, the Bruce Lee film 'Enter the Dragon', dubbed into Portuguese for the Brazilian market. Noting that they seemed to be having no difficulty following the dialogue, I commented on how good their Portuguese must be. They looked at me, first with bafflement, then derision. 'That's not Portuguese', one of them said. 'That's Spanish.' They could not be persuaded otherwise. This kind of encounter will perhaps make us step back momentarily, and think again about how language and languages are usually conceived of. At the very least, it suggests that those commentators who regard the concept of separate, discrete languages as no more than a social construct (Gardner-Chloros 1995; Makoni and Pennycook 2007; Larsen-Freeman and Cameron 2008, among a good number of others) are not simply theorizing in the abstract but describing something quite fundamental in language *practice*. It also reinforces the feeling (*pace* Edwards) that the notions of code-switching and code-mixing, like that of 'borrowing' words from one language to another, cannot adequately describe the behaviour of bilinguals like these. As García (2009: 47) remarks: 'the concept of translanguaging makes obvious that there are no clear cut borders between the languages of bilinguals. What we have is a languaging continuum that is accessed.'

11.4 Sense and nonsense

One can employ the communicative resources of a language without having any great degree of competence in that language. One can employ the communicative resources of a language without being aware that one is doing so. Certainly one can employ the communicative resources of a language without necessarily understanding the language: think of the Latin mottos still used by schools, city councils and even football clubs (Tottenham Hotspur's is *Audere est Facere*), even though very few British people now learn any Latin at all. Or of, say, Nigerian or Turkish Muslims learning to read and recite Koranic verses and pray in Arabic, even though they may understand scarcely a word of the language. There is a fast-food chain in the United Kingdom ungrammatically called *El Mexicana*: perhaps its owners decided that the masculine definite article *el* signalled 'Spanish-ness' or 'Mexican-ness' to the average monolingual Briton more reliably than the grammatically correct, but less immediately identifiable, feminine article *la*.

Communicative effect, then, does not depend (or does not solely depend) upon linguistic correctness or linguistic competence; and this is one way of understanding the use of the nonsensical or borderline-comprehensible English found, for example, in advertising and on branded clothing in Japan. Similarly, the slight oddness, to a native English speaker, of football club names such as *Sport Boys* (Callao, Peru) or *The Strongest* (La Paz, Bolivia) is unimportant. The point is to suggest Englishness, and therefore index footballing tradition and authenticity, in the minds of South Americans – not to pass linguistic-cultural tests set by native speakers.

Many football clubs were founded around the world at a time, in the early decades of the twentieth century, when English speakers were more naturally thought of as the cultural owners of football than would perhaps be the case today. Their founders, even when they were not British, quite often chose quasi-English-sounding names in order to suggest a link with the mother country of football. South American clubs named in that period include *Chaco For Ever* (Rosario, Argentina, 1913); *Racing Club* (Buenos Aires, Argentina, 1903); and *Always Ready* (La Paz, Bolivia, 1933). European quasi-English club names usually fall rather less jarringly on the native English ear, though not always. *Athletic Bilbao*, yes. *Go Ahead Eagles* (formerly *Be Quick*), perhaps not.

Even graphemic hints can be enough to achieve this, as in the names of businesses in France such as *Croissant Jean's* and *Bar le Clap's* (Picone 1996: 180). The fact that the English possessive is incorrectly used and might not even be pronounced is neither here nor there; the instantly recognizable {apostrophe plus s} suffix has no function other than to suggest a fashionable Englishness. In the same way, the so-called metal Umlaut (as in *Mötley Crüe* or *Motörhead*) has no linguistic function, but carries the social semiotic function of indexing a hardcore style of music, presumably through its supposed Teutonic associations. A related principle governs the use of more-or-less Irish-looking script to spell the name, in English, on the signs of the faux-Irish pubs that can now be found in depressingly large parts of the world.

Of course, the use of English or 'English' in advertising and other public discourse jars with many people. This is how one British publication reported on resistance to the phenomenon in Germany:

> Advertising in Germany is particularly prone to Anglicisms. 'There is the illusion that using English shows you are livelier, younger and more modern,' says Holger Klatte of the German Language Association, founded in 1997 to preserve and promote Goethe's mother tongue. Zalando, an online clothes shop, is a typical offender with its 'Must-haves', 'Basics' and 'Shop by Style'. (*The Economist*, 29 June 2013)

So far, so unexceptional. As we know, 'lively', 'young' and 'modern' are precisely the kind of connotations which English often carries, and as such can be expected to appeal to advertisers and brand managers, despite what the German Language Association might think about it. What follows, though, is rather stranger:

> Most English slogans used in Germany fall flat because they are so garbled, says Bernd Samland of Endmark, a brand consultancy. A recent survey by his firm showed that only one-quarter of the English slogans used to advertise cars were understood by those polled. Most bewildering was Mitsubishi's 'drive@earth'.

This appears to miss the point entirely. If most English slogans 'fall flat', why on earth would advertisers insist on using them? (And see the related discussion of unconventional spelling in advertising in Chapter 12). As the article in fact goes on to note, the carmaker Audi has had great success in English-speaking markets with the slogan *Vorsprung Durch Technik.* Of course most British people are unlikely to know exactly what it means (it's something like 'in the lead through technology'). The linguistic or semantic meaning is, though, next to immaterial, just as it is with 'drive@earth'. The point is that 'German-ness' in the context of cars (rather than heavy metal, this time) indexes reliability, quality, technical excellence. The German therefore functions, as English often functions, 'not as a system of signs, but as a sign itself' (Cheshire and Moser 1994, cited in Edwards 2012: 191). Whether the slogan is understood, whether it is garbled, whether it is grammatically correct – none of these things alters the semiotic charge it delivers through its desirable 'otherness'.

Not only does it not necessarily matter if the language is incorrect or odd-sounding: in strict linguistic terms (rather than social semiotic terms) it does not necessarily have to mean anything at all. Take the name of a hotel restaurant, advertised on a billboard in Tashkent, Uzbekistan:

FIGURE 11.1 *Sign outside a hotel in Tashkent, Uzbekistan.*

Example 11.7

Le Vita Crystal

How is this, as a text, to be interpreted? From a linguistic point of view, we can say that the words are European, clearly – indeed, Latinate. From its position we might guess that *Le* is probably the French masculine, singular, definite article; though it could conceivably be Italian or Spanish. Whatever it may be, it does not agree grammatically with *vita*, which is Italian or Latin for 'life' or 'living' and is feminine. *Crystal* is an English noun: but here it is placed after the noun, as if it were an adjective belonging to a Romance language. The picture on the billboard (also part of the text, of course, in the way we discussed in Chapter 11.1) shows a neatly-laid dining table, with white tablecloth, napkins, cutlery, plates, glasses and so on, so the allusion must be to fine glassware. But is there also perhaps an allusion to Cristal champagne, popularly associated with 'bling' and supposedly glamorous high-rollers? Perhaps *Vita* is meant to make us think of the film *La Dolce Vita*, associated with (European) glamour and style. Assuming *Le* is indeed the French 'le', there is perhaps a nod towards the prestige of French cuisine. But what does it *mean*? Crystal life? Life in crystal?

The answer, we would suggest, is that it is not actually supposed to mean anything specific, any more than it is intended to be translated or analysed in the way that we are doing here. The meaning resides in the associations or connotations of the words, in the way they index European style and sophistication and, through the use of English, the elite world of international business. What is important, then, is not their literal meaning but their perceived *provenance* (Kress and van Leeuwen 2001). This transplanted quasi-Europeanness certainly marks the 'distribution of a discourse across space and time' (Scollon and Scollon 2003: 195), but the discourse is remoulded in the process. To complain that it is ill-formed or 'doesn't make sense' is to miss the point – which again takes us back to the student election posters we talked about in Chapter 2. In essence, *Le Vita Crystal* does not contain any particular semantic proposition, and does not belong to any particular language – but it is nevertheless an act of linguistic communication which we might call, following Canagarajah (2013a), a piece of translingual practice. The hotel in which the Tashkent restaurant was situated, meanwhile, rejoiced in the name of *Le Grande Plaza*.

11.5 Repertoires

Before we leave this topic we should look briefly at a related area, one that applies directly to multilingual situations, but not only to them. We have noted that, in certain contexts, speakers can avail themselves of (some of) the resources of a language without necessarily having great competence in it. One concept which has proved useful in discussion on the affordances of multilingualism, as well as on community and culture (see Chapter 3), is that of repertoires (see e.g. Blommaert 2010). By this we mean the different language competencies that speakers have in relation to different topics and social contexts and/or communities. Blommaert (2010) uses himself as an example to illustrate the principle, providing a bar chart of the different levels of competence he thinks he has when using the four languages in his repertoire in different communicative contexts. For instance, while with regard to academic communities, and specifically his own discourse community, he is probably as competent in English as in his first language of Dutch, when shopping in a supermarket or talking to a doctor in Britain he is 'fairly inarticulate' (2010: 104). Everybody experiences this phenomenon, whether with different languages as such, or with different discourses as discussed in Chapter 3. We could also include in the category of repertoires things like genre and other semiotic resources (some people are hopeless at telling jokes; some people are excellent at giving formal speeches; some are hopeless at one and excellent at the other). We are better, linguistically, in certain contexts than in others.

To a large extent our repertoires are formed by our life experience, or lack of it; and it has sometimes been seen as the principal role of the school to supply those elements of repertoire which children have not been exposed to at home. In Indonesia or China, say, this means teaching the national language (Bahasa Indonesia, Putonghua) to children who at home speak a regional language. In Britain and similar countries, in practice, it has usually meant teaching the standard language and formal register (Bourdieu's *langue légitime*) to children who at home speak dialectally or have little exposure to higher register language. The social and political implication of this, that there is some kind of deficit inherent in working-class speech, has not of course gone unnoticed: Bernstein's (1971) famous description of 'restricted code' and 'elaborated code', much misunderstood, was heavily criticized in its time for supposedly seeming to privilege middle-class speech norms over those of the working class.

The word 'restricted', we might feel with hindsight, was probably not the best one Bernstein might have chosen. It remains true, though, that it is the circumstances of one's life that will dictate the content and range of one's repertoires. Fiona was chatting to a group of young girls in inner-city Haringey in north London; during the course of the conversation one of them wanted to refer to the chimney stack of a nearby derelict factory; it transpired that none of them knew the words *chimney stack*, and not all were sure about *chimney*. They had never before, presumably, had the need to refer to such things. This is a very specific lexical gap; more generally, a speaker might be exposed only to a certain register of language. I (Tim) knew a Spanish-speaking South American who learned his English over the course of several years as an illegal immigrant in London, during which period he rarely emerged from the confines of the fried chicken shop in Hackney, staffed entirely by migrants from various parts of the world, where he worked and lived. His English was fluent, precise and locally accented, as one might expect. However, although he did not seem to realize it, his register was limited to the basilectal (i.e. furthest away from the standard) and his everyday speech was embellished very liberally indeed with swear words. Upon returning to his home country he managed to obtain a job in a tourist hotel, on account primarily of his fluency in English: it was there that I heard him cheerfully offer a group of newly-arrived British tourists a cold drink as they 'must be fucking gasping'.

11.6 Conclusion

We all have different competencies; we all know different amounts of different languages; we all change and adapt our way of speaking as it suits us or seems appropriate. Despite the contempt of such linguistic *ultras* as Skutnabb-Kangas (e.g. 1996) for the very thought of monolingualism (as we shall see in the following chapter), even the supposedly 'monolingual' – unfortunately, it is a very inflexible term – have access to other codes, registers, discourses, styles, depending on their life experience and personal circumstances. But while Skutnabb-Kangas overstates her case, there remains an irreducible core of truth in it. Variety in repertoire is the very essence of language practice; but where speakers have access to multiple linguistic resources (in the sense of other linguistic systems), the affordances of language are likewise multiplied. As we noted in Chapter 4, there is nothing about monolingualism which makes it the base or default position for language competence, if by being monolingual we mean being able to speak only a discrete, named language which can at any and every moment be differentiated from all other discrete, nameable languages. As Blommaert (2008: 84) insists, 'the old monolingualist assumption that people are "naturally" monolingual' needs to be questioned; not least because it is after all an assumption derived from a dominant language ideology, and has the insidious effect of turning upon its head the experience that most speakers in the world have of language use, even if it is not the case for most speakers in, for example, Britain and the United States. It follows that those who can use different codes, will do so – and not always in a regularly structured, schematized or systematic way. The question to be asked about code-switchers, translanguagers, then, is not 'Why do they do that?', but 'Why would they *not* do that?' (see Woolard 2004).

This is not to say that there are no norms in code choice, or that everyone simply makes up everything as they go along, like the monk Salvatore in *The Name of the Rose* (whom we mentioned in Chapter 4), regardless of whether anyone understands them or not. Social norms certainly exist – but as we saw in our discussion around the election posters in Chapter 2, in highly diverse environments these norms are typically not fixed, and are subject to the constant shifting and remaking of speech, language and discourse communities. The concept of translanguaging and related theoretical constructs offer us a way of thinking about language use which foregrounds the idea of language and languages as creative communicative resources over that of language as structure and languages as discrete systems. In this way the discipline of linguistics allows us to approach more nearly the multilingual reality of the world as most people *experience* it, even if this differs from the way people are taught traditionally to *understand* it. The next chapter looks more closely at the particular question of how language is in fact represented in public discourse, how it is understood and how it is talked about. Concentrating mainly on the United Kingdom as a case, we consider how some language issues have been raised in the public domain, and what this might tell us about the fundamental importance of doing linguistics.

Suggested reading

Blommaert, J. (2010), *The Sociolinguistics of Globalization*. Cambridge: Cambridge University Press.

A fascinating discussion of the changing ways in which language and communication operate across the globe. The author provides many interesting examples and case studies to demonstrate how sociolinguistics can adapt to accommodate the present-day realities of constant global movement and change.

Canagarajah, S. (2013), *Translingual Practice. Global Englishes and Cosmopolitan Relations*. London and New York: Routledge.

A theoretically-oriented book which some will find inspiring and others, perhaps, provocative. It is, at heart, an appeal for the world of hegemonic standard English (with particular reference to the university) to open up and welcome the kind of mixed-code practice which has become so common in globalized interactional contexts.

Edwards, J. (2009), *Language and Identity*. Cambridge: Cambridge University Press.

An all-round consideration of the relationship between language and identity by a long-time specialist in the field, covering areas such as religion, gender, naming, ethnicity and nationalism.

Rampton, B. (2006), *Language in Late Modernity: Interaction in an Urban School*. Cambridge: Cambridge University Press.

A detailed analysis of children's (often mixed) language use in an urban school in the United Kingdom, this influential book combines sociolinguistic data and sociological theory to illuminate the workings of, for example, cross-cultural interaction and social class itself.

12

Myths and moral panics? linguistics and the public domain

12.1 Introduction

You've probably at some point come across an email circular or news story which claims an entertaining or lurid origin for common phrases or words. Thus for example the assertion from the *Mail Online* that the phrase 'gone to pot' dates back to a time when boiling to death was a legal punishment[1]; or the anonymous internet article 'Life in the 1500s' which claims among other things that *threshold* derives from the fact that in medieval England the lintel of a house door functioned to hold back the 'threshes', which were supposedly bundles of straw or rushes used to cover an earth floor. In fact, there is no evidence at all for the 'gone to pot' theory; 'thresh', meanwhile, comes from an Old English word for 'tread' or 'trample', and where the 'hold' part of the word comes from has never been established. These stories are examples of what is known to linguists as 'false etymology'. Ignorant of the real origins of a word or phrase, or simply frustrated with the fact that its origins are unknown, someone, somewhere decides to invent a plausible-sounding etymology for it.

Very often, for some rather mysterious reason, false etymologies claim that the word in question is an acronym, even though this is not actually a particularly common source of new words, outside technical and military coinages such as *scuba* and *radar*. Hence *posh* has been claimed over and over again, without a shred of evidence, to come from 'Port Outward, Starboard Home'. (It is in fact possibly derived from a Romany word). So hoary is this myth that a book debunking these popular etymologies (Quinion 2005) actually bears 'Port Outward, Starboard Home' as its title – yet still the story is repeated. A more recent UK suggestion, ingenious but utterly devoid of merit, is that *chav* comes from 'Council House And Violent'. Equally mysteriously, but rather more disturbingly, false etymologies are developed to suggest that certain 'innocent' words and phrases actually have their origins in slavery. Hence it is claimed with regularity on US websites that *nitty gritty* once described the detritus that collected in the hold of a slave ship, and that *picnic* originated as a term for a lynching party.[2] On the internet these preposterous etymologies can spread like wildfire, and in the way that they are distributed, vouched for and believed to be authentic, they have something in common with urban myths. Indeed, they take on a life of their own. I (Tim) last heard the specious etymology for *nitty gritty* repeated by an anti-racism education worker in an interview on BBC Radio Five Live in August 2013; the BBC interviewer, sounding shocked, solemnly undertook never to use the phrase again.

The manufacture of false etymology is related to 'folk etymology', a technical term in linguistics which refers to the process by which speakers alter a foreign word to make its content seem more native-like and immediately accessible. Hence the Anglo-Norman *creveis* (modern French *écrevisse*) becomes 'crayfish', presumably on the grounds that it is a creature that lives in water and is therefore to some extent fish-like. Similarly, the archaic *shamefast,* 'bound with shame' becomes 'shamefaced' by association with the word 'face', where one would expect emotions to be shown, and what Italian-Americans (probably) called the *girasole* or 'sunflower' artichoke turns into 'Jerusalem artichoke'. Essentially, folk etymology is the art of the fanciful guess. There is no harm in this; indeed, it is rather endearing in its human desire to bring the alien and incomprehensible within the ambit of what is familiar and knowable. Other forms of linguistic ignorance, though, can potentially end up doing damage: and it is linguistic ignorance that is the topic of this chapter.

As the popularity of internet false etymology shows, everyone has an opinion on matters of language, or as Goethe had it: 'Everyone thinks that because he can talk, he can therefore talk about language' ('Ein jeder, weil er spricht, glaubt auch über die Sprache sprechen zu können'). Few people, though, actually study language as a subject in itself. So while public debate on the subject is to be welcomed unequivocally, too often contributions to what we might call the language conversation are clouded by misunderstanding about what language is and how it works. In this chapter we look at some examples of the public discourse around language and go on to consider some of the common-sense things that everyone 'knows' about language and about language learning. We will try to show some of the difficulties and risks inherent in ill-informed intervention in language-related issues, and foreshadow Chapter 13 by suggesting that language is an important enough phenomenon to deserve a place of its own in the school curriculum.

12.2 Is speaking a dialect a 'bad habit'?

In February 2013, a school in Middlesbrough, in the north-east of England, was suddenly and briefly in the headlines when it was reported that it had sent a letter to pupils' parents listing a number of dialect words which were to be banned, on the grounds that the pupils should be using only 'proper' or standard English. The *Daily Telegraph* reported on the matter thus:

> **Middlesbrough primary school issues list of 'incorrect' words. A primary school has banned pupils from using northern phrases such as 'nowt' and 'yous', in an attempt to ensure they are not discriminated against in job interviews when they are older.**
>
> Children at Sacred Heart Primary School in Middlesbrough will be corrected on their use of dialect, irregular grammar and pronunciation after they were found to have picked up bad habits. Parents have been asked to monitor their children's mistakes, after they began to appear 'regularly' in speech and written work. The school, led by head teacher Carol Walker, has produced a list of 11 banned words and phrases, including 'I dunno', 'gizit ere' and 'he was sat there'. According to the rules, the word 'yous' – often used as a plural by people in the North East – is prohibited, along with the phrase 'it's nowt'. A letter to parents explaining the decision states the latter should be pronounced 'it's nothing', while 'the word you is never a plural.'
>
> 'Tomorrow', which was increasingly spelt 'tomorra' by pupils in line with their accents, was highlighted, as was 'letta' (letter) and 'butta' (butter). Other examples of common mistakes include 'I done that', 'I seen that' and 'could of' instead of 'could have'. 'Gizit ere', the list explains, should be 'please give me it', while 'school finishes at free fifteen' should be 'school finishes at three fifteen'. Mrs Walker, who was born in nearby Stockton-on-Tees, said:
>
> 'I don't want the children to be disadvantaged. Using Standard English in applications and job interviews is important. You don't want the children to lose their identity, but you do want them to be able to communicate properly with people and be understood. We are going to teach them the rules. If they decide not to use these rules with friends that is fine, but I want them to know that when they are filling in application forms and speaking in a formal situation they should use standard English.'
>
> Mrs Walker said the school had noticed a decline in spelling and grammar, with children reading less for pleasure. An increase in social networking and texting, as well as spending time around the dialect and broad accents

> of friends and family in Middlesbrough, was also believed to have had an effect. The children, aged up to 11, are said to be embracing the policy, while staff at the school are ensuring they always say 'yes' instead of 'yeah'.
>
> Mrs Walker said problems had arisen as children increasingly could not distinguish between 'standard English and the English of the street'. She added: 'I think some people do judge – maybe that's the wrong word – but they make decisions about people on the way they speak, whether they are from the North or South. It's not that either speak wrongly, but that they speak differently'. Mrs Walker, who has been head teacher at the urban primary for 12 years, emphasized the aim was not to wipe out the Teesside accent but to teach children standard English.
>
> Cheryl Fortune, a mother of two boys at the school, said it had been welcomed by parents. 'When I saw it I was a bit shocked. I thought my kids are only eight and five, so it's a bit extreme,' she said. 'My eldest son said "yeah" last night and my youngest said "it's yes," so he corrected him. I can understand why the school has done it – to encourage people to speak properly. At the end of the day, they're children. Now is the time to make an impression on them. I don't think we will ever lose our accent – you can't mistake it – but I want my boys to have the best upbringing possible and that includes knowing how to speak properly.'
>
> *Daily Telegraph*, 5 February 2013

There is a perfectly good point here, of course. Children do indeed need to know how to use standard English (assuming we can agree on what that might be) and how to express themselves in such a way that they will be understood beyond their immediate geographical area. However, the school management's approach to the perceived problem generated a series of confusions that only succeeded in fogging the issue thoroughly, while suggesting to the children that their way of speaking was a bad habit in need of correction. In Chapter 13, which deals specifically with language in the school context, we will argue that an informed, linguistics-based approach would have been more effective and appropriate here than an edict banning particular usages. But for the moment, let us look more closely at some of what was reported by taking a few of the more striking aspects of the *Telegraph*'s story, and commenting on each in turn.

Correct; mistakes

> One can correct incorrectly spelt words, and to spell a word wrong is without doubt a mistake. But *mistakes* is used here to cover the simple use of dialect. In such a case, there is no mistake in the form of the language used. If there is a mistake, which in itself is arguable, then it is a

sociolinguistic, not a linguistic one: the use of dialect (that is, linguistically correct, but non-standard language) in a context where standard English is expected.

Irregular grammar

As we saw in Chapter 2, the grammar of dialect speakers is not irregular – it is regular (i.e. rule-governed). It's just that not all the rules are the same as those of standard English.

'It's nowt' . . . should be pronounced 'it's nothing'

Nowt is not a mispronunciation of *nothing.* They are two different words, one being a dialectal usage widespread in the north of England (cognate with the archaic 'nought'), the other being the standard English term.

The word 'you' is never a plural

The word *you* can obviously be a plural – for example in *You are both wrong.* In some dialects of English the plural is marked in the morphology of the word: *yous/youse* is common in Ireland and Liverpool, for example, as well as the north-east of England; *y'all* is found in many southern parts of the United States. What is actually meant here, it would appear, is that in standard English the plural *you* is not marked with the ending *–s*, but is identical to the singular form.

Letta and *butta*

The gist of the school's worry here appears to be that the children write the word as they pronounce it. But this is not an argument for banning local pronunciation; rather, it is an argument for teaching the children that written and spoken forms are often different, and that writing, in English (as we saw in Chapter 8), does not simply mirror the spoken word. A moment's reflection will confirm that speakers of Received Pronunciation (RP) do not pronounce such words as they are spelt, either: that is, they don't finish the words with a /r/ sound, but with a vowel, in their case /ə/, just as the Middlesbrough children do with their more open vowel. No one argues on this account that RP-speakers should be banned from saying words with an RP accent. So if pupils at, say, Eton College do not write 'letta' but 'letter', it is not because they spell the word as they pronounce it, but because they have been taught that English orthography has its own rules and does not consist simply of transcribed speech sounds. The solution to the problem lies in linguistically informed teaching of writing, not in banning certain ways of speaking.

'Could of' instead of 'could have'

Similarly, to write *could of* for *could have* is an error which might have been produced by any RP-speaker, for in connected speech where *of* or the verb auxiliary *have* are unstressed, they tend both to be pronounced /əv/. Hence *could have* or *could've*, pronounced /'kʊdəv/, could quite reasonably be rendered *could of* in writing if the writer was unaware of the correct form. The problem is not one of intrusion of dialect into standard English, but of incorrect orthography, or insufficient grammatical awareness.

[A] decline in spelling and grammar, with children reading less for pleasure. An increase in social networking and texting, as well as spending time around the dialect and broad accents of friends and family in Middlesbrough, was also believed to have had an effect.

Several different aspects of literacy and oracy are here conflated and treated as if they were all part of the same phenomenon. But as we note below, speaking with a 'broad accent' is not the same as speaking a dialect; and in any case, neither ought to lead to a decline in accuracy of spelling and (written) grammar, provided children are made aware that writing does not automatically reflect speech. Equally, social networking and texting are valuable contexts for the development of literacy skills, as long as children are made aware that different writing contexts require different registers and styles. And what is social networking anyway, if not reading (and writing) for pleasure?

Using standard English in applications and job interviews

Here, 'standard English' is insufficiently differentiated from the RP accent. It is perfectly reasonable to teach children that they should as a general rule use standard written English when filling in an application form, and adjust the register of their speech to suit a particular context such as a job interview. But very many people, of course, speak standard or near-enough standard English with a regional accent, whether that accent be from Middlesbrough, Edinburgh, Chicago, Bridgetown or Bangalore, and modify their style to suit their surroundings. Some of the children's supposed errors do indeed involve deviations from the grammar of standard English, but others, like 'free fifteen' are matters solely of pronunciation, not dialect form.

Yeah/yes; I dunno

What appears to have happened here is that perfectly normal English contractions have been taken for non-standard or dialectal forms. This is simply a matter of register; casual speech is casual speech, regardless of one's accent or dialect, and casual speech exists in standard English (and in standard-English-with-RP) just as it exists in all other varieties. Again, it would seem that 'speaking correctly' is being conflated with writing correctly.

My eldest son said 'yeah' last night and my youngest said 'it's yes,' so he corrected him

The home and the school are what in sociolinguistics would be described as different domains, requiring different registers of language. Even if we accept that *yes* is always appropriate for school – and that is very far from being a given – few would argue that *yeah* is generally inappropriate in the intimate domain of the home. The younger son seems, however, to have picked up from his school the idea that *yeah* is always wrong.

In sum, most of these are not problems of right or wrong language at all, linguistically speaking. Some are problems of orthography; note how in paragraph two, there is a shift from referring to writing to referring to speaking without any differentiation at all, so that writing 'letta' is held to be the same *kind* of error, as it were, as saying 'free fifteen'. Others are matters of sociolinguistic appropriacy. Now, the school clearly shows some understanding of the crucial importance of appropriacy in language usage. The headteacher goes out of her way to insist that she does not wish to stop the children speaking naturally when they are with their friends: the aim is purely to instil an awareness of standard English. So she points out that it is not a case of speaking rightly or wrongly, but differently – but this vital insight, the key to the whole matter, is not followed up on or made explicit. Then there is a highly ambiguous reference to rules ('We are going to teach them the rules. If they decide not to use these rules with friends that is fine') which almost seems to imply that the way the children speak with their friends has no rules. As we saw in Chapter 4, with the example of the Jamaican Patois speaker Marlon, this is a very widespread belief, and one which speakers themselves often internalize.

12.3 The beginnings of a moral panic?

The Middlesbrough school might, of course, have been a one-off case. But in the months that followed this story, similar examples began to appear with some frequency in the British media, often containing similar features such as the issuing of a list of 'banned' words, a complete failure to distinguish between slang, dialect, accent and the use of informal register, the conflation of speaking correctly with speaking as if writing, and the attribution of declining standards of literacy to over-exposure to electronic media and games. As the seeming fashion took hold, these examples included the new management of a school in south London (see Figure 12.1) banning a selection of informal contractions, dialectal usages, slang, fillers and stylistic features, all of which ended up being lumped together and described simply as 'slang'.[3]

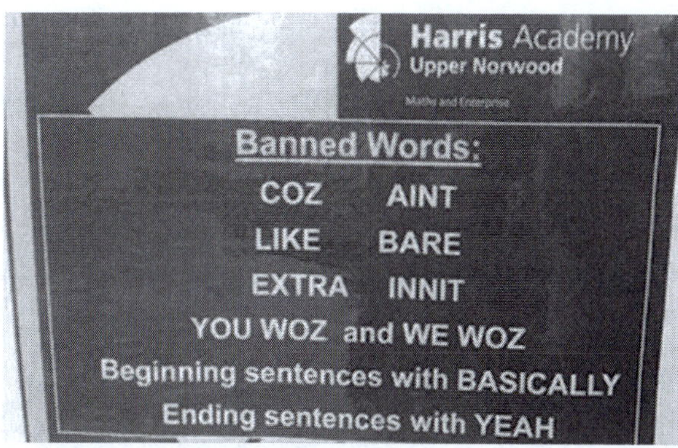

FIGURE 12.1 *A sign-board outside the gates of a South London school in 2013.*

As we saw in Chapter 10, category assignment plays a crucial role in how we think about such things. Placing regional dialect in the same category as slang not only does a disservice to dialect speakers, but reveals ignorance or laziness on the part of the school authorities and, worst of all, helps obstruct and confuse clear and rational thinking about how language is used.

In the Black Country in the English midlands, meanwhile, a school's war on 'dialect' usage, in another category error, turned out also to include informal contractions and regional pronunciations. Again, predictably, the whole was couched in terms of worries about 'correctness' and bundled up with a rationale about standards of *writing*:

> The headteacher of a Black Country school has defended banning the local dialect from classrooms, saying it will help raise literacy standards. John White, said that failing to ban the dialect from Colley Lane community primary school, in Halesowen, would put the prospects of his 600 pupils at risk. . . . The 10 banned phrases include 'you cor' rather than 'you can't'. Other banned phrases include the more widely-used 'somfink' instead of 'something'; 'gonna' rather than 'going to' and 'ain't' rather than 'are not'. . . . White said: 'We'd been looking at our literacy standards and we wanted to talk to parents about some of the confusion that happens when

> children are talking to their mates in the playground. When it comes to phonics and English lessons it can be very confusing for the children. When they are reading phonics, it's incorrect, so we think it's better for them this way. . . . We're not stopping them talking to their friends in the playground how they want to,' White added. 'We're just saying that in the classroom we'll correct them.'
>
> *The Guardian*, 15 November 2013

The reference to phonics is perhaps what can help us to disentangle some very muddled thinking about language on the part of the school authorities. The headteacher in this case is reflecting the mistaken assumption, prompted by current government insistence on what is known as synthetic phonics as the panacea for supposedly low levels of literacy in schools, that words should be pronounced as they are written. If the children do not do this, then they must be 'corrected'. But as one imagines any 15-year-old pupil who had studied the 'Spoken Language' element of the English language GCSE (see Chapter 13) could have pointed out, of course phonics is not a true reflection of English spelling, and English just does not work like that. As various reports show (Hodgson et al. 2013; UKLA 2012), most teachers are very well aware of this, even if their managers – not to mention politicians – are not. It is hardly surprising that the children (and their parents) are confused.

These stories are a rather depressing illustration of the problems caused when well-meaning attempts are made to address language issues from a position of very limited knowledge about language. The schools' supposed aim of improving their pupils' language use is fatally undermined by their own lack of language awareness, seen in the persistent conflation of written form with spoken; of non-standard usage with sub-standard usage; of casual (ie., low register) speech with incorrectness; of slang with dialect; of standard English form with RP accent; and so on. In the end, in attempting to tackle what they perceived as a problem, these schools have confused matters to the extent that they seem to be suggesting that the very use of dialect forms or regional pronunciations is a danger to literacy and therefore a bad habit, to be corrected. This is not just muddle-headed and wrong: it actually takes us inexorably back to the insistence of Halliday et al. (1964), quoted in Chapter 2, that to make a child feel ashamed of the way they talk is to do them a real injury, and MacRuairc (2011), for example, has been far from alone in pointing out how the implicit or explicit imposition of 'school' language on working-class children causes real resentment, emotional upset and alienation from the school and its value system. Not unnaturally, too, when this kind of story appears in the media, it looks like a very inviting bandwagon for MPs, self-appointed guardians of the language and 'standards' campaigners of various stripes to jump aboard, thus compounding the problem further with simplistic and strident assertions which professional linguists are hard pressed to rebut (assuming they are even invited to do so).

When the language of children is addressed in the confused and uninformed way that some British schools and media outlets are now doing, it is tempting to suggest that we are no longer dealing with a matter of education, but witnessing the beginnings of a full-blown moral panic (see Barton 2000). Debates about the use and teaching of standard English and the place of accent and dialect have gone on for a very long time. There were heated discussions in the 1980s and 1990s, for example, around the time of the design of the National Curriculum (see Chapter 13), leading to a flurry of both academic and popular books about the subject (e.g. Honey 1989, 1997; Cameron 1995; Bex and Watts 1999; Milroy and Milroy 1985). A wealth of research was built up which dealt with the subtleties of the relationship between standard English and children's use of non-standard forms (e.g. Williamson and Hardman 1997). It seems, though, that we are fated to return to the public debate time and again, with its basic terms unaltered and with the same fundamental misunderstandings left intact: one is forced to the conclusion that, as Williams (2007) carefully demonstrates, there will always be political (and media) resistance to anything which does not fit a certain set of ill-informed prejudices. Despite the best efforts of a number of 'popularizing' language specialists and academic linguists, especially on radio, 'the standard of public discourse on linguistic topics is lamentably low' (Cameron 1995: xiii). That was true in 1995, and it remains so today.

12.4 Subverting and disregarding

Let's now look at another example of good intentions being derailed by a lack of language awareness – not on the part of a school this time, but of those whose job it is to inspect schools.

> **Firms' names set bad example, says Ofsted.** School inspectors in England have attacked companies for setting children a poor example by having names that 'subvert' and 'disregard' standard spelling and punctuation rules. In its latest report on literacy in secondary schools, Ofsted warns that, by using these names, businesses give the impression that spelling, grammar and punctuation do not matter. 'Those in the wider world – employers, for example, or representatives of national or local government – complain about falling standards of literacy,' the inspectorate's report states. 'The blame is then directed towards schools, although examples are legion of

businesses that subvert standard spellings and syntax in their trade names and slogans, and of official publications and signage that disregard standard rules of punctuation.'

The Guardian, 24 April 2013

'Subvert' and 'disregard' are a curious pair of words to put together. What this appears to be is a conflation of two different concerns on the part of the school inspectors' body. One of these concerns is quite legitimate, and the school inspectors are right to raise it: to 'disregard standard rules of punctuation' through simple ignorance or carelessness is indefensible. A 20 mph 'school safety zone' near a large school in east London, for example, is advertised by official signs showing a snail apparently named Sam and the slogan *Sam say's 20 is plenty!* It would be difficult to argue that this does not set the children in the school a bad example.

However, to 'subvert standard spellings and syntax' – or for that matter punctuation – is a different matter altogether. The company that produced a range of dolls and christened them *Bratz* is surely not sending to pre-teen girls the message that spelling does not matter, but that it *does* matter. As we saw in Chapter 3 with regard to how we signal membership of communities through language, the word is spelt in this way for a reason. The *-z* plural ending of course references written usages like *sistaz* and *boyz* and as such is intended to index desirable qualities such as urban hipness, edginess and cool – which is presumably why it is so popular in the names of provincial nightclubs (there is a *Honeyz* in Skegness, a *Playerz* in Fuengirola, a *Moverz 'n' Shakerz* party night in Llandudno). A rather similar, if more politicized semiotic effect can be obtained in Spanish by using *k* (which does not figure in the standard Spanish alphabet) in place of *c*, as in *okupado* ('squatted') seen graffiti-ed on the door of a building in Seville. The inspectors appear to be missing the crucial point that of course the reader notices that such spelling is non-standard, and that of course they think it matters. If they did not notice, or it did not matter, then what would be the point of the exercise? If you call your doughnut range *Krispy Kreme*, it is in order to draw attention to it – a principle embraced by the makers of Weetabix, too, as far back as the 1930s, though the inspectors perhaps do not object to such venerable and familiar 'subversions'. We might also consider neologisms (i.e. newly coined words) used in advertising, such as the barber's shop run by a group of young black men in east London whose window slogan is *We barb to impress.* The back-formation of a verb *to barb* from the noun *barber* is entirely logical and immediately comprehensible. It is hardly indicative of 'falling standards of literacy'; rather, it shows ease on the part of the writer with the syntax of English and confidence that the clientele at whom it is aimed will similarly easily 'get it'.

To place *disregard* for, or ignorance about the rules of writing and syntax in the same category as *subversion* of those rules is to make yet another fundamental category error (see Chapter 10), rather in the same way as we saw the mis-labelling of dialectal and informal usages as 'slang', above. Writing, particularly, is a hugely fertile space in which to develop new meanings; the apparent rigidity of scripts and spelling rules provides a framework within which skilled communicators or networks of communicators can improvise, adapt and innovate. Many schools are, and all schools should be, in the business of increasing their pupils' awareness of the many different kinds of writing they see around them, whether it be standard, non-standard, 'subversive' or just plain incorrect. For the Ofsted school inspectors to complain that non-standard writing in the public sphere is automatically wrong and damaging reveals a lack of knowledge about, or even interest in, the way writing can be used creatively to convey a message which is larger, subtler or more complex than that encoded in the simple meaning of the words themselves.

12.5 Speaking foreign tongues

It is not only ideas about the quality of English, or how English should be taught, that can become muddled. The same is abundantly true of ideas about the learning and teaching of other languages. Here we are concerned principally with the context of the United Kingdom, and to some extent also with other English-speaking countries. There are a number of themes which tend to be given an airing in the press and in public debate whenever the question of MFL (modern foreign language) teaching is raised, and while here we try to separate the themes for the sake of convenience, it should be kept in mind that they are very closely intertwined. First is the deep-rooted conviction that the British, or English speakers in general, are bad at or uninterested in learning languages; next its corollary, that abroad 'everyone speaks English'; finally, the oft-repeated assertion that the earlier children begin to learn another language, the easier and more effective the process will be. We shall suggest that, while all these notions contain more than a kernel of truth, they are based on some questionable assumptions and need to be hedged around with a good many caveats and reservations.

We should note before we proceed that, strange as it may sound, the very notion of what is a modern foreign language is at times rather unclear. When the phrase 'modern languages' was first coined, it was meant simply to differentiate between modern languages and classical ones: Latin and ancient Greek. However, changing cultural assumptions and political imperatives have combined over the years to produce an illogical and uncomfortable divide between MFLs and so-called 'community' languages. Quite how the division is arrived at, no one is able to say with any precision, and some groups and institutions do not recognize such a division at all, regarding it (rightly) as implying a hierarchy of languages. The Department for Education's website includes Urdu along with Arabic, Spanish, Mandarin, Russian and other 'major European and world languages' as examples of MFLs that schools may choose to teach – the phrase 'community language' is not used at all.[4] The teachers' magazine website www.teachsecondary.com will tell you that community languages are 'languages spoken by members of minority groups or communities within a majority language context', and gives as an example Urdu – though plainly this definition would also cover every language spoken in the United Kingdom apart from English. CILT (the National Centre for Languages) on its website states that it campaigns alongside other interested groups and organizations to place 'community' languages on an equal footing with MFLs, but does not define what they are, other than to state that they are *not* 'the more common, often western European languages taught in our education system and taken advantage of by employers'.[5] The incoherence of the sentence perhaps reflects the incoherence of the notion itself. The inescapable conclusion of this position, that French, say, is not a 'community language' in London despite there being some 400,000 French citizens (and many other French speakers) living there,[6] is a nonsense – as is the idea that Bengali, say, is not a modern foreign language despite its being demonstrably modern, foreign and a language.

The distinction is not really that difficult to pin down at all, of course, for all that it ties some anxious language education professionals up in knots. The root of the division lies in brute sociolinguistic realities, and specifically in the notion of language prestige as discussed in Chapter 4. Bengali tends to be relegated to the ranks of 'community languages' and is not much taught at schools because it has low prestige; French is a 'proper' MFL and has traditionally been taught in schools because it has high prestige. The prestige or lack of it derives, it need hardly be said, from history, economics, power, ideology and the social status perceived to attach to each language's speakers: *linguistically*, it is quite impossible to say that a hierarchy of languages exists. And of course, as was also noted in Chapter 4, prestige varies according to time and place. Bengali is afforded high prestige in South Asia in part because of its distinguished poetic and literary tradition (including the Nobel Prize-winning Rabindranath Tagore). In Britain this tends to count for little, and it is seen primarily as the language of a low-status minority group (in the same way that Spanish often is in the United States). That this is not always said, openly and explicitly, by educators and language-teaching professionals might conceivably be due to sociolinguistic ignorance; much more likely, it can be put down to historical tradition, or a simple reluctance to offend.

12.6 Are we bad at languages?

Whether we are dealing with high prestige or low prestige languages, there is no doubt that it is a struggle to sell language learning to schoolchildren. In fact, school (and university) language teaching in Britain has dropped precipitately in recent years. In the decade between 2001 and 2011, for example, the proportion of English school students sitting for a GCSE qualification in a language fell from 78 per cent to 40 per cent, with a 56 per cent decline in the two most common languages, French and German (though there was something of a rally in 2013). Some other languages – notably Putonghua (Mandarin Chinese) and Spanish – have fared rather better, relatively speaking, but the actual numbers studying them are low (CILT 2013; and see Edwards 2012: 210–2 for a discussion of the position in other English-speaking countries). Part of the way through this already steep decline, in 2004, the British government actually made languages optional after the age of 14, where they had previously been compulsory to the age of 16. Between then and 2011 the number of pupils taking a GCSE in French virtually halved. Evidently, the students voted with their feet.

In attempting to explain why so many British teenagers drop language study at the first possible opportunity, we must first note that the *choice* of language is of paramount importance. Should one opt for French, German, Spanish, the newly fashionable Putonghua, a 'community' language, or something else? Classroom language learning is after all a fairly arduous and difficult business, and one would like the benefits to justify the effort invested. But essentially, curriculum planners or teenagers themselves just have to take a guess as to which language is likely to afford the greatest benefits, such is 'the unpredictability, especially in English-speaking countries, of a pupil's future language needs' (Hawkins 1999: 124). And it is indeed in English-speaking countries that the problem rears its head. Politicians and language-teaching lobbyists are fond of pointing out that other Europeans are much more interested than the British in learning languages, but of course for most of them, the answer to the question 'which language?' is staring them in the face. Only one language is guaranteed to be useful and perhaps even indispensable in virtually any profession one cares to name, virtually anywhere. Other languages (Putonghua, Hindi-Urdu, Spanish) may have more native speakers, but no language in human history has ever had anything close to English's reach and appeal as a global lingua franca. For those who already speak English – as a birthright, as it were – there is no such 'banker' choice available. The purported enthusiasm of other nations for foreign languages, in other words, is to at least some extent actually an enthusiasm for English, or the perceived advantages it confers.[7] A change in political or economic circumstances would doubtless bring about a change in attitude; as Bailey

(2006) reminds us, up until the beginning of the eighteenth century, the English tended to consider themselves good at learning other languages, even supposedly preferring other languages to their own native tongue. It is usually solid circumstance that dictates language attitudes and language choice, as we have remarked elsewhere, rather than any more abstract concerns.

Since the 1980s a vocal and politicized lobby has argued consistently for individual multilingualism as a good in itself. Here, the language used about language can become heated, as when Skutnabb-Kangas and Cummins (1988: 13) describe monolingualism as 'an ideological cramp . . . an illness, a disease which should be eradicated as soon as possible because it is dangerous for world peace'. This discourse is perhaps most visible in the United States, where the metaphor of monolingualism-as-disease has even found its way onto bumper stickers and T-shirts reading 'Monolingualism is curable'. Leaving aside the sickness metaphor temporarily, elsewhere Skutnabb-Kangas takes aim from another angle with an indictment of the 'ideology of monolingual reductionism/naivety/stupidity' (1996: 177). It's strong stuff; and in our experience when we have discussed these notions in class with postgraduate students, the (usually British or American) monolinguals in the group tend to feel embarrassed, defensive or both. But of course Vietnamese-Americans or Dominican-Americans or whoever it may be tend to speak English for practical reasons, rather than for the sake of personal intellectual development, ideological rigour or a commitment to world peace. If one already speaks English, then to remain monolingual is on most grounds a perfectly reasonable and rational choice. As a general rule there is no *need* to learn any other language in the United States, any more than there is in Britain, for the sound sociolinguistic reason that English 'serves across domains' (Edwards 2012: 199).[8]

Politicians, educators and language professionals in English-speaking countries therefore have their work cut out trying to explain why language learning is so necessary. As Hawkins (1999) notes, it was probably a bad mistake for British schools to start to promote the speaking of another language as a useful skill, rather than an integral part of a rounded education, as the supposed usefulness is often simply not that clear. St John's University (based in Queens, New York – an area of enormous linguistic diversity) promotes language learning thus:

> In a world that is increasingly interdependent, we can no longer afford to remain monolingual. Success depends in large measure on the ability of an individual to function as a member of a global village whose members speak a variety of languages. Learning foreign languages is no longer a pastime: it is a necessity. . . . In large metropolitan areas such as New York, knowing a foreign language seems almost an essential aspect of urban living.[9]

Now, language learning is useful and beneficial in all sorts of ways: there is plenty of evidence to suggest, for example, that it can enhance intercultural understanding and personal development, and some have suggested that it has cognitive-intellectual benefits, though not everyone agrees (see Edwards 2011: 135). But to suggest that to speak another language is 'almost essential' for life in New York (or London or Sydney or Vancouver) is simply wrong, no matter how multilingual these cities might be. If it really were the case, then languages would have obvious appeal, and the foreign language teachers of the anglophone world would not be plunged in communal despair. It may well be true that English speakers are 'bad at languages' – but they're bad for a reason, and the reason is a pretty good one.

12.7 The 'Early Start' movement

Is it, then, the case that in the rest of the world, 'everyone speaks English?' It is true that English is extraordinarily widespread. There are perhaps some 400 million native speakers of the language, and perhaps 400 million users of English as a second language (in countries where English has some special or official status); plus a fast-increasing 600–700 million users of English as a foreign language, according to the cautious averaging of various estimates by Crystal (2006). And yet, away from the domains of urban centres, hotels and airports, among older or less educated people, or when the subject under discussion is an unfamiliar one, the supply of English can dry up very rapidly indeed. As Crystal goes on to remind us, '[i]f one quarter of the world's population are able to use English, then three-quarters are not' (2006: 425). We should not lose sight of how complex and subtle language distribution and spread can be – a result of the mixture of history, politics, economics, geography, war, culture, trade and transport links and much else besides (see Ostler 2005). Many other languages have huge regional influence, such as Russian in central Asia and (mainly for older speakers) eastern and central Europe; Arabic in the Middle East and beyond; Spanish in the Americas; French in large swathes of north and sub-Saharan Africa, though its appeal is declining. Even given the astonishing reach of the 'global lingua franca', and even in rich European countries like France and Germany, it actually takes little effort to find people who have no English at all. In India and the rest of the subcontinent, there are millions of fluent speakers and everyday users of English, but a British native speaker would understand a good number of them only with difficulty, so 'Indianized' is the variety of English that they speak. Meanwhile, in Japan, Korea and many other east and southeast Asian countries, English has until very recently been taught almost exclusively as a written language, with the result that even well-qualified graduates are sometimes barely able to speak the language at all.

This has not escaped notice. And with the growing perception that competence in English is one of the key life skills to acquire, there has been a strong and fast-growing trend towards the ever-earlier teaching of a foreign language – which in practice, in most places, is almost *always* English. In fact, it is now more or less routine in the wealthier regions of the world to begin teaching English at primary school. In Europe, with strong EU encouragement, the trend is towards starting mandatory teaching at the age of 6 or 7 (Enever et al. 2009), and the adherence to the philosophy of early language learning is often reinforced by parents who, anxious that their offspring not lose a competitive advantage, send them to paid-for after-school classes. This has been the case for a long time in traditionally competitive east Asian countries such as South Korea, Taiwan and Japan, but it is now becoming the norm for the middle classes in much of central Europe. And this is not to mention newly-rich China, where the market for private teaching is worth at least three billion dollars per year and Disney English, an offshoot of the US leisure corporation, offers to teach children as young as 2 years old, helped by Peter Pan and Little Mermaid-themed teaching materials (*Guardian Weekly*, 13 June 2010).

Such sustained investment and commitment should mean that fast-growing competence in English is guaranteed in much of the developed world. If you read the advertisements for early language learning providers, you would be excused for thinking that it was, indeed, a safe bet. This is how one company offering child language tuition sells itself online:

> Young children are uniquely suited to learning a second language. The developing brain is hard-wired to acquire language. Never again will it be this natural or this easy! . . . Exposing your child to a second language while young allows him or her to optimize his or her learning potential, helping to shape the brain at its most flexible stage. Young children are uniquely suited to learning a second language. Learning a second language at a young age is cognitively as easy as learning a first language.
>
> Young language learners can acquire native-like fluency as easily as they learned to walk, in contrast to an adult language learner. Where adult learners have to work through an established first-language system, studying explicit grammar rules and practicing rote drills, the young learner learns naturally, absorbing the sounds, structures, intonation patterns and rules of a second language intuitively, as they did their mother tongue. The young brain is inherently flexible, uniquely hard-wired to acquire language naturally.

> Older learners lose the ability to hear and reproduce new sounds by age 8–12, according to experts, resulting in a permanent foreign-sounding accent in any language. Younger learners benefit from flexible ear and speech muscles that can still hear the critical differences between the sounds of a second language, as well as reproduce them with native-like quality.[10]

This is generally rather ill-conceived, and takes a pick-and-mix approach to a very large body of academic research in linguistics and language acquisition, managing to muddle up various different parts of different fields and misrepresent them in the process. However, not all of it is actually, objectively, completely *wrong* (we will leave aside for now the intriguing reference to 'flexible ear and speech muscles' which apparently stop working at the age of twelve). It all chimes, certainly, with the one thing that everyone 'knows' about children and language learning: the earlier you start, the better. In reality, though, the ingrained belief among governments and the general public that children learn languages more easily is not one that is shared wholeheartedly by researchers in linguistics (see e.g. Singleton and Ryan 2004). As so often happens when ideas filter through from academic research, via the media, to the public domain, there have been some misrepresentations and misunderstandings and some vital caveats and nuances have been lost.

As a very general rule children seem to find the process of picking up the language or languages spoken around them less difficult and frustrating than adults do: this much is true. However, there are some very specific provisos to bear in mind. The most important of these is that the academic finding that children learn a language without conscious effort relates principally to *first* language acquisition – that is, the learning of the mother tongue in the first few years of life. Now, if another language is also spoken around them, then children will tend to acquire that language effortlessly, too (or even many languages, as among the famously multilingual Tukano people of the Amazon or the Siane of New Guinea – see Wardhaugh 2010: 94–5). To this extent it is true that 'learning a second language at a young age is cognitively as easy as learning a first language', as the advertisement claims.

However, classroom second language learning will not produce anything like the same results, for the environment – even if it is a 'total immersion' one – is radically different (Marinova-Todd et al. 2000). In a classroom there is less naturally-occurring language (lessons are managed by teachers); less need to speak the target language to your companions (in Poland, say, you could just use Polish); much less exposure to the language and reinforcement of what has been learned (at the end of the class, you switch back to the normal language environment for the rest of the day). Apart from anything else, as many adults can attest who lived abroad as children and picked up the language from the locals, what is quickly learned in childhood is often just as quickly forgotten when the environment changes. And while it is true that children do appear to have the edge over adults in developing a native-like accent when learning a second language, pronunciation is of course only one area of language learning; in other areas, such as the understanding of tricky points of grammar, or the ability to paraphrase, adults have much more success (Scovel 2000, 2006). Add to this the reality that in many countries training of primary language teachers is inadequate or absent; that specially designed materials are often unavailable; and that teachers are themselves seldom expert speakers of the target language, and it is clear that early start policies are far from guaranteed to deliver the kind of long-term advantage that many governments and parents assume.

In reality, it may well be that the single most reliable outcome of early start language learning is the development of a positive attitude to the language and its speakers, and/or to language learning in general. This is without doubt worthwhile; but why invest such a great deal of effort and money for such a modest guaranteed outcome? Part of the answer, in non-English-speaking countries at least, is that for ambitious national governments as for ambitious parents worldwide, English has symbolic status. Commitment to English is a token of progress, aspiration, ambition and modernity (see e.g. Inal 2009). And because everyone thinks they know, or fears that everyone else knows, that an early start is best, governments and parents alike compete to secure the earliest start possible, terrified of being left behind. Enever et al. (2009: 6) remark: 'Uncritical acceptance of the view that "early is better" under all circumstances can lead to hasty policy decisions to begin early, with huge implications for national resources.' Quite so. But is anyone listening? One begins to suspect that, even if the anxious parents and governments were assured by linguists that the advantage gained from the 'Early Start' was often negligible, they would stick with it just the same.

12.8 Conclusion

Sometimes, then, ignorance of how language works can be harmless; sometimes it can be harmless and expensive; sometimes it can cause real psychological damage. Astonishingly, it can even lead to physical harm. In 2002 the *Los Angeles Times* reported on a new trend in South Korea:

> **SEOUL:** In a swank neighborhood renowned for designer boutiques and plastic surgery clinics, anxious parents drag frightened toddlers into Dr. Nam Il Woo's office and demand that he operate on the children's tongues. It is a simple procedure: just a snip in a membrane and the tongue

> is supposedly longer, more flexible and – some South Koreans believe – better able to pronounce such notorious English tongue-teasers as 'rice' without it sounding like 'lice.' 'Parents are eager to have their children speak English, and so they want to have them get the operation,' said Nam, who performs about 10 procedures a month, almost all on children younger than 5, in his well-appointed offices in the Apkujong district here. 'It is not cosmetic surgery. In some cases, it really is essential to speak English properly'.[11]

As the story goes on to point out, of course linguists dismiss the idea that Koreans find it difficult to distinguish /l/ and /r/ because their tongues are shorter than Americans' tongues (or indeed, because they do not have flexible enough 'ear and speech muscles'). As we saw in Chapter 6, the problem is purely one of phonology. In English /l/ and /r/ are separate phonemes, and in Korean they are not: therefore Koreans are not accustomed from an early age, as Americans are, to notice and reproduce the difference between the sounds. A competent language teacher – which means one whose skill-set includes a working knowledge of phonetics and phonology, apart from anything else – would have little difficulty in diagnosing the problem and developing a set of teaching materials designed to help learners overcome it. The real mystery is this: what are the parents thinking, to say nothing of the doctor? Why is such basic knowledge about language not considered part of general knowledge, like what it is that clouds are made of, and how blood circulates in the body? As a subject of study, linguistics is surely of the very first importance in helping us to understand how we think and communicate, and how the social world is organized: to be ignorant of linguistics is to be ignorant of one of the fundamental attributes of being human. But how is the situation ever to be overcome? In the next chapter, Language at School, we will argue among other things that language awareness as an approach, and most particularly linguistics as a body of knowledge, should have an automatic place in the school curriculum.

Suggested reading

Bauer, L. and Trudgill, P. (eds) (1998), *Language Myths*. Harmondsworth: Penguin.

Do women really talk more than men? Are some languages 'primitive'? Is it illogical to use the double negative? An informative and entertaining collection of essays, written by prominent linguists for a lay audience, which takes aim at a number of the most embedded and hard-to-shift myths about English, and about language.

Cameron, D. (2012a), *The Myth of Mars and Venus: Do Men and Women really Speak Different Languages?* Oxford: Oxford University Press.

In challenging one of the most prevalent language myths, Cameron considers how and why it originated and, using an evidence-based argument, shows why it is an unhelpful and even dangerous way to view gender, gender identity and gender politics. It is written in an engaging style which makes it not only an informative read but a good one too.

Garrett, P. (2010), *Attitudes to Language.* Cambridge: Cambridge University Press

A compact survey of the field of language attitudes, including sections on how such attitudes are measured, how we react to other people's speech styles, and the role of language attitudes in professional contexts. Sharply written and thorough.

13

The subject that isn't a subject: Language at school

13.1 Introduction: What should everyone know about language?

At a recent celebration lunch for a friend, I (Tim) fell into conversation with a personable couple, now semi-retired, who had had interesting and varied careers. As quite often happens, the subject of language dominated our conversation. In fact, from the moment it was discovered what I did for a living, I was peppered with questions. *How many languages are there in the world? What has happened to the cockney accent? Is Welsh going to die out? Is text message-speak having an impact on standards of literacy? What's the hardest language to learn?*

Everyone is a language user, and almost everyone is curious about at least some aspect of language. For most people, therefore, the subject is an inherently interesting one (as long as the linguist present has the sense to know when enough is enough), and there is nothing odd about this kind of encounter. It does, though, raise a much larger question. How can it be that people like the lunch companions above – who were demonstrably intelligent, highly educated, well-travelled and well-read people – have gained comparatively little exposure to the kinds of concepts of language that are necessary in order to answer, or even to discuss, questions like these? Is it that language is not taught at school as part of the basic curriculum, the knowledge of the world that everyone needs? The answer, as we shall see, is that it is and it isn't. Language has a place in schools, certainly. But in this chapter we address a fundamental failing in the educational experience, in Britain and elsewhere, and one that has been debated and commented on by language professionals for decades: that is, the virtual absence of the *study of language* as a school subject. This curricular gap leads to the kind of misunderstanding and 'dialogue of the deaf' that we looked at in the previous chapter; it also accounts for the holes in the general knowledge of what must be a broad sector of society, as suggested in our anecdote above. To gain at school a solid understanding of how language works is to have one's intellectual horizons broadened for life; the study of language would also have a direct impact on the life of the school itself, mitigating some of the everyday problems and issues associated with language that schools experience, and which we shall discuss further in due course. Apart from anything else, it would open up the possibility of using such issues (things like the use of dialect and slang by pupils, as we saw in Chapter 12) as material for fruitful, informed classroom discussion, rather than treating them as problems of school management.

Of course, many schools do this kind of thing already – the problem is that consistency is lacking right across the sector. (In this chapter we are concerned primarily with the British context, and indeed primarily often with England: but of course you might like to compare it with other contexts that you are familiar with). In Britain, concepts like Language Awareness (LA) and Knowledge about Language (KAL) have had some kind of presence in the curriculum for some time, even while the goalposts keep being moved and politicians blow hot and cold. KAL is, for example, now embedded as a requirement in the English and Modern Foreign Language (MFL) sections of the secondary National Curriculum for England – until 2014, at least – though it might be argued that the conception of it suggested by the Department for Education (DfE)'s guidelines is a highly restricted one.[1] The 'embedding' approach reflects one of the ways in which the perceived language problem in the curriculum has been tackled. It might be considered a watered-down version of an earlier vision, which conceived of language as a 'bridging' subject (Hawkins 1999), using the insights offered by MFL and English teachers – who have not always seen eye-to-eye – to form strands running through and across the curriculum at every level. Of course, this also implies training of non-specialist teachers if it is to work to its full potential, which is one of several reasons why governments and some teachers have been lukewarm about it. Another common suggestion has been the introduction of a discrete language module in the curriculum, establishing language as a free-standing subject in its own right. This has not transpired either, though the introduction of the A Level English Language qualification might be considered, again, a dilute version of it.

This is, then, far from being a new discussion and we do not pretend to be pioneers in the field. As far back as the early 1990s, in the very first issue of the journal *Language Awareness,* a leading figure in the LA movement was explaining rather wearily that he did not wish to restate the case for the study of language in the curriculum, as it had been stated so extensively already (Hawkins 1992). There have been many missed, or more often, spurned opportunities to introduce a substantial element of the study of language into schools, and organizations such as the Association for Language Awareness (ALA) and the Committee for Linguistics in Education (CLiE) continue to press the case for it – from rather different perspectives – whether in the form of a curricular strand or a stand-alone subject. While there have been partial successes (such as the introduction of English Language A Level and the embedding of KAL in the National Curriculum referred to above), too often efforts to solve the 'language problem' have foundered on the indifference, reluctance or even hostility of successive governments. Sometimes, ironically, it would seem that the hostility to what is suggested by professional linguists derives from the very ignorance and prejudice (around matters such as the teaching of standard English, for example – see Williams 2007) that the suggestions are designed to dispel. In this chapter we wish to add our voice to the case for language study in schools, in the same spirit as that in which this book is offered: that is, with the aim of encouraging as many people as possible to take an interest in language and to acquire the basic knowledge and terminology to be able to take part in informed debate about language. The root of the problem, after all, is fairly easy to identify: language is a critically important element in all our lives, but few people have actually studied it.

13.2 How is language dealt with at school?

The muddled state of language in the curriculum has been evident for a long time. Part of the back cover 'blurb' of Carter (1990), an edited collection of essays intended to help teachers prepare for an earlier (and in the end abortive) roll-out of KAL, reads thus:

> Knowledge about language has been identified as one of the key areas of the National Curriculum requirements for English; it has also generated considerable controversy and caused some confusion amongst teachers, many of whom remain insecure about their ability to deliver this strand of the curriculum effectively.

Here the twin, interlinked problems at the heart of the question are laid out with some clarity: first, language in the curriculum is bound up with English; second, many English teachers, reasonably enough, are not or do not feel themselves to be experts in *language* as a field of study.

It is worth reflecting on the implications of this. The two fundamental resources for human understanding and articulating of the world, it might be argued, are number and language. Modern societies accept that these should be taught at school, along with other central areas of human knowledge and culture – history, literature, geography, chemistry, biology, physics and so on. But the way in which language is usually taught is, when you come to think of it, rather odd. There are 'language-y' subjects, such as English and foreign languages, but the extent to which these actually deal with language per se is typically very restricted indeed. In UK state schools, for a good part of the last 30 years, it has often not even included much in the way of the study of grammar. The way English-related subjects and qualifications are labelled is also a source of dire confusion, as we detail in the next section.

So when language is explicitly presented at school as a subject of study, it is invariably presented under the aegis of either English or a foreign language, not as language per se. This invisibility persists through the rest of the curriculum, where elements of language study are present, but are often disguised or left unnamed. In history students might be invited to compare historical accounts of the same event and analyse them from the perspective of authenticity and reliability, which is of course a form of discourse analysis akin to the analyses we have done in previous chapters. Hence students might look at the vocabulary used, the modality of verbs, the ideological perspective suggested by the author's choice of lexis and so on – without ever realizing that 'discourse analysis' is what they are doing. Meanwhile, historical topics such as the Norman Conquest are often taught with no reference to their linguistic effects, by historians who are themselves monolingual (Hawkins 1999). In geography, students might (perhaps) learn that certain countries consist of groups of speakers of disparate languages, just as they might learn what their highest mountain range or principal export is. This is sociolinguistic knowledge, but is rarely named as such. Anywhere in the curriculum they might be told that saying or writing something in such-and-such a way is inappropriate to the context, but this is unlikely to be explained in technical terms of register, domain or genre. You will recall from the previous chapter that students might even be forbidden to use their own regional dialect in the school – but one wonders if it is ever properly explained to them what a regional dialect is, and how it differs from the use of slang, or the dialect known as standard English. Apart from in a handful of cases, which we discuss below, language *as language* is rarely foregrounded.

But we can go further than this. As the study of language as a coherent body of disciplinary knowledge does not exist in schools, it follows that there is no requirement to have qualified teachers to teach it. Some teachers of English and MFLs will of course have had some training in linguistics, but there is no expectation that this will be the case, and such teachers are probably relatively few (the CLiE is attempting to identify them at the time of writing). Most degrees in English are still focused on literature; degrees in foreign languages tend also to be literature-heavy, and aim, in addition, to produce expert users of the particular foreign language, whichever one it may be, not experts in language; PGCE courses, by their very nature, are not set up to offer training in disciplines other than pedagogy. This leads to a very curious state of affairs. History teachers are obliged to be specialists in history, maths teachers to be specialists in maths, physics teachers to be specialists in physics and so on; *but language teachers are not required to be specialists in the discipline of language itself.*

Part of the problem, we suggest, lies not only in the disparate places in which language work in the curriculum is located, but in the equally disparate ways in which it is named.

13.3 The naming of language

It used to be common in the 1990s for certain Middle Eastern universities, seeking British teachers of English, to stipulate in their newspaper advertisements that applicants must hold a good degree in English. The practice seems now to have died out: presumably the penny finally dropped when one promising new recruit too many proved themselves rather more adept at post-structuralist critique than they were at identifying a past participle. It is hardly surprising that the universities were misled, though, for the naming of qualifications in the area of language is notoriously confusing. Not only might employers be quite mistaken about what it is that prospective employees have studied, but school students might be surprised and dismayed by the actual content of the course they have signed up for (see Goddard and Beard 2007).

The way that language-related subjects are named in fact seems to reflect the elusive, almost tangential nature of language study in the curriculum. In Britain, as has been noted, there is no such school subject as Language (or Knowledge about Language, or Linguistics, or whatever we might label it), and much of the language-specific work in the curriculum is covered in English classes. This general model applies to very many countries worldwide: while perhaps a handful of countries do offer language as a stand-alone part of the curriculum (Denmark and Serbia are two: there may be others), typically the idea of language is tied to the national language or the official language of the region. Sometimes this is quite explicit: to take the example of *lenguaje* in Spanish-speaking countries, it is assumed almost everywhere that the chief aim of the subject of this name is to develop pupils' abilities in the Spanish language. This might be bundled up in the curriculum with literature (as in Spain) or with 'communication' (as in Chile and Peru), and there may or may not be extensive teaching of grammar, but the principle remains the same.

Lenguaje is not really language, but Spanish. In the English-speaking world, meanwhile, and perhaps even more confusingly, English is not really language. In countries like the United States and Britain, and many post-colonial, English-as-a-Second-Language countries such as India and Pakistan – and this is what bamboozled the Middle Eastern universities referred to above – 'English' also denotes the study of English literature, especially at university level. In other words, the distinction is elided between the language itself and a canon of cultural products (which may of course vary from place to place) that have been written in the language.

As we mentioned, one relatively recently introduced Advanced level course is dedicated to at least some extent to the study of language from the perspective of linguistics, rather than solely to English. This has to be seen as a step forward (and it has been welcomed by the CLiE), but in the naming of the course, confusion still reigns. While it could perhaps conceivably have been called Language, it is actually called English Language, presumably because this area of the curriculum falls under English and is taught by English teachers. Meanwhile, though, a new version of the English Language GCSE introduced in 2010 is a different creature entirely: the only aspect of it that might be considered to be concerned chiefly with language per se is a module comprising 10 per cent of the total and called 'Spoken Language Study'. Naming aside, the content of this module deserves a brief comment. Assuming they opt for this course it is here, typically, that pupils will first formally come across linguistics-related notions such as dialect and accent, slang, register and so on: no other part of the curriculum requires them. For the AQA board, in 2012–13 the topics offered for discussion in this area included social attitudes to spoken language, spoken genres and multimodal 'talk', in which pupils were encouraged to look critically at the language of internet chat rooms. Useful and imaginative though this is, it forms a very small part of the syllabus. The other 90 per cent consists mainly of developing written and spoken communication skills in English. The fact that two quite different courses have the same name can lead to problems for those pupils who go on to make the transition to the A Level English Language mentioned above where the emphasis is more on areas such as discourse analysis and language acquisition as well as sociolinguistics, rather than skills development (see Goddard et al. 2013; Goddard and Beard 2007). The GCSE English, meanwhile (to add even further to the chaos of designations), ignores the sociolinguistic element altogether.

The other curricular area concerned with language is, naturally, the study of languages other than English. Here the situation is scarcely less chaotic, for as we saw in Chapter 12, there is no universally recognized subject area of 'languages'. There are MFLs, sometimes called simply modern languages, community languages and classical languages, each label having its own connotations. Then there is the vexed topic of EAL (English as an Additional Language). Should it be included alongside English, on the grounds that it is, after all, concerned with the teaching of English? Or perhaps it could be located alongside the other languages, on the grounds that it consists primarily of teaching the content of a language to people who do not speak it already? Or should it stand alone, as being essentially unlike either of the others?

Whatever these subject areas and qualifications are called, and whatever they consist of, the point is that they do not offer a course in the study of *language*; and the only one which leans to some extent in that direction, the A-Level English Language, is available only in post-compulsory settings (i.e. sixth forms, Further Education colleges and the like). This means that for students who do not opt for this course – the vast majority, of course – their exposure during the whole of their school career to linguistics-related critical thinking about language, or even English, is extraordinarily limited. The position is summed up by Goddard et al.:

> UK English curricula and their associated assessments currently show little evidence of opportunities for learners to reflect critically on language, virtual or otherwise. GCSE assessments are predicated on standard English, a concept which remains largely unanalysed in any documentation. There is little or no recognition of language varieties even within the UK, let alone any of the larger scale Englishes that operate in different parts of the world. Attitudes to language, language as cultural history and as a performance of identity, language as symbolic capital, language play, discourses and power – these areas are not systematically studied until post-16, and yet even quite young students have their own experiences to draw on and have something to say. Goddard et al. (2013: 91–2)

13.4 A history of setbacks and small successes

A problem that has exercised language professionals for decades is how to bring together the conflicting designations, academic traditions and groups of teachers in order to bring out the commonality inherent in their spheres of operation and establish the importance of language and language awareness right across the curriculum. In 1976, for example, the National Congress on Languages in Education (NCLE) was created with the aim of beginning to harmonize the activities of teachers of English as L1, as L2, teachers of MFLs, community languages and classics. While the early stages were marked by suspicion and lack of comprehension between MFL teachers and academics, who had led the initiative, and those from the world of (L1) English (Hawkins 1999), a good deal of progress was made thereafter and there was optimism about embedding LA in the curriculum. 'LA was viewed as an enabling field, designed to facilitate people's access to one another through language, to make available the language to talk about language, and to reduce jargon. Its starting point was the removal of barriers, which was to remain its essence' (Donmall-Hicks 1997: 22). In the end, however, LA was excluded from the first National Curriculum when it was drawn up, government funding was withdrawn and the project's impetus petered out.

From the perspective of L1 English teaching, a similar fate met the Language in the National Curriculum (LiNC) project (Carter 1990) in the early 1990s; the materials prepared by the project team in order to train English teachers to teach language were never published (Donmall-Hicks 1997). Work that had fed into it, such as the 'Language for Learning' project carried out for the National Foundation for Educational Research (Gorman et al. 1990), which focused on language (not just English) study in every curricular area, largely fell by the wayside. Even well before all this there had been attempts to lock language study into the curriculum, such as a seminar chaired by M. A. K. Halliday which gave rise to 'Language in Use' (Doughty et al. 1971). This also attempted to bring a linguistics lens to bear on social language problems such as the perceived under-performance of African-Caribbean children in reading and writing, an area which Le Page (1981), too, considered ideally suited to a 'language studies and linguistics' approach (and for a whole series of valuable sociolinguistic discussions see Stubbs and Hillier 1983). There have been some successes since, as has been noted, but the way ahead is unlikely to be smooth. Language specialists in schools typically remain as firmly entrenched in their own 'silos' as ever, and language is still virtually never presented as a body of knowledge. The two problems are, it goes without saying, closely related.

If a pattern can be discerned in this history of repeated failure and limited success, it is that political (and hence financial) support for attempts to introduce LA/KAL tends to be contingent upon how far the politicians agree with the opinions of the professional linguists regarding how language performance might be improved. The touchstone appears always to be the ability of children to write (and to some extent to speak) using standard English grammar (Clark 2010). And as Clark rightly notes, the politicians tend to be wedded, or perhaps suspect that the public is wedded, to the idea of teaching standard grammar in isolation (as opposed to through a contextualized, LA-informed approach) even though linguists and educationalists have told them it doesn't work, and even though it is not at all clear that public and government concern about children's literacy is even justified (Barton 2000). As long as the professionals continue to come up with what is considered, politically speaking, the 'wrong' answer, then, projects continue to founder (and see Williams 2007).

This is not to suggest that there is hostility to grammar teaching as such among linguists (most of them, anyway). Rather, as the response of the CLiE to government consultation on National Curriculum English in 2011 makes clear, it is that people who have had training in linguistics tend to have a wider, more nuanced and theorized conception of what grammar actually is:

> Grammatical analysis is different from teaching 'correct' grammar, which consists of a rather arbitrary list of do's and don'ts. We accept the need for children to learn Standard English and the 'etiquette' of formal writing and speaking, but this is only a small part of the language development that takes place during the school years. 'Teaching grammar', in our sense, is not about split infinitives and double negatives, but about the structure of words and sentences. Grammatical analysis is as relevant to casual non-standard speech as it is to formal standard writing: *I ain't saying nothing* has just as much grammatical structure as *I am not saying anything*, and exploring the differences should be an important part of education.[2]

Unfortunately, however, as we noted in Chapter 2, this kind of thing – which to linguists is unexceptional and indeed self-evident – is for some people just too much to swallow. An ideologized view of grammar therefore prevails in which 'grammar' is taken to mean standard grammar, and linguistic insights such as the above are, if not rejected outright, then accepted only partially and grudgingly. So KAL made its way into the National Curriculum, but in a reduced form, and the teaching of standard English grammar retains its central place in the official conception of what language study should consist of.

We might add that the scepticism shown by successive governments in this area is probably shared to a fair degree by the public. As was pointed out by Cameron (1995) with regard to the intense public debate about language matters at around the time of the LiNC project, while laypeople tend to care deeply about rightness and wrongness in language, linguists dismiss this approach as 'prescriptive' and insist instead on investigating and describing how language is actually used (this is the 'descriptive' approach which informs all of the modern academic discipline of linguistics). The result is 'an exchange carried on very much at cross-purposes, if indeed there is any exchange at all' (Cameron 1995: xi) and a widespread public perception that academic linguists not only do not care overmuch about correctness but sometimes even appear to revel in the 'abuse' of the English language. Certainly not every professional linguist who is invited to comment on television or radio covers themself in glory. There can be an occasional air of condescension towards the layperson's very real concerns about language, and Cameron's (1995) book is partly aimed precisely at this lack of comprehension or empathy on the part of the professionals. However, ironically enough, it would seem that the overriding contributory factor in public, and with it media and government, resistance to using the insights of linguistics at school is the very lack of exposure to such insights. It is a closed, vicious circle.

13.5 What should be the scope of linguistics at school?

There is another aspect of the language at school issue, though, which links all these problematic discourses and goes to the heart of what this book is about. This is that it is not always clear, to the public, to politicians, to teachers, to parents, to pupils, what is meant by the term 'linguistics'. This is probably not unconnected to the fact that linguists often do not agree among themselves. As we saw in the General Introduction and in Chapter 6, some boil the discipline down to a number of core areas, the traditional domains of phonetics, phonology, morphology, syntax, semantics and (perhaps) discourse. This core body of linguistic knowledge has sometimes been represented as the only true, 'scientific' or formal linguistics (see Blommaert 2013; Agha 2007). Even within these core areas, the variety of the subject matter is immense: from abstract Chomskyan theories of grammar which essentially form a branch of psychology, to predicate logic, free and bound morphemes, turn-taking in conversation, acoustics and speech sounds. Even then not everyone agrees on what goes where. Should semantics and phonology be included under 'grammar', for example, as many Chomskyans would suggest?

Beyond this core, however, assuming we can agree roughly what it looks like, lies an extraordinary depth and diversity of language-related topics, some of which we have touched upon in this book. Drawing on such fields as sociolinguistics, anthropological linguistics, historical linguistics, linguistic ethnography and psycholinguistics – to mention only a very few – it is easy to compile lists of compelling subject matter that one might argue should be discussed in any balanced school curriculum. How do infants acquire language? Do all cultures possess the notion of formality in speech? Why do regional accents exist? How many words are there in English, or for that matter in the other home languages represented in the school? How does the brain understand language? Who invented the alphabet? What is the oldest language in the world? – the kind of questions, in fact, with which we began this chapter, and which cannot be answered without some basic knowledge of linguistic terms and concepts. The English Language A Level does cover some of this kind of ground (the Cambridge International 2014 syllabus for the subject, for example, includes topics such as English as a global language, child language acquisition, and spoken language and society). However, as we have noted, it is an optional course at post-compulsory level, and most people therefore never come across its content or the approach it embodies. As things stand, all of this area of fundamental knowledge is a closed book to most schoolchildren, and hence adults, in Britain today.

Taking a broad view of linguistics, in other words, we can represent it not just as knowledge about language (let alone knowledge about grammar) but *indispensable knowledge about the world*. If the public and the government are to be persuaded of the case for linguistics in schools, they will need to be persuaded that the subject is not solely a theoretical one. Of course, the core areas of 'traditional' linguistics need to be taught, and can be taught in a way that makes them exciting and relevant. This should not really need saying. But few linguists in fact advocate studying *only* traditional linguistics, or studying it in the way that one might do at university. As Goddard and Beard (2007: 9) are careful to note about the English Language A level, it 'was never an attempt simply to do H[igher] E[ducation] Linguistics at school level'.

By the same token, we must recognize that linguistics has a reputation for being not only heavily theoretical, but dry and difficult. As we pointed out in our Introduction to the book, many people who have to take a compulsory element of linguistics as part of a university course come to it with a mixture of trepidation and resentment, and cannot see how the formal linguistics they are anticipating – in which sentence diagrams and the like seem to loom large – will be of any use to them (and see Freeman and Freeman 2004 for the United States). They may already have had some exposure to Chomskyan linguistics and the arcane and, to the outsider, unfathomable debates that rage around it (Harris 1993), and have come to the conclusion that this is not for them. If linguistics seems forbidding to many postgraduates, it is of course bound to be even more so to secondary school pupils. It seems clear that in order to bring language study to life, an integrated and unified path needs to be taken, in which the core material of traditional, descriptive linguistics is linked systematically to the social and cultural context in which language is produced.[3]

13.6 Language problems vs. learning experiences

In Chapter 12 we showed how misapprehensions about language and ignorance of even the basics of linguistics had led some school authorities to issue bans on the use of certain words by their pupils. Had any of the headteachers involved had any background in linguistics, of course, the question of a ban would never have arisen; more than this, though, the notion of what is or is not acceptable speech could have been turned into a fruitful subject for classroom discussion or a class project (see e.g. MacRuairc 2011; McCallum 2012). What is slang? How is it different from dialect, or informal register? Do we write in the same way we speak? – sometimes, always or never? What is standard language? Why and how do we adjust the way we use language from one context to another? Where an integrated approach is taken, using the broad definition of linguistics outlined above and the contextualized approach it implies, perceived language problems turn into learning opportunities.

One example of this is the way in which it has become commonplace for schools serving multilingual communities to claim that they view their children's languages not as a problem, but as a resource. In the absence of staff trained in linguistics, though, such lofty sentiments often struggle to rise above the cliché of posters in the reception area saying 'Welcome' in 20 different languages. Indeed, we might argue that such an approach is not only tokenistic, but reductive. Given the foundation provided by sound linguistic and sociolinguistic knowledge, *all* pupils' language would be treated as a resource by *all* schools, for there is linguistic diversity in all student bodies, not just multilingual ones. Language variation according to gender, age, social background, self-identification and multiple other factors will always provide rich pickings for the teacher who is confident and experienced enough in the field of language study to bring such things into the classroom. Equally, many other questions which have provoked disagreement and uncertainty among teachers and public alike lose their sting when viewed through a linguistics lens – that is, as matters to be debated in an informed manner, rather than as problems needing resolution (and a policy handed down from on high). Should standard English be accepted as a 'given'? Should it be explicitly taught? In what contexts should it be required of pupils? Should the MFL classroom be a 'target language only' environment? Should children from linguistic minorities be allowed to speak their own language to each other in the classroom? There are countless areas where informed discussion about language could contribute to the curriculum and to the life of the school, and indeed, this already happens in many places. The task facing all those who are concerned about language and about education is to find ways, small or large, to begin to make this happen in a consistent way, right across the sector.

13.7 Conclusion

While the presence of KAL/LA in the National Curriculum is to be welcomed, this presence, as we have shown, is a very limited one, and its impact might prove to be similarly limited. It seems probable that if the organized study of language at all ages and across the curriculum is ever to become 'more than an idle dream' (Hawkins 1999: 140), then it will need to have the kind of theoretically informed leadership, support, recognition and visibility that being a free-standing, compulsory subject would provide. Of course, this raises immediate problems: where are the linguistically trained staff to come from? What elements of the curriculum will have to be changed or removed in order to accommodate this new subject? We do not pretend to know the answers, but we do feel that linguistic ignorance in society at large is a damaging enough phenomenon for answers to be sought.

M. A. K. Halliday, advancing an argument for bringing linguistics into the school rather than leaving it confined to university departments, commented that 'linguistics is everywhere because language is everywhere'.[4] Indeed so. As was pointed out by the earliest campaigners for LA, the point of the exercise is to sensitize children to the sea of language in which, without ever really noticing it, they swim (Halliday 1971; Svalberg 2007). If adults are to become linguistically literate, if we can put it like that, then they need to start the process at school. It is never too early to begin the critical business of learning to notice language.

Suggested reading

Carter, R. (2012), *Linguistics and the Teacher.* Abingdon: Routledge.

This edited collection was first published in 1982 and has recently been reissued in response to current debates. The fact that the discussions, by leading scholars, remain highly relevant is testament both to the fact that their work is significant and that, as we have seen in this chapter, progress in introducing linguistics into mainstream education has unfortunately been agonizingly slow.

Denham, K. and Lobeck, A. (eds) (2014), *Linguistics at School: Language Awareness in Primary and Secondary Education.* Cambridge: Cambridge University Press.

This recent publication clearly demonstrates contemporary concerns about the need for linguistics in mainstream education, not just in the United Kingdom, but in many different parts of the world. Like us, it argues for linguistics to be part of the school curriculum as well as a central component in teacher education.

McCallum, A. (2012), *Creativity and Learning in Secondary English*. Abingdon: Routledge.

Although this book is essentially about creativity, the author invites teachers to make use of the analytical approaches and the insights provided by the kind of linguistics that we have been discussing in this book when thinking about and developing teaching activities. It usefully combines theoretical discussion with practice-oriented suggestions for use in the classroom.

14

Communicating at the sharp edge: Linguistics and the workplace

14.1 Introduction

I've think I've realised a lot just by talking all this through. (north London GP)

We start this chapter with a comment from a GP who works in a busy practice in Tottenham, a highly multicultural part of north London. We interviewed her because we were curious to find out whether and how language might affect the successful outcome of a consultation and how she herself dealt with language-related issues in the course of her work. The comment came just as we were winding down the discussion which was based around a series of questions we had sent her ahead of the interview so that she would have time to reflect on them. What her comment indicates is just how useful it can be to put language centre stage. By using a linguistics lens (rather than just a medical one) to discuss some of the many communication problems she experienced during patient consultations, she began to develop new insights into possible reasons behind these problems and ideas of how she might approach them differently. We return to this later.

This chapter focuses specifically issues in the workplace which are related to language but which are rarely understood from a linguistics perspective. This is not surprising given the lack of attention that the study of language receives in formal education, as we discussed in the previous chapter. If you have never been properly introduced to the tools, frameworks and concepts that linguistics provides, then you will naturally be unaware of the way in which such knowledge can be used as a resource for understanding particular workplace problems, some of which you may not even recognize as being primarily to do with *language* at all. The examples we use to examine the relevance of linguistics in workplace settings concern themes such as terms of address and how they can affect interpersonal relations at work. We look at problems associated with multilingualism that people like the GP above face every day and discuss some of the ways these are dealt with in practice. We also show how linguistics research can shed light on workplace interactions and how linguists, working with other professions, can directly impact on workplace practices.

We start, though, with an example that everyone will be familiar with: the case of the offshore call centre and its recent fall from grace.

14.2 The abrupt decline of the offshore call centre

In the 1990s and early 2000s, it became common for large service-sector companies in the western world in areas such as banking, telecommunications and utilities, to move their customer service call centres 'offshore'. In practice this meant moving them to those parts of the developing world where a good knowledge of the relevant language could be assumed and staffing costs were low. Traditionally English-as-a-Second-Language countries such as India and the Philippines were favoured by largely British and American corporations, while France, for instance, drew on such countries as Senegal (Moriset 2004). Naturally, some problems were anticipated. Chief among these was the question of linguistic intelligibility, particularly in pronunciation, and particularly in countries like India, where local pronunciation norms differ can differ very markedly from the norms of the 'core' (Phillipson 1992) countries, even where speakers have been educated mainly or wholly through the medium of English. It was also assumed that some cross-cultural knowledge would be needed.

In response to these perceived training needs, there has been a mushrooming of training providers within the countries concerned offering both pre-service and in-service courses, and even including courses to prepare would-be call centre operatives before they apply for a job in a highly competitive market. These courses tend to concentrate on areas of performance such as achieving a 'neutral' accent, or in a few cases on the acquisition of a British or American accent; in any case, the goal is to eliminate, as far as possible, the phonological influence of the mother tongue. In addition, the providers often offer 'cultural awareness' or 'cultural sensitivity' training, whereby trainees are coached in the supposed national characteristics of the target countries, their psychology and preferred styles of interaction. Famously, though possibly anecdotally, Indian call centre employees have been briefed on day-to-day developments in the popular British TV soap opera *EastEnders*, or on current weather conditions in the United Kingdom, in order to cater for the presumed favoured themes in British small-talk. Certainly some call centre workers in Senegal were encouraged to take their lunch break in front of the lunchtime TV news from Paris, which is conveniently in the same time zone as Dakar (Moriset 2004).[1]

Regardless of how much training was provided, however, customers have never taken to the experience of the offshore call centre conversation. Complaints have been constant, and as wages in the 'periphery' countries have risen, the perceived benefits of the system seem to have dwindled away. By 2007, when Lloyds Banking Group repatriated their centres, the retreat from overseas was well under way. By 2013, many UK-based companies were making a point of highlighting in their advertising that all their call centres were now based in Britain: they included Co-op Banking, Royal London Group, Sainsbury's Bank, Midland Telecom and NatWest. While some companies have persisted (for now) with the offshore model, the bubble has definitively burst. Why did it not work? What is wrong with the call centre model? Or to put it another way, why would so many customers object to talking to someone in India or the Philippines? A possible answer to this might lie in the way the call centres were conceived of, and what this tells us about the companies' understanding of the nature of language and human interaction.

A glance at the content of the training courses available for call centre operatives reveals that, as suggested above, their principal preoccupation is intelligibility; there is much repetitive drilling in particular problem sounds, which are often of course the sounds that do not feature in the phonemic inventory of the operative's native language, as we saw in Chapter 6. Then there is much attention to the 'staging' of each telephone conversation, and practice of supposedly appropriate set phrases to say at each point ('Is there anything else I can help you with today?'). Some companies provide complete 'scripts' to guide the operative through common scenarios. (And do so even for native speaker operatives in Britain – see Cameron 2000). There are at least two problems here, and you might think that both are probably known instinctively by speakers of any language in the world. First, as we have shown throughout this book, language consists of much more than the utterance of intelligible phrases, just as culture is more than television programmes and talking about the weather. Second, interaction is more than a series of intelligible set phrases uttered in a prescribed order and manner.

Take first the question of speaking 'neutrally' (Cowie 2007). The assumption which underlies the demand for employees to speak in a neutral accent is that such an accent is accessible and intelligible to all, and upsets no one.

But accent, as we have noted, is also concerned with identity (so can mark or index things like social class, age, in-group affiliation, ethnic heritage and geographical provenance): ways of speaking are also ways of belonging, in the way that we talked about in Chapter 3. Ordinary native speakers of English in Britain intuitively understand that there is no such thing as a neutral British English accent,[2] whether the speaker's first language is English or not – and an ostensibly neutral accent is therefore rightly perceived as something manufactured. As a deception it is not in the same league as the fake 'English' names that operators are often required to assume (Nadeem 2011), but it is hardly a firm basis on which to build a relationship of trust with your customers, either. As we suggested in Chapter 4, mutual intelligibility is not only a question of usage and pronunciation, it is also a matter of co-operation and adjustment to achieve successful communication; and this is something to which English speakers, accustomed to their language being spoken in a vast variety of ways, are perhaps particularly attuned. Indeed, the principle applies as much to native speaker interaction as to that between native speaker and non-native speaker, and as a general rule, people 'can be trusted to make the same necessary adjustments that a university professor from Chicago must learn [in order] to converse with a miner from Rotherham' (Jibril 1982: 98). In short, the notion of the neutral accent is not only unwelcome but unnecessary. The outsourcing history of the banking conglomerate Santander illustrates very neatly how misconceived it is. Having relocated its British call centre activity to Bangalore and Pune in 2003, in 2010 Santander moved back to Britain and opened new call centres in Leicester, Glasgow and Liverpool – the last two in particular being cities renowned in Britain and even beyond for their distinctive and easily recognizable accents. Clearly the company no longer thought that a neutral accent was what the customer wanted to hear.

To prescribe a supposedly neutral accent is to misunderstand how speech works and what 'else' it does, apart from the obvious. More than this, to attempt to manage interaction through the use of scripts is to misunderstand in a fundamental way what human communication is, for it sets out to reduce its complex, multilayered nature down to the transmission of an intelligible message in order to effect a transaction. Any linguist could have told the companies that this was unlikely to be a profitable strategy. Indeed, their own employees might have told them so, had they troubled to ask them: Cameron (2000: 339) notes that even British call centre operatives complain bitterly about the 'artificiality' and 'inauthenticity' of the persona that the imposed script forces them to adopt. It is no surprise, then, that the message might sound even less authentic when it comes from a non-native speaker, from a different culture, speaking to you from an unidentified country and using an accent that cannot be placed. Even if the accents had been convincingly native-like, it is to be suspected that the outcome would have been the same, and the customers would still have complained. A script is no substitute for genuine communication, however routine and even routinized the communicative event may be. And while intelligibility is vital, it remains only a single feature of the complex, context-dependent, intensely social phenomenon that is linguistic communication. In essence, ignorance of how language works, in other words an absence of language awareness, led the companies to attempt to commodify language, and the attempt failed.

14.3 Language at the sharp edge

Call centre work is, of course, to some extent a special case, the operative's job consisting of 'little else but language-using' (Cameron 2000: 327). However, as we have already suggested, language, in its many different guises, plays large in the workplace. We all experience it and some of our examples in earlier chapters have illustrated it (e.g. Example 10.1 in Chapter 10). During the writing of this book we spoke informally to a number of different people about whether and how language as an issue played out at work and we received a lot of anecdotal feedback. For instance, at an elderly people's care home, one particular staff member, a Jamaican woman, always addressed residents by their title and surname, as in Mrs Conway or Mr Johnson, rather than using their first name, because she wanted them to feel properly respected as elders (see 14.2.1 below for more on terms of address). At the other end of the scale is the example of the secondary school teacher who, trying to use the speech styles of his teenage students, crossed a line when he used a particular phrase in the wrong context, an act which nearly led to a fight. What these two examples show is how language use, as we have seen throughout this book, has an enormous impact on social relations. Two of the people we spoke with work in fields where language issues arise every day, particularly issues relating to multilingualism. One was the GP with whom we opened this chapter and the other was a senior police officer from Slough, a town some 20 miles to the west of London. Given their interest in discussing their problems with us and our interest in hearing what they thought, we decided to interview them more formally. Both of them work in extremely linguistically and culturally diverse environments and both reported very similar problems regarding their interactions with their 'clients'. Neither of them had received any input on language as such in their training although communication skills of the type 'how to listen', 'how to ask questions' or 'the importance of eye contact' were included. The GP remarked, as already pointed out, that the interview had helped her realize things about the language behaviour of her patients that she hadn't thought of before. She went on:

> *During training we were told about the importance of communicating effectively, but I'd never really thought much about language as such.*

Likewise, the police officer told us that the subject of language as such was never mentioned in his training, other than in the context of dealing with people who are unable to speak English. In fact the official advice given for this particular situation, as it was in the case of the GP also, was simply to phone the commercial interpreting service, Language Line (and we will have more to say about this shortly).

Courses in communications skills are all very well, of course, but true language awareness, as we have argued throughout this book and particularly in the previous chapter, needs to be rooted in awareness of the discipline of language study. That is to say, communication training is doomed to be ineffective unless it is built on a properly theorized and linguistically informed foundation (and this is why offshore call centres have run into trouble, despite all the call centre training providers). In the following sections we look at two very different kinds of workplace problem, and consider to what extent an awareness of language and linguistics might have been helpful in avoiding or resolving them.

14.3.1 *Terms of address*

As we noted in Chapter 10, to choose a term by which to address someone can seem a small thing. However, it is potentially fraught with difficulties, involving complex calculations of social context, relationship, identity, positioning of self and other, and much else besides, as discussed in Chapter 7. It is perhaps in a bid to negate such complexities that some employers take it upon themselves to mandate certain terms of address and forbid others. In 2003 the city council of Bristol (in the west of England) banned the use of, among other terms of address, 'love' and 'dear'. According to the BBC:

> Receptionists and security staff at the city council have been told not to use local terms of endearment because they are unprofessional. Instead of greeting people with traditional Bristolian pet names such as 'my lover', 'my babby' and 'my treasure', workers must address them as sir or madam. But the decision has puzzled the city's residents, who fear the council may be 'sanitising' their distinctive local dialect.[3]

Meanwhile, in Australia, the Northern New South Wales Local Health District banned 'mate' and 'love' among other words, but, following complaints and a certain amount of online ridicule, 'conceded that such language may be acceptable in situations where staff members have established an ongoing relationship with a patient'.[4]

Let's consider briefly what might lie behind decisions like these, and indeed, why public reaction to them should be so strong (and the story therefore so newsworthy). In essence what these cases and others like them represent is an attempt to control language choice. That is to say, while in any given linguistic interaction, by the very nature of things a choice of terms of address always exists, in these cases it was thought desirable to curtail this choice – and in the Bristol case, even to impose an approved set of terms ('sir' or 'madam'). Linguistic control or reduction of choice, though, quite clearly indexes control over people's management of their own relations with others, and to claim that only 'sir' and 'madam' represent 'professional' usage is to privilege or foreground one aspect of a relationship above all the others which might exist at any given moment. Presumably this is why the Australian health board eventually made its concession: competent speakers of any language on earth know instinctively that certain forms of language will be appropriate in some cases and not in others, or at certain points in the development of a relationship and not in others. To remove from people their discretion in choosing a term of address is to rob them of their agency in creating and maintaining relationships with others in the course of their work, and to treat them as linguistic-cultural incompetents, or potentially such. While it is perfectly reasonable to offer guidance or instruction to those who are newly arrived to a particular social context, such as nurses trained overseas (Hearnden 2010), it is something else to deny to natives, so to speak, the exercise of their linguistic-cultural competence. In a small way, it is analogous to the deployment of the call centre 'script'; in attempting to ensure uniform standards and maintain efficiency, the mandating of terms of address manages to miss the very essence of human communication, and thereby strikes a false note every time.

In short, most people know when 'mate' or 'love' (or indeed, 'my treasure') is appropriate and when it is not. If they do not, then (as the example in Chapter 10 showed), they are likely to be quickly put right. These management teams are therefore perhaps responding to an uneasy awareness, derived ultimately from sociolinguistic research, that so-called institutional talk carries an inbuilt power asymmetry (Harris 2003), and that people in positions of authority in institutional contexts can display a tendency to 'talk down' to their interlocutors, rather as if they were children, or can be felt to be doing so. This applies particularly to contexts such as hospitals and nursing homes for the elderly (see Backhaus 2013), where a particular style of speaking has been identified by researchers and labelled as 'elderspeak' (Kemper 1994) or 'patronizing communication' (Ryan et al. 1995). To wish to respond is of course commendable; but as we have pointed out before, language policy formulated by people with no background in language study is liable to be, at best, a blunt instrument. And here is the nub: if a basic knowledge of social linguistics could be assumed (e.g., if language were to be taught as a core curriculum subject at school, as we suggested in Chapter 13, or if linguistically informed work on language and communication formed an integral part of professional training), then people would arrive equipped to understand. Council staff, medical professionals, caregivers and management alike would come to the issue armed with the basic sociolinguistic understanding that, for example, language attitudes vary according to gender, age and social background; that it is in the normal way of things that sometimes standard language is appropriate, and sometimes dialectal usage; that small variations in speech can carry strong messages about power relations; and so on. Such a foundation would, on the one hand, ensure that instructions were not simply empty rules and regulations, but had a clear purpose; and on the other, give staff the confidence to be able to challenge clearly ill thought-out blanket regulations concerning things like terms of address.

14.3.2 Language in legal settings

As we noted in Chapter 4, the diglossia introduced into England in 1066 had the long-term effect of making English speakers think of their language in terms of everyday, short (Germanic) words and rarefied, long (Latinate) words. Hence making something easy to understand is often thought of as saying it in the shortest words possible. The irony in this is that of course, if the English speaker is trying to make things easy for a speaker of a Romance (i.e. Latinate) language such as Italian, French or Romanian, he or she would probably be better off using the longest, hardest words they could think of, these being for that person closest to their common, everyday words. Rather than 'Do you want to go to the cinema with me?' you might come up with something like 'Do you desire to accompany me to the cinema?' and so on. The lesson of this is that to make things easy is not necessarily easy: some linguistic knowledge might be required.

The example we use to illustrate this point comes from the transcript of a police interview, collected by one of the authors, with a Portuguese-speaking detainee whose level of English, as became clear during the interview, was minimal. The example is of the police officer giving the caution, a legally required utterance informing a detainee of his rights. As an utterance, the caution has the qualities of writtenness in the sense we discussed in Chapter 8, rather than spokenness. It is formulaic in that it is a frequently repeated statement as far as the police are concerned, and largely familiar to the population at large via the many police dramas on TV. People know, or assume they know, what it means. This kind of understanding is what Pavlenko (2008: 13) is referring to when she talks about 'conceptual competence', competence in the sociocultural meanings as well as the implications of the utterance – something that visitors to a country are unlikely to have. In fact, as the act of telling someone about their rights following an arrest is not universally practised, it may not even figure in many people's minds. (And Pavlenko's discussion above analyses one such case).

In our own example, the officer following the advice provided in the UK Police and Criminal Evidence Act to lower the register when issuing the caution to a foreign language speaker, falls into the linguistic trap that we discussed above with his reformulated version as we now show in Example 14.1. The case, which involved a suspect parcel that had been delivered to the detainee's address, was subsequently dismissed by the judge when it came to trial.

Example 14.1

(P = police officer; D = detainee; the caution in bold, the paraphrase in italics)

P:	**You do not have to say anything, but it may harm your defence if you do not mention when questioned something which you later rely on in court. Anything you do say may be given in evidence.** Do you understand?
D:	No
P:	Did you get a parcel from the postman? We are investigating this.
D:	No, I don't understand.
P:	I will clarify the caution. *If this business goes to court, before a judge,* do you understand?
D:	Yes
P:	*And you say nothing at this moment, keep silent, and then say something at that time, it may go against you. You do not have to speak to us now,* do you understand?
D:	Yes
P:	*But if you don't speak to us, but speak if this matter goes to court and say something that you could have told us now, it may look bad.* Do you understand?
D:	No

If this were not a serious case, the progression of the interview would be amusing. However, for the two participants, it must have been anything but. Despite the officer's best intentions in seeking to ensure that the detainee has understood his rights, it is obvious that he has failed miserably. There are, of course, glimmers of hope along the way with the positive responses to the question asking whether the detainee had understood. However, in each of those cases it is unclear exactly what he had understood (though we might guess that his positive responses referred to the last said thing – *before a judge* and *You do not have to speak to us now*); apparently not the meaning of the caution itself, nor the officer's reworking.

From a purely linguistic perspective, to explain the caution is no easy thing, as it is not simply a matter of replacing 'hard' words with 'easy' ones (which as we have already noted, is in itself an exercise which requires some knowledge of how language and languages work). It is, in fact, a process of unpacking what is a syntactically, rather than lexically, complex statement typical of formal written language as we saw in Chapter 8. The first sentence alone has six clauses in it, if we include the elided 'when questioned' instead of its unelided form 'when you are questioned' and 'in court' for 'when/if you are in court'. Even a proficient speaker of English might have to work a bit to unravel the different elements and their interrelatedness, but, as we have pointed out, 'natives' are likely simply to accept the utterance as a whole, understanding it as a set piece with conceptually established meanings.

In the reformulated version, the officer, seemingly aware of problems that might be caused by the instances of elision in the original, starts off by expanding the elided elements. For example *in court* becomes *if this business* (and later, *matter*) *goes to court*; *when questioned* becomes *if you don't speak to us*. He also tries to clarify what he suspects might be unknown vocabulary such as *in court,* which he re-glosses as *before a judge,* or *harm your defence,* which becomes *may look bad, may go against you*. Unfortunately though, what the police officer did not seem to realize was that in his attempt to simplify, he had, for this particular detainee with his particular linguistic background, rendered it equally (though differently) difficult and opaque. This is because the officer adopts the strategy of using what, to the English speaker, would be easy to understand idiomatic, colloquial language characteristic of spokenness. However, the phrases *go against you* and *look bad*, not to mention *this business,* are unlikely to have illuminated the situation for the Portuguese speaker whereas the less colloquial original terms might have been more accessible once unpacked from their syntactic complexity.

Perhaps most disturbingly, in this example, the police officer fails to get across the issue of the detainee's rights, which, as we have already pointed out, may be, to him, an entirely alien concept in the legal process. Cotterill's (2000) discussion of the caution and the different ways in which police officers present and represent it demonstrates the difficulty of the task.

> It is probably inevitable that police officers find the apparently straightforward task of reading the rights problematic, since they are in fact being asked to carry out a series of fairly complex and challenging linguistic tasks, tackling a range of issues which have preoccupied academics for many years. (2000: 20)

Example 14.1 comprises part of the analysis undertaken by an expert witness in producing a report to be used as part of the defence being prepared by the legal team involved in the case. This kind of work is a part of what is called forensic linguistics, a field which is becoming an established resource for those involved in legal practice from the police on the ground to high court judges. It uses the three key linguistic approaches of discourse analysis, language description and linguistic ethnography in its analytical work, and in so doing sheds light on communicative activity in legal settings. For instance, Cotterill's work above helps improve the approach that the police adopt in clarifying the caution, chiefly by raising their language awareness. Heffer's (2010) analysis of courtroom interactions shows how much of the process involves co-constructed story telling rather than the kind of rigorous testing of evidence that is popularly thought to take place. The case from which Example 14.1 is taken involved assessing the detainee's level of English to comment on the likelihood or otherwise of his having properly understood the questioning during the police interview (see English 2010). Such studies, and there are many more such (see Coulthard and Johnson 2010), can be highly informative to those involved directly in the process and can raise their awareness about the social, cultural and linguistic factors that the legal process involves and the issues that can arise if such factors are not taken into account.

This last can perhaps be best exemplified by the high profile cases that Malcolm Coulthard (see e.g. 2005) has been involved in such as that of the posthumous acquittal, 46 years after his execution, of the wrongly convicted Derek Bentley. In the appeal, Coulthard was able to demonstrate, using analysis of police and witness statements and drawing on information that corpus analysis can provide, that the authorship of Bentley's own statement was in doubt. In 2002, meanwhile, his work contributed to the conviction of the murder of a teenage girl whose alibi was challenged by the linguistic analysis of a series of text messages.

What the development of forensic linguistics shows is the potential linguistics has for making a real difference in professional fields that are not ostensibly linguistics-based. The development of academic programmes in forensic linguistics bears witness to its increasing reach and it is now not unusual to find police officers among the students attending such programmes. This has to be considered progress and is something that could, and in our opinion, should be integrated into other professional programmes such as in Social Work, Nursing and even Education itself, as we argued in Chapter 13. In fact, one of our former students, who was studying for a degree in Social Work and who had taken our second-year module in Language and Society as an outside option, commented that the knowledge of sociolinguistics and linguistics that she had gained from our course was starting to have a positive impact, not only on her studies but on her professional work as a community youth worker in east London. She explained that the language awareness that she had developed helped her have, for instance, a better understanding of reasons behind her clients' speech styles and the linguistic choices that they made, recognizing them now as acts of identity rather than acts designed solely to annoy!

14.4 Managing multilingualism at work

This leads us on to our final consideration, that of multilingual work environments. It is rather striking that, in Britain at least, professional training for those at the sharp edge of dealing every day with people who speak no English, or do not speak it as a first language, often contains little or nothing in the way of reflection upon language. Indeed, the north London GP we spoke to, working in one of the most linguistically diverse areas on earth, felt that her training in communication with patients had entirely missed the point:

> *We had stuff about listening, communication, being open, being patient-centred, but how can you do that when it's a non-English speaker? There was no training on language, no training on how to use the English language in different ways.*

In many areas linguistic diversity appears to be dealt with strictly at a surface level, often by provision of commercial interpreting services, and in particular Language Line, which is accessed by phone, and can provide remote or face-to-face interpreting. This is seen as a vital lifeline, of course – 'the Language Line service has become as much part of our toolkit as a pen' commented the police officer referred to earlier – but guidance on how to use the service, assuming it exists at all, is decontextualized from any wider issues of language, culture and communication and the practice therefore carries its own problems. Our GP reported that she had had no training in how to use Language Line's remote interpreting service, even though she used it sometimes a dozen or more times a day, and in any case had had no training in sociocultural issues, so that even when she was able to communicate with a patient in this way she was often unsure what sort of questions it would be acceptable to ask. She continued:

> *You're talking to a telephone, you lose all of that non-verbal communication, you're talking to an interpreter, who's a phone. Those vital cues that are going on, you're missing them, what you've learned as a doctor you can't use; it's very frustrating. Language is a major frustration.*

A face-to-face interpreter present at the scene is naturally preferable to a disembodied voice, but again, where there has been no training in how to manage this kind of communication, there are obvious problems. The police officer told us:

> *A situation I see often when younger officers are interviewing a person with an interpreter present is that they are drawn toward the interpreter and begin to direct their questions at them rather than the interviewee. This undermines the officer and looks poor.*

Then there is the question of conflicting interpretations of dialectal usage:

> *I once interviewed a suspect who didn't speak English. I arranged for an interpreter to be present during the interview and the suspect had also elected to have a solicitor present. As it happened the solicitor also spoke the same language as the suspect and was able to understand his answers without translation. A situation arose where the solicitor disputed the translation that was provided by the interpreter. It was (apparently) an issue of dialect rather than the basic language and of course I was none the wiser either way.*

These are, of course, anecdotal reports: one doctor and one policeman do not constitute a representative sample of informants. However, some of these very concerns have been considered in research by, for instance, Kredens and Morris (2010) whose discussion raises concern over the great variability of interpreters and interpreting services. Their comments on the kind of telephone interpreting referred to above confirm the experiences of our two informants:

> Telephone-based remote interpreting, while a most welcome development, is not without its problems, most of which have to do with the absence of

> the non-verbal cues that normally facilitate turn-taking and also enable the interpreter to make decisions about pragmatic aspects of the message. (2010: 456)

They go on to point out that the interpreter may find herself having to take on a counselling role or one of managing the situation:

> Additionally, it often happens that individuals requiring police assistance are emotionally distressed. In such cases, the interpreter may actually have to intervene by taking over, whether explicitly or implicitly, the task of assuaging the caller's agitation in order to be able to obtain relevant information. (2010: 456)

They also discuss the sometimes damaging consequences that can result from poor interpreting and poor understanding of the role of the interpreter by the interpreter herself. Concern about what was actually being discussed between the interpreter and the patient was also expressed by our GP. In response to our question about her confidence in the interpreting service she replied:

> *Not confident because you have no idea – I mean you might ask 'yes' or 'no' to make it simple and then you'll hear a good 40 or 50 seconds going on between the patient and the interpreter and it's like – how can that be? I just wanted to know 'yes' or 'no' and then they'll come back with something that you didn't really ask about.*

The problem of interpreter's interpretation is something that I (Fiona) have also come across in my own work as an expert witness whereby faulty translation and the practice of paraphrasing have caused serious problems in the collection of witness evidence. Examples include 14.2 below in which neither the police nor the detainee were aware of the misrepresentation of what the police officer actually asked, and hence the inaccurate response (*I don't know*) given by the detainee.

Example 14.2

> The police officer asks in English: '*He didn't take the knife off you?*'
>
> The detainee asks the interpreter in Turkish: '*What is he saying?*'
>
> The interpreter then summarizes, in Turkish, what he himself has decided to be the gist of the line of questioning rather than the question itself. '*If he didn't have knife on him would it be possible if you stabbed yourself?*'
>
> To which the detainee answers in English: '*I don't know.*'

Or look at how a poor translation can entirely change the meaning of what is actually said, in the next example from the same interview.

Example 14.3

> The detainee says, in Turkish: '*When I was running away he came by me and grabbed me. At the time, I pulled my knife out. I felt something entering me. I felt something painful.*'
>
> This is then interpreted for the police officers as follows:
>
> *'When I was running away they caught up and I pulled a knife. At the point that I pulled a knife I felt something enter me.'*

In this case, the consequences of the interpreter's mistakes both misled the police in their understanding of the events that took place and greatly disadvantaged the detainee, whose actual account, rather than the interpreted one, might have given the police a very different impression. The phrase *he came by me and grabbed me,* for instance, offers a very different account than the interpreter's version, *they caught up.* Meanwhile *Pulling a knife out* has a very different connotation to *pulling a knife.* You only have to ask yourself which action would worry you most: if someone *pulled a knife out* or if they *pulled a knife.*

For those who are interested in following these themes up, Gunnarsson (2013) includes a huge bibliography of work done on multilingual workplaces worldwide, often with a focus on power relations and related sociological issues. Our intention here is not to add to this literature, but to point to the way in which an absence of linguistically informed language awareness training, whether received at school or as part of normal professional development, meant that these professionals were always struggling to contextualize the language issues they came up against, or even to identify them as language problems per se. Two final examples will perhaps illustrate this. The GP, reflecting on the number of isolated, housebound, older Turkish women who presented at her Tottenham practice with depression, commented that she would have liked to prescribe them English language classes. This is an insight which recognizes that the clinical problem is in large part a language problem, and the language problem is embedded in cultural practice; but such things were never mentioned in her training (which she completed in 2000), and she was left to struggle towards it alone. The police officer, meanwhile, mentioned that he would welcome some training in how to deal with deaf people, as he was unsure of the 'protocol or etiquette involved', as he put it. He had had some training in how to deal with the disabled, as one might expect: but the concept of sign language users being first and foremost a *language* community was quite new to him, and might have shed an entirely new light on things.[5]

As we have already remarked, a training in communication skills for professionals is no bad thing. However, it is no substitute for a properly constituted base of knowledge about language; indeed, such a base is an indispensable precondition for it, if it is to be truly effective. The study of language, as we have argued throughout the third part of this book, gives one the terms and concepts with which to be able to analyse and talk about language with confidence. This is not to say, of course, that no one can understand anything language related without a specific course of study. As we noted above, most people know when to use terms like 'mate' or 'love'; equally, most people will instinctively understand the police officer's final comment:

> *I find those we come into contact with who have a selective approach to how much English they understand ever more trying. Tell someone they are under arrest and they can't speak English. Tell the same person they are no longer under arrest and they will probably understand and respond in English.*

However, as the work with non-native speakers in detention, or Blommaert's (e.g. 2005) work on the interactions between immigration officials and migrants both demonstrate, such 'common-sense' assumptions can sometimes blind us to other ways of understanding a situation.

14.5 Conclusion

This chapter has used examples of workplace environments where the issue of language is very much foregrounded in the work activity. However, as we have shown, even in such contexts, where language plays a crucial role in achieving successful outcomes, very little attention is paid to it either in initial or ongoing professional training. Of course, issues of language and communication are fundamental to all workplaces, from the linguistic and cultural diversity of the urban construction site, most clearly characterized by the London 2012 Olympics building project, through the day-to-day service encounters in shops and call centres, to global business interactions, as discussed in, for example, Gimenez (2002), and the non-verbal communicative interactions in the operating theatre (Bezemer et al. 2014) or the literacy practices at university (e.g. Lillis 2001; Turner 2010); in fact anywhere people get together to work.

A superficial, common-sense view of language which lacks, for instance, the kinds of understanding that sociolinguistics can provide or the insights that a social semiotic approach to discourse analysis can bring, or simply the terms of reference made available by language description, can result in misunderstandings and miscommunications which affect workplace relationships and, in turn, can have both small and large impacts on workplace effectiveness, as Clyne (1994) concluded in his detailed study of intercultural discourse in the workplace.

Of course people in the workplace cannot be expected to undertake the kind of study that we have discussed in our examples, nor should they be expected to be linguists in their own right. However, with a more finely-tuned understanding of what lies beneath the language issues they encounter and a better understanding of the kinds of things that can lead to problems, they might be able to better handle these kinds of situation. What our examples have shown is how the work of the linguist can illuminate problematic workplace situations which involve communicative interaction. We suggest that if professional training programmes, both initial and in-service, drew on this kind of work, people like our GP and police officer would be better equipped to understand and respond to the problems they experience.

In the next, concluding, chapter we draw together the strands of this book in our final push in making the case for linguistics.

Suggested reading

Coulthard, M. and Johnson, A. (2007), *An Introduction to Forensic Linguistics.* Abingdon: Routledge.

As we have discussed this aspect of linguistics in the workplace in some detail, we think that this excellent introduction to forensic linguistics may be of interest to readers. It is not only a good example of the value of linguistics in legal settings and beyond but a fascinating read in its own right.

Forey, G. and Lockwood, J. (eds) (2012), *Globalization, Communication and the Workplace: Talking Across the World.* London: Bloomsbury.

This edited collection considers the importance of language and language awareness in the global workplace. Although it focuses particularly on call centre interactions, it also considers other work settings where communication across cultures is a fundamental aspect of working practices.

15

So why do linguistics?

15.1 Introduction

This book has been about noticing. It has sought to draw attention to the kind of texts that surround us, the language practices that we engage in and the language issues and questions that confront us wherever we may live and whatever language(s) we speak. It has shown how a linguistics lens can be used to bring into focus phenomena that otherwise might pass unnoticed or be taken for granted, and in so doing has highlighted the value of the study of language in its own right.

15.2 Why this book and why now?

Over the last couple of decades we have had the good fortune to live in a highly diverse city, and to work with colleagues and students from all over the world, at a time of enormous demographic and social change. Change of this kind has been apparent throughout Europe and far beyond during these years, bringing with it, as is natural and inevitable, changes in patterns of language and communication. It is unsurprising, then, that we should have observed changes in language. But more than this, we have noticed a great many different voices addressing the subject of language itself, often in the form of mutually antagonistic discourses. Substantial inward migration to Europe, along with recent economic instability and occasional eruptions of social unrest (such as outbreaks of rioting in France, Sweden and England) have tended to create anxiety among many: this much is natural. What has struck us more and more forcibly, though, is how often anxiety about rapid social change has been expressed through anxiety about language, standards of literacy and related issues. Language seems to assume the role of social lightning rod at periodic intervals, and this has been the case throughout history. Deep-rooted concern about social order might manifest itself as concern about linguistic order, for example in the form of grammar (Cameron 1995). Certainly, few generations have ever thought that language standards have risen during their own lifetime, a point made forcefully by the American, Thomas R. Lounsbury, in his *The Standard of Usage in English* as long ago as 1908 – and he had very many predecessors. In a similar vein, of course, complaints might be made about, say, dress codes (skirts are too short or codpieces too protuberant) or the perceived lack of public politeness (youths spit in the street, smartphone users don't look where they're going). But over the last few years we seem particularly to have been on a language binge.

This renewed focus on language has taken many shapes. In Britain there have been media reports about primary schools where there were no native English speakers; government declarations that literacy levels were declining in comparison to, say, South Korea or Finland; complaints that text messaging and other forms of digital communication were harming pupils' ability to write properly; the banning by schools, hospitals and town councils of certain words and phrases from their premises; claims that Poles and other new migrants spoke better English than native speakers and were therefore winning out in the jobs market; worries about the marked decline in foreign language teaching in schools and universities; and widespread bafflement that white, suburban youths were beginning to sound like their black, inner-city counterparts.

We, too, worry about language, but our concern takes a different form. While we are delighted that language is being talked about in the public sphere, we are dismayed that the insights provided by linguistics are often either absent from these discussions or simply ignored, despite the best efforts of professional linguists. Because the study of language is rarely foregrounded, we think it necessary to spell out what makes it such a rich resource for exploring and explaining. In this chapter, then, we take a final opportunity to show why knowing about language is so important and we make a number of claims about why we think it is worth doing linguistics.

15.3 First claim: Linguistics opens up different ways of thinking

Linguistics is 'the study of the links between sound and meaning' (Harris 1993: 5), an intentionally tiny definition which encompasses a vast range of human experience. The science of linguistics (if indeed it is a science, or if some or all of it is) has often been considered one of the central intellectual developments of recent centuries, a tool for understanding that which makes humans truly unique. From fundamental building blocks such as the identification of meaningful contrast (to recognize *shoe* /ʃu:/ we must know it is not the same as *Sue* /su:/) and the notion of the arbitrariness of the linguistic sign (there is nothing inherently cat-like in the word *cat* – we have to agree on what it signifies by convention), linguistics has expanded in influence, reach and explanatory power to an extraordinary degree. Linguistics certainly offers systems for categorizing and labelling (creating language typologies, for example, as we saw in Chapter 5, or classifying phonemes as in Chapter 6), but it can do much more than this.

To adopt a linguistics lens is to look again, and think again not just about why people say what they say, but how they say it; how they learned to say it in the first place; how people understand it, or fail to understand it; how other people might say it; how it might have been said in other languages and at other times; with what other genres or modes it might be expressed; what social norms and constraints underlie the speaker's communicative choices; and so on, practically ad infinitum. The analytical frameworks that linguistics provides offer an approach to language and communication that promotes inquiry, reflection and the kind of critical, creative thinking that is fundamental to dealing with the complexities of social interaction in the world today.

15.4 Second claim: Linguistics is (or should be) general knowledge

We can identify at least two levels at which linguistic knowledge must be considered basic knowledge about the world. One is the level of knowledge about language itself. This means not just the rules of the grammar and orthography of the language that one happens to speak, or even its various styles and conventions. This much tends to be taught at school, wherever in the world it may be (though perhaps not if you are a speaker of a minority language). Rather, we mean the essential information that linguistics offers us about language per se: what a phoneme is, for example; how speech sounds are made; how words and sentences are formed; how we manage to extract meaning from sounds; how spoken syntax differs from written syntax.

Second, we refer to what might loosely be called sociolinguistic information: at the micro level, how language varies according to such features as gender, age, social status, group identification and so on; at the macro level, the basics of how many languages are spoken in the world and by whom, the distinction between languages and dialects, the notion of standard language (rather than 'correct' language). Add to this some of the principles of child language acquisition (most people will bring up children at some point in their lives – a little understanding would save a lot of worry and confusion), and perhaps second language learning (most people will speak another language) and you have a kind of toolkit, a body of essential linguistic knowledge. By essential, we mean analogous to what most people tend to know, even if not in great detail or with great precision, about how the human body works, for instance, the chronology of historical periods or how the oceans and continents are distributed across the globe. We would further argue, as we did in Chapter 13, that the most appropriate place for this knowledge to be imparted is the school – and it can be started early. Why should it be that we are taught so little about what defines us as human beings, indexes and shapes our individual identity, and provides the principal means by which we understand and interact with the world?

15.5 Third claim: Linguistics empowers

A defining characteristic of modern linguistics is its insistence on the primacy of description (how things are said) over prescription (how things should be said). In equipping us with the tools to be able to talk about language in an informed way, it offers a possibility of seizing back power from self-appointed experts, amateur language police and other prescriptivists, and challenging them on what they imagine to be their own territory. This applies just as much to a nurse who might wish, quite appropriately, to call someone 'love' (Chapters 10 and 14) as it does to those school children in Middlesborough (Chapter 12) who naturally use their own distinctive dialect, or to minority language campaigners who insist on the right to have their children educated in their mother tongue in the face of the hostility and condescension of speakers of the dominant language (Chapter 4). I (Tim) as a schoolboy was told repeatedly and aggressively by one of my teachers that my West Yorkshire speech was ugly, sloppy and lazy. Knowing then that this was somehow not right, but being quite unable to explain why, I wish now that I had had the insights of linguistics at my disposal. What a knowledge of linguistics would have told me is that the teacher's prejudice was based on misguided notions of correctness and appropriacy. Correct spoken English is not synonymous with written English, as we discussed in Chapter 8, and speaking in a non-standard way does not mean speaking in a sub-standard way. What is more, there is nothing inherently proper or aesthetically pleasing about Received Pronunciation. It is just another accent, albeit one which has succeeded in acquiring social prestige.

15.6 Linguistics is fun

We hope that it has become evident that doing linguistics is not a dry-as-dust pursuit but instead an activity that is as varied in its objectives as it is in the types and sources of its material. We go further, though, and suggest that doing linguistics is fun because it adds a new dimension to our everyday interactions and experiences. Linguistics, by making us more aware of the communicative world, makes us notice what we might otherwise take for granted.

Blommaert and Jie (2010: 58) have joked that linguistic ethnographers 'are notorious for collecting rubbish', and we would agree with this, though what counts as 'rubbish' is, of course, in the eye of the beholder. We cause great amusement, not to say bemusement, to those who happen to be with us when we stop in our tracks to take a photograph of a flyer stuck to a lamp post; when we are as delighted with the newspaper used to wrap a souvenir presented to us by an overseas student as we are with the gift itself; or when we suddenly go 'shush' to a companion so that we can jot down a fragment of overheard conversation. But for the linguist, these seemingly insignificant things can provide insight into the communicative practices that they exemplify. *This* is what it means to be an active noticer of language. An old sheet of newspaper might be written in an unfamiliar script, or a combination of different scripts and/or languages. This might point to the linguistic make-up of a community or tell us something about how multilingual societies work. A conversation overheard while queuing at the post office, in which the speakers mix two or three different languages in a seamless flow, might raise questions about language choice or behaviour. Are they conscious that they are doing it? Are they native speakers of one, all or none? Equally, a happened-upon flyer advertising a warehouse party might provide an example of a newly coined word or transgressive spelling indicative of current youth usage. Once you get your eye in (or your ear) then there's no stopping. Doing linguistics can become a lifelong addiction. Beware!

15.7 Doing linguistics

To finish off with we invite you to do a bit of linguistics yourself. It is a photograph (Figure 15.1) that one of us took while out shopping one day and is an example of textual interaction in the public domain. We want to leave it with you to analyse using the approaches that we have introduced in the book. What kind of communication is it? Who produced it and why? What does it do? What does it tell you? Why is it interesting? We are sure you will generate further questions of your own as you go along.

FIGURE 15.1 *Public domain text for analysis.*

15.8 Final remarks

There are three points that we feel it worth making before we finish. The first concerns the sources of our data, the second relates to the debates we have engaged in and the third concerns the kind of linguistics that we have presented.

It is in the nature of linguistic ethnography to use observed phenomena, things that one has personally encountered; as we have just noted, this is what it means to be an active observer of language. Hence our examples have been collected from the situations that we have found ourselves in: our university classrooms, the different places that we have visited, the people that we have met and, perhaps most prominently, the city in which we live and work, London. We make no apology for this. London is arguably the most linguistically diverse city in the world, at least at the moment, and we would be foolish not to take advantage of such an intensely rich environment. The opportunities it provides for observing language in society have allowed us to consider what it means to live in a global community. This is not to say that 'doing linguistics' can only take place in the context of an ethnically diverse city; linguistic observation can happen in any situation anywhere in the world, from the intimacy of the family circle to the noisy chatter of a school playground, from the interactions in a fast-food restaurant to the negotiations at a global economic summit.

We have also concentrated much of our discussion on British language issues. To some, this may seem to lend a rather UK-centric orientation to the book. However, we are confident that readers will be able to locate the debates within their own specific contexts and see the similarities as much as the differences. The point is that the linguistic phenomena and the debates that they generate can be found, in one form or another, everywhere in the world. Our aim has been to draw attention to them and suggest ways of usefully engaging with them.

We should also reiterate one last time that there are other ways of approaching linguistics which differ to a greater or lesser extent from our own. In writing this book we had to make choices about what to include and what to leave out. We could not include everything, nor could we say everything there is to say about the things we did include. Nevertheless, we hope that what we have presented here gives some insight into what linguistics can do in terms of understanding the world around us.

15.9 Conclusion

With this book we have extended an invitation to all those with an interest in language to engage with the discipline of linguistics, perhaps even go on to study it, and add their voices to discussions about language from a properly informed position. In essence, we believe that to know something about language helps to explain the world in which we find ourselves. This is nothing new, but with increasing globalization, movement of populations and instant global communications, such knowledge is ever more necessary. After all, in understanding others, your main resource is language.

We said right from the outset that the aim of this book was not to teach you linguistics but rather to show what you can do with it. We have tried to make the case for linguistics by showing its potential in describing, analysing and explaining social phenomena and by sharing the enjoyment that is to be derived from observing the world through a linguistics lens. Now you have reached the end of the book, we hope that you can see why we think it is so important and we hope that you will now feel inspired and equipped to go out and do some linguistics of your own. Have fun!

Notes

Chapter 1

1 Keynote address at the Interdiciplinary Linguistics Conference, Queen's University, Belfast, October 2011.

2 The programme follows first response members of the emergency services (police, ambulance and fire) on urgent call-outs. See: http://www.channel5.com/shows/emergency-bikers

3 Though some highly inflectional languages (e.g. Spanish) also use a similar form, as in *voy a cantar*. (I'm going to sing).

4 As we go to press, some six months later, we notice that Russell Square has now replaced 'shall' with 'will'. Somebody has obviously had a word.

5 This use of the term originates in the fields of linguistics, semiotics and social semiotics (Halliday 1978; Hodge and Kress 1988; Kress 2010). See P. Cobley (ed.) (2010), *The Routledge Companion to Semiotics*. London: Routledge, for an excellent overview of this complex and broad field.

6 An identification sign to mark out territory or ownership, sometimes used to indicate incursion into a rival's patch.

7 At the time of writing, the graffiti 'Slave Labour', painted on a wall in the London Borough of Haringey by the anonymous artist Banksy, was removed, section of concrete wall and all, and originally put up for auction by a Miami art dealer. The outcry, both local and across the sea, was substantial, leading to a police investigation and its eventual removal from sale. However, it appeared that no crime had been committed as it was the owners of the building on which the graffiti had been painted who removed it. It went back on sale, this time in a London auction house, with the bidding reported to start at £900,000 despite the fact that Banksy him/herself never admits attribution. As a work in someone's house it has lost both its co-text (the wall of a 'pound' shop) and its context (pre-Olympics, poor borough, etc.). Is it then the same work?

8 P. Hennessey (2009), *The Junior Officers' Reading Club*. London: Penguin, p. 282.

Chapter 2

1 M. G. Santos (2006), *Inside: Life Behind Bars in America*. New York: St Martin's Press, p. 143.

2 D. Cordingly (2007), *Cochrane the Dauntless*. London: Bloomsbury, p. 67.

3 Not shown here for reasons of anonymity.

4 And this was very late on, when the long process of vernacularization was already at an end. Indeed, the connection between standardized language and state power is inescapably suggested by the date of Nebrija's work: he presented his grammar to Queen Isabella in 1492, by some distance the most momentous year in Spanish history.

Chapter 3

1 Malinowsky (1923), 'The Problem of Meaning in Primitive Languages', in Charles K. Ogden and Ian A. Richards (eds), *The Meaning of Meaning.* London: Routledge, pp. 146–52.

2 Though it is also important to point out that how you say 'please' matters too. A flat or down-tone 'please' can denote irritation or reluctance to be polite.

3 Face is a concept that is used in politeness theory (e.g. Brown and Levinson 1987) in analysing how politeness works within a culture or between different communities.

Chapter 4

1 http://www.ndtv.com/video/player/the-big-fight/the-language-debate/113596 [accessed 5 April 2013].

Chapter 5

1 Which qualities do not, then, translate easily or elegantly into languages of other types. The British *Economist* reported on 16 November 2013 that the third plenum of the Chinese Communist Party's 18th Central Committee had announced, among other policy planks, 'the three represents' and 'the six tightly revolve-arounds'.

Chapter 6

1 Oxford World Classics edition, 1998, p. 203. This kind of usage crops up repeatedly, too, among the lower social classes (especially servants) in Fielding's *Tom Jones* (1749).

2 A more recent example of a shibboleth has given its name to the 'Parsley Massacre' of 1937, in which thousands of Haitian immigrants to the neighbouring Dominican Republic were slaughtered. It was said – it might be an apocryphal story – that in order to distinguish the Haitians from indigenous black Dominicans, the soldiers of the Dominican dictator Trujillo held up a sprig of parsley, in Spanish *perejil*. If the French patois-speaking Haitians were unable to pronounce the *r* sound in the Spanish manner, producing instead the characteristic French uvular trill, they were killed.

3 Lynn Visson, *London Review of Books*, 7 November 2013.

Chapter 7

1 Of course this version of what has traditionally been 'The Irish Joke' in a British context, in which the Irish come out badly, is here told from an Irish perspective and has been inverted in gentle revenge.

Chapter 8

1 In case readers don't recognize these names, David Beckham is a world famous football player (now retired) celebrated not only for his skill on the field (he played for clubs such as Manchester United and Real Madrid) but also for his celebrity life. His wife, Victoria, is famous in her own right for having been a member of the late 1990s pop group, The Spice Girls, and more recently as a successful fashion designer.

2 http://www.bbc.co.uk/news/uk-22183566 (accessed 01 April 2013).

3 Grouting is what you do when you fill in the gaps between ceramic or terracotta tiles that have already been stuck to the wall or floor with a kind of paste known as grout.

4 It is also worth pointing out the use of phonological variants (e.g. *da* plan for *the* plan) of the kind we discussed in Chapter 1.

Chapter 9

1 He has given us permission to use both examples, of course.

2 Colour versions of all examples can be seen on the accompanying website.

3 See accompanying website.

4 We have blanked out the full names for reasons of anonymity.

5 Fowler, G. A. (2012), _Facebook: one billion and counting', Washington Post, 04 October 2012. http://online.wsj.com/news/articles/SB10000872396390443635404578036164027386112 [accessed 14 January 2014].

6 Iftikhar A. Khan (2013), 'Sun and Crescent Most Sought-After Election Symbols', *Dawn,* http://dawn.com/news/795743/sun-and-crescent-mot-sought-after-election-symbols [visited 19 November 2013].

Chapter 10

1 As with all our images, colour versions can be found on the accompanying website.

2 Written by Damon Rose, former editor of the BBC website for disability, Ouch!, 2004. http://news.bbc.co.uk/1/hi/magazine/3708576.stm

3 Real names have been changed to ensure anonymity.

4 In some societies (e.g. South Korea) first-name use is retained for family and intimate friends and its misuse can have a similar effect to choosing the wrong referential pronoun (*tu* or *vous*) in French as we discussed in Chapter 5.

5 See Wigglesworth and Yates (2007), 'Mitigating Difficult Requests in the Workplace: What Learners and Teachers Need to Know'. *TESOL Quarterly* 41 (4): 791–803 for discussion of how such resources are used by native speakers compared with non-native speakers.

Chapter 11

1 As with 'translanguaging', Edwards is less than impressed with the notion of 'super-diversity'. '[A]n obviously unnecessary term, coined to suggest a non-existent development' (Edwards 2012: 42–3). We do, though, feel that it helps capture something that has changed demographically and culturally in the last decade or so, and particularly in London.

2 As Wang et al. (2014) note, in discussions of globalization, linguistic diversity and sociolinguistic complexity there has often been a bias towards the urban context, even though the 'margins', to use their word, can provide equally rich pickings.

3 How, indeed, can we tell the difference? Gardner-Chloros (1995: 73–4) suggests three tests that you might think would be helpful: integration (in terms of pronunciation or word structure) with the surrounding language; the displacement of an already-existing synonym in the surrounding language; and grammatical category. But, as she notes, actually these tests are *not* reliable: in the real world of messy language use, sometimes you just can't be sure.

4 In linguistics, *calque* is the term for a loan translation, that is to say a word or concept borrowed from another language, but then translated into the borrowing language, as in the Spanish *ratón* (mouse), used in Spanish for a computer mouse.

5 For a more general discussion of the whole, complex relationship between language, religion and identity, see Edwards (2009: 99–125).

6 What to make of the T-shirt slogan celebrating the Montreal Canadiens ice hockey team (seen in France), *Vite sur tes patins – Skate with les Canadiens*? Perhaps it indexes bilingual Canadian identity; perhaps it attempts to call such a thing into being.

Chapter 12

1. http://www.dailymail.co.uk/news/article-2388615/Are-pulling-leg-The-surprisingly-sinister-origins-commonly-used-phrases.html [accessed 11 August 2013].
2. http://news.bbc.co.uk/1/hi/uk/1988776.stm [accessed 26 April 2014].
3. http://www.dailymail.co.uk/news/article-2459502/Harris-Academy-London-bans-slang.html [accessed 15 November 2013].
4. http://www.education.gov.uk/schools/teachingandlearning/curriculum/secondary/b00199616/mfl/languages [accessed 16 November 2013].
5. CILT (National Centre for Languages) (2013), http://www.cilt.org.uk/ [accessed 9 August 2013].
6. According to estimates made by the French Consulate in London. http://www.bbc.co.uk/news/magazine-18234930 [accessed 26 April 2014].
7. A TV ad for a language school in Peru in 2014 showed a montage of bilingual signs from around the world (Arabic/English, Chinese/English, Russian/English etc.) and ended with the slogan: 'Sabes inglés, sabes todos los idiomas' – if you can speak English, you can speak all languages. No other language has this kind of *passe-partout* quality, and that is primarily why speakers of other languages are enthusiastic about learning it. It is misleading and rather unfair to demand that English speakers demonstrate the same level of enthusiasm for learning French, say, or German – never mind Norwegian or Finnish.
8. He also notes laconically that 'it has always been difficult to sell languages in Kansas: wherever you go, for many hundreds of miles, English will take you to McDonalds, get you a burger, and bring you safely home again' (Edwards 2012: 196).
9. http://www.stjohns.edu/academics/graduate/liberalarts/departments/languages/why.stj [accessed 16 April 2013].
10. http://www.languagestars.com/program-overview/programs/parents-and-tots/14-programs/curriculum/66-the-benefits-of-learning-language-young.html [accessed 12 August 2013].
11. http://www.tomcoyner.com/a_snip_of_the_tongue_and_english.htm [accessed 16 August 2013].

Chapter 13

1. For MFLs, for example, the DfE website has the following 'Key Concepts': 'Knowledge about language: (a) Understanding how a language works and how to manipulate it. (b). Recognising that languages differ but may share common grammatical, syntactical or lexical features'. A later explanatory note also offers: 'Knowledge about language: Pupils should explore and learn about standard structures and patterns'. Later still, there is a very brief

mention of intercultural understanding and of diversity – by which seems to be meant the varieties of a language used in different countries, though 'cultural differences' in language is the rather ambiguous phrase used. http://www.education.gov.uk/schools/teachingandlearning/curriculum/secondary/b00199616/mfl/programme/concepts [accessed 10 November 2013].

2 http://www.phon.ucl.ac.uk/home/dick/ec/clietop.htm [accessed 20 November 2013].

3 See Andrews (2006) for one example of how an integrated, LA-informed approach can be used to produce stimulating learning and teaching materials.

4 Keynote address at the Interdiciplinary Linguistics Conference, Queen's University, Belfast, October 2011.

Chapter 14

1 It has been noted in some detail that the way call centres work tends towards the use of prepared scripts, a manufactured persona and the 'commodification of language' (Cameron 2000). Unsurprisingly, the intriguing phenomenon of the offshore call centre has attracted close attention from academics and commentators interested in questions of language, culture and identity (see e.g. Forey and Lockwood 2012; Hamp-Lyons and Lockwood 2009; Friginal 2007 for the Philippines; Rahman 2009 for Pakistan).

2 Received Pronunciation is often referred to in Britain as a 'neutral' accent. This may be true in terms of geography – while many RP-speakers are from the south-east of England, not all are – but in other ways it is as loaded with markers as any other accent in the United Kingdom.

3 http://news.bbc.co.uk/2/hi/uk_news/england/bristol/somerset/3151033.stm [accessed 1 January 2014].

4 http://www.northernstar.com.au/news/mate-and-love-banned-from-hospital-corridors/1655503/ [accessed 01 January 2014].

5 Sign languages are of course fully-formed, natural languages, with all the abstraction and cultural complexity that that entails, not systems of imitating things through the use of your hands. Users of sign languages are therefore part of a particular language community, just like speakers of German or Arabic. Failure to understand this no doubt explains the widespread bafflement among hearing people when media reports appear of deaf people who are reluctant to have their children undergo operations which will allow them to hear (and thereby join a different language community). Such basic linguistic knowledge, as we argued in Chapter 13, really should be part of everyone's general education.

References

Ackroyd, P. (2011), *The History of England. Volume One: Foundation.* London: Macmillan.

Adams, J. N. (2003), *Bilingualism and the Latin Language.* Cambridge: Cambridge University Press.

Agha, A. (2007), *Language and Social Relations.* Cambridge: Cambridge University Press.

Andrews, L. (2006), *Language Exploration and Awareness: A Resource Book for Teachers.* London and New York: Routledge.

Archibald, E. (2010), 'Macaronic poetry', in Saunders, C. (ed.), *A Companion to Medieval Poetry.* Chichester: Wiley-Blackwell, pp. 277–88.

Atkinson, M., Kilby, D. and Roca, I. (1982), *Foundations of General Linguistics.* London: Unwin Hyman.

Austin, J. L. (1962), *How to Do Things With Words.* Oxford: Oxford University Press.

Backhaus, P. (ed.) (2013), *Communication in Elderly Care: Cross-Cultural Perspectives.* London: Bloomsbury.

Bailey, R. (2006), 'English among the languages', in Mugglestone, L. (ed.), *The Oxford History of English.* Oxford: Oxford University Press, pp. 334–59.

Bakhtin, M. (1986), *Speech Genres and other Late Essays.* Austin: University of Texas Press.

Barthes, R. (1977), *Image, Music, Text.* London: Fontana.

Barton, D. (2000), 'Moral panics about literacy'. University of Lancaster, Centre for Language in Social Life, Working Paper No. 116.

—(2007), *Literacy: an introduction to the ecology of written language*, 2nd edn. Oxford: Blackwell.

Barton, D. and Papen, U. (2010), *The Anthropology of Writing.* London: Continuum.

Barton, D., Hamilton, M. and Ivanic, R. (2000), *Situated Literacies.* London: Routledge.

Bauer, L. and Trudgill, P. (eds) (1998), *Language Myths.* Harmondsworth: Penguin.

Baxter, J. (2002), 'Jokers in the pack: why boys are more adept than girls at speaking in public settings'. *Language and Education* 16(2): 81–96.

Bazerman, C. (1988), *Shaping Written Knowledge.* Madison: University of Wisconsin Press.

Berger, J. (1972/2008), *Ways of Seeing.* London: Penguin Classics.

Bernstein, B. (1971), *Class, Code and Control: Volume 1 – Theoretical Studies towards a Sociology of Language.* London: Routledge & Kegan Paul.

Bex, T. and Watts, R. (eds) (1999), *Standard English: The Widening Debate.* London: Routledge.

Bezemer, J., Cope, A., Kress, G. and Kneebone, R. (2014), 'Holding the scalpel: achieving surgical care in a learning environment'. *Journal of Contemporary Ethnography* 43: 38–63.

Biber, D. (1988), *Variation Across Speech and Writing.* Cambridge: Cambridge University Press.

Bizzel, P. and Herzberg, B. (eds) (1990), *The Rhetorical Tradition.* Boston: Bedford.

Blackledge, A. and Creese, A. (2008), 'Contesting "language" as "heritage": negotiation of identities in late modernity'. *Applied Linguistics* 29(4): 533–54.

Block, D. (2006), *Multilingual Identities in a Global City: London Stories.* Basingstoke and New York: Palgrave Macmillan.

Blommaert, J. (2005), *Discourse.* Cambridge: Cambridge University Press.

—(2008), 'Multi-Everything London'. *Journal of Language, Identity and Education* 7: 81–9.

—(2010), *The Sociolinguistics of Globalisation.* Cambridge: Cambridge University Press.

—(2013), *From Fieldnotes to Grammar: Artefactual Ideologies of Language and the Micro-methodology of Linguistics.* Tilburg Papers in Culture Studies No. 84.

Blommaert, J. and Jie, D. (2010), *Ethnographic Fieldwork: A Beginner's Guide.* Bristol: Multilingual Matters.

Bolinger, D. (1980), *Language the Loaded Weapon: The Use and Abuse of Language Today.* Harlow: Longman.

Bond, M. (1999), *Paddington Treasury.* London: Harper Collins.

Boorman, C., Pickett, J., Proszynska, N. and Roberts, A. (2013), Unpublished student project University of Manchester. http://www.manchester.ac.uk/discover/news/article/?id=9856 [accessed 15 January 2014].

Bourdieu, P. (1991), *Language and Symbolic Power.* Cambridge: Polity Press.

British National Corpus, version 3 (BNC XML Edition) (2007), Distributed by Oxford University Computing Services on behalf of the *BNC Consortium.* URL: http://www.natcorp.ox.ac.uk/.

Brown, P. and Levinson, S. (1987), *Politeness: Some Universals in Language Usage.* Cambridge: Cambridge University Press.

Brown, K. and Ogilvie, S. (2009), *Concise Encyclopedia of Languages of the World.* Oxford: Elsevier.

Brown, G. and Yule, G. (1983), *Discourse Analysis.* Cambridge: Cambridge University Press.

Burgess, A. (1992), *A Mouthful of Air. Language and Languages, Especially English.* London: Vintage.

Cameron, D. (1995), *Verbal Hygiene.* London and New York: Routledge.

—(2000), 'Styling the worker: gender and the commodification of language in the globalized service economy'. *Journal of Sociolinguistics* 4(3): 323–47.

—(2012a), *The Myth of Mars and Venus: Do Men and Women Really Speak Different Languages?* Oxford: Oxford University Press.

—(2012b), *Verbal Hygiene,* 2nd edn. Abingdon: Routledge.

Canagarajah, S. (2009), 'The plurilingual tradition and the English language in South Asia', in Lim, L. and E. Low (eds), *Multilingual, Globalizing Asia. Implications for Policy and Education* (AILA Review Vol. 22). Amsterdam and Philadelphia: John Benjamins, pp. 5–22.

—(2013a), *Translingual Practice. Global Englishes and Cosmopolitan Relations.* London and New York: Routledge.

—(2013b), 'Agency and power in intercultural communication: negotiating English in translocal spaces'. *Language and Intercultural Communication* 13(2): 202–24.

Carter, R. (ed.) (1990), *Knowledge about Language and the Curriculum*. London: Hodder & Stoughton.

—(1999), 'Standard grammars, spoken grammars: some educational implications', in Bex, T. and R. Watts (eds), *Standard English: The Widening Debate*. London and New York: Routledge, pp. 149–66.

—(2012), *Linguistics and the Teacher*. Abingdon: Routledge.

Carter, R. and McCarthy, M. (1997), *Exploring Spoken English*. Cambridge: Cambridge University Press.

Cenoz, J. (2008), 'Achievements and challenges in multilingual education in the Basque Country', in Cenoz, J. and D. Gurter (eds), *Multilingualism and Minority Languages* (AILA Review Vol. 21). Amsterdam and Philadelphia: John Benjamins, pp. 13–30.

Cheshire, J. and Moser, L.-M. (1994), 'English and symbolic meaning: advertisements in the Suisse Romande'. *Journal of Multilingual and Multicultural Development* 17(1): 451–69.

Cheshire, J., Fox, S., Kerswill, P. and Torgersen, E. (2008), 'Ethnicity, friendship network and social practices as the motor of dialect change: linguistic innovation in London'. *Sociolinguistica* 22: 1–23.

Chik, A. (2010), 'Creative multilingualism in Hong Kong popular music'. *World Englishes* 29(4): 508–22.

CILT (2013), http://www.cilt.org.uk/ [accessed 08 August 2013].

Clark, U. (2010), 'Grammar in the curriculum for English: What next?' *Changing English* 17(2): 189–200.

Clyne, M. (1994), *Intercultural Communication at Work: Cultural Values in Discourse*. Cambridge and New York: Cambridge University Press.

Cohen-Tannoudji, C., Diu, B. and Laloë, F. (1977), *Quantum Mechanics*, trans. Susan Reid Hemley, Nicole Ostrowsky and Dan Ostrowsky. Paris: Hermann & New York: Wiley.

Cooper, R. L. (1989), *Language Planning and Social Change*. Cambridge: Cambridge University Press.

Cotterill, J. (2000), 'Reading the rights: a cautionary tale of comprehension and comprehensibility'. *Forensic Linguistics* 7(1): 4–25.

Coulthard, M. (2005), 'The linguist as expert witness'. *Linguistics and the Human Sciences* 1: 39–58.

Coulthard, M. and Johnson, A. (2007), *An Introduction to Forensic Linguistics: Language in Evidence*. London: Routledge.

—(eds) (2010), *The Routledge Handbook of Forensic Linguistics*. Abingdon: Routledge.

Coupland, J. (ed.) (2000), *Small Talk*. Harlow: Longman.

Cowie, C. (2007), 'The accents of outsourcing: the meanings of "neutral" in the Indian call centre industry'. *World Englishes* 26(3): 316–30.

Creese, A. and Blackledge, A. (2010), 'Translanguaging in the bilingual classroom: a pedagogy for learning and teaching?' *The Modern Language Journal* 94(1): 103–15.

Crowley, T. (2003), *Standard English and the Politics of Language*, 2nd edn. Basingstoke: Palgrave Macmillan.

Crystal, D. (1987), *The Cambridge Encyclopedia of Language*. Cambridge: Cambridge University Press.

—(2004), *The Stories of English*. London: Allen Lane.
—(2006), 'English worldwide', in Hogg, R. and D. Denison (eds), *A History of the English Language*. Cambridge: Cambridge University Press, pp. 420–39.
—(2008), *Txtng*. Oxford: Oxford University Press.
Cutting, A. (2011), *Missions for Thoughtful Gamers*. Pittsburgh: ETC Press.
Dalby, A. (1998), *Dictionary of Languages*. London: Bloomsbury.
Davies, N. (2011), *Vanished Kingdoms. The History of Half-forgotten Europe*. London: Allen Lane.
Deutscher, G. (2005), *The Unfolding of Language*. London: William Heinemann.
Deutschmann, M. (2003), *Apologising in British English*. Doctoral Thesis, Umeå: Umeå University.
Dewey, M. (2007), 'English as a lingua franca and globalization: An interconnected perspective'. *International Journal of Applied Linguistics* 17(3): 332–54.
Domingo, M. (2014), 'Transnational language flows in digital platforms: A study of urban youth and their multimodal text making'. *Pedagogies: An International Journal* 9(1): 7–25.
Domingo, M., Jewitt, C. and Kress, G. (2014), 'Multimodal social semiotics: Writing in online contexts', in Pahl, K. and J. Rowsel (eds), *The Routledge Handbook of Contemporary Literary Studies*. London: Routledge.
Donmall-Hicks, B. (1997). 'The history of Language Awareness in the United Kingdom', in van Lier, L. and D. Corson (eds), *The Encyclopedia of Language and Education (Volume 6)*. Dordrecht: Kluwer, pp. 21–30.
Doughty, P., Pearce, J. and Thornton, G. (1971), *Language in Use*. London: Edward Arnold.
Eades, D. (2000), 'I don't think it's an answer to the question: silencing Aboriginal witnesses in court'. *Language in Society* 29: 161–95.
Edwards, J. (2009), *Language and Identity*. Cambridge: Cambridge University Press.
—(2011), *Challenges in the Social Life of Language*. Basingstoke: Palgrave Macmillan.
—(2012), *Multilingualism: Understanding Linguistic Diversity*. London: Bloomsbury.
Enever, J., Moon, J. and Raman, U. (eds) (2009), *Young Learner English Language Policy & Implementation: International Perspectives*. Reading: Garnet Education/IATEFL.
English, F. (2010), 'Assessing non-native detainees' English language proficiency', in Coulthard, M. and A. Johnson (eds), *The Routledge Handbook of Forensic Linguistics*. Abingdon: Routledge, pp. 423–39.
—(2011), *Student Writing and Genre*. London: Bloomsbury.
Evans, S. (2011), 'What Paddington tells us about German v British manners'. *BBC News Europe*, http://www.bbc.co.uk/news/world-europe-13545386#story_continues_1 [accessed June 2012].
Evans, N. and Levinson, S. C. (2009), 'The myth of language universals: language diversity and its importance for cognitive science'. *Behavioral and Brain Sciences* 32(5): 429–92.
Fairclough, N. (2001), *Language and Power*, 2nd edn. Harlow: Longman.
Fairclough, I. and Fairclough, N. (2012), *Political Discourse Analysis: A Method for Advanced Students*. Abingdon: Routledge.
Ferguson, C. A. (1959), 'Diglossia'. *Word* 15: 325–40.
Firth, J. R. (1950), 'Personality and language in society', in *Transcriptions of the Philological Society*. Reprinted in J. R. Firth, *Papers in Linguistics, 1934–1951*. Oxford: Oxford University Press.

Fischer, S. R. (2005), *A History of Language.* London: Reaktion Books.
Fishman, J. A. (1965), 'Who speaks what language to whom and when?' *La Linguistique* 2: 67–88.
—(1974), 'Language modernization and planning in comparison with other types of national modernization and planning', in Fishman, J. A. (ed.), *Advances in Language Planning.* The Hague: Mouton, pp. 79–102.
—(1991), *Reversing Language Shift. Theoretical and Empirical Foundations of Assistance to Threatened Languages.* Clevedon: Multilingual Matters.
—(1992), 'Conference summary', in Fase, W., Koen, J. and S. Kroon (eds), *Maintenance and Loss of Minority Languages.* Amsterdam and Philadelphia: John Benjamins, pp. 395–403.
—(ed.) (2001), *Can Threatened Languages be Saved? Reversing Language Shift, Revisited: A 21st Century Perspective.* Clevedon: Multilingual Matters.
Foucault, M. (1972), *The Archaeology of Knowledge.* London: Tavistock/ Routledge.
Freeman, D. E. and Freeman, Y. S. (2004), *Essential Linguistics.* Portsmouth, New Hampshire: Heinemann.
Friginal, E. (2007), 'Outsourced call centers and English in the Philippines'. *World Englishes* 26: 331–45.
García, O. (2009), *Bilingual Education in the 21st Century: A Global Perspective.* Oxford: Wiley-Blackwell.
García, O. and Li, W. (2014), *Translanguaging: Language, Bilingualism and Education.* Basingstoke: Palgrave Macmillan.
Gardner, R. C. and Lambert, W. E. (1972), *Attitudes and Motivation in Second-Language Learning.* Rowley: Newbury House.
Gardner-Chloros, P. (1995), 'Code-switching in community, regional and national repertoires: the myth of the discreteness of linguistic systems', in Milroy, L. and P. Muysken (eds), *One Speaker, Two Languages: Cross-disciplinary Perspectives on Code-switching.* Cambridge: Cambridge University Press, pp. 68–89.
Garrett, P. (2010), *Attitudes to Language.* Cambridge: Cambridge University Press.
Gee, J. P. (1996), *Social Linguistics and Literacies: Ideology in Discourses,* 2nd edn. London: Taylor and Frances.
—(2007), *What Video Games Have to Teach Us About Learning and Literacy.* Basingstoke: Palgrave Macmillan.
—(2010), *An Introduction to Discourse Analysis,* 3rd edn. New York: Routledge.
Gillen, J. and Hall, N. (2010), 'Edwardian postcards: illuminating ordinary writing', in Barton, D. and U. Papen (eds), *The Anthropology of Writing.* London: Continuum, pp. 169–89.
Gimenez, J. C. (2002), 'New media and conflicting realities in multinational corporate communication: a case study'. *International Review of Applied Linguistics* 40(1): 323–43.
Goddard, A. and Beard, A. (2007), 'As simple as ABC? Issues of transition for English language A Level students going on to study English Language/Linguistics in higher education'. *Higher Education Academy English Subject Centre,* Report Series No. 14.
Goddard, A., Henry, A., Mondor, M. and van der Laaken, M. (2013), '"Have you ever been to England? You know, they speak really weird English there": Some implications of the growth of English as a global language for the teaching of English in the UK'. *English in Education* 47(1): 79–95.

Goffman, E. (1967), *Interaction Ritual*. London: Allen Lane.

Gorman, T., White, J., Brooks, G. and English, F. (1990), *Language for Learning*. London: Schools Examinations and Assessments Council, Department for Education and Science.

Graddol, D. (2006), *English Next: Why Global English May Mean the End of 'English as a Foreign Language'*. London: British Council.

Greenberg, R. D. (2004), *Language and Identity in the Balkans*. Oxford: Oxford University Press.

Grice, H. P. (1989), *Studies in the Way of Words*. Cambridge, MA: Harvard University Press.

Gu, M. (2011), '"I am not qualified to be a Hongkongese because of my accented Cantonese": mainland immigrant students in Hong Kong'. *Journal of Multilingual and Multicultural Development* 32: 515–29.

Guillot, M.-N. (2012), 'Film subtitles and the conundrum of linguistic and cultural representation: a methodological blind spot', in Hauser, S. and M. Luginbühl (eds), *Contrastive Media Analysis: Approaches to Linguistic and Cultural Aspects of Mass Media Communication*. Amsterdam: John Benjamins, pp. 101–22.

Gumperz, J. J. (1962), 'Types of linguistic community'. *Anthropological Linguistics* 4(1): 28–40.

Gunnarsson, B.-L. (2013), 'Multilingualism in the workplace'. *Annual Review of Applied Linguistics* 33: 162–89.

Hall, C. J. (2005), *An Introduction to Language and Linguistics: Breaking the Language Spell*. London and New York: Continuum.

Halliday, M. A. K. (1971), Foreword to Doughty, P., Pearce, J. and G. Thornton (eds), *Language in Use*. London: Edward Arnold.

—(1978), *Language as Social Semiotic: The Social Interpretation of Language and Meaning*. Baltimore: University Park Press.

—(1989), *Spoken and Written Language*. Oxford: Oxford University Press.

—(1993), 'Towards a language-based theory of learning'. *Linguistics and Education* 5: 93–116.

Halliday, M. A. K. and Hasan, R. (1976), *Cohesion in English*. Harlow: Longman.

—(1989), *Language, Context and Text: Aspects of Language in a Social-Semiotic Perspective*. Oxford: Oxford University Press.

Halliday, M. A. K., McIntosh, A. and Strevens, P. (1964), *The Linguistic Sciences and Language Teaching*. London: Longmans.

Hamp-Lyons, L. and Lockwood, J. (2009), 'The workplace, the society and the wider world: the offshoring and outsourcing industry'. *Annual Review of Applied Linguistics* 29: 145–67.

Harris, J. (2008), 'Primary schools and Irish revitalisation', in Cenoz, J. and D. Gurter (eds), *Multilingualism and Minority Languages* (AILA Review Vol. 21). Amsterdam and Philadelphia: John Benjamins, pp. 49–68.

Harris, R. A. (1993), *The Linguistics Wars*. New York and Oxford: Oxford University Press.

—(2006), *New Ethnicities and Language Use*. Basingstoke and New York: Palgrave Macmillan.

Harris, S. (2003), 'Politeness and power: making and responding to requests in institutional settings'. *Text* 23(1): 27–52.

Harvey, P. (1987), 'Lenguaje y relaciones de poder: consecuencias para una política lingüística'. *Allpanchis* 29(30): 105–31.

Hasan, R. (1989a), 'The structure of a text', in Halliday, M. A. K. and R. Hasan (eds), *Language, Context and Text: Aspects of Language in a Social Semiotic Perspective*, 2nd edn, pp. 52–69.

—(1989b), 'The texture of a text', in Halliday, M. A. K. and R. Hasan (eds), *Language, Context and Text: Aspects of Language in a Social Semiotic Perspective*, 2nd edn, pp. 70–96.

Hawkins, E. (1992), 'Awareness of language/knowledge about language in the National Curriculum in England and Wales: An historical note on twenty years of Curricular Debate'. *Language Awareness* 1(1): 5–17.

—(1999), 'Foreign language study and Language Awareness'. *Language Awareness* 8(3/4): 124–42.

Hearnden, M. (2010), *Nursing across cultures: The Communication Needs of Internationally Educated Nurses (IENs) Working with Older Adults*. Saarbrücken: Lambert Academic Publishing.

Heffer, C. (2010), 'Constructing crime stories in court', in Coulthard, M. and A. Johnson (eds), *The Routledge Handbook of Forensic Linguistics*. Abingdon: Routledge, pp. 199–217.

Heller, M. (2007), 'Bilingualism as ideology and practice', in Heller, M. (ed.), *Bilingualism: A Social Approach*. Basingstoke: Palgrave, pp. 1–22.

Heugh, K. (2013), 'Multilingual education policy in South Africa constrained by theoretical and historical disconnections'. *Annual Review of Applied Linguistics* 33: 215–37.

Hodge, R. and Kress, G. (1988), *Social Semiotics*. Cambridge: Polity.

Hodgson, J., Buttle, H., Conridge, B., Gibbons, J. and Robinson, J. (2013), *Phonics Instruction and early Reading: Professional Views from the Classroom*. Report for the National Associated of Teachers of English, http://www.nate.org.uk/index.php?page=8&paper=11 [accessed 20 January 2014].

Holliday, A. (2011), *Intercultural Communication and Ideology*. London: Sage.

—(2013), *Understanding Intercultural Communication: Negotiating a Grammar of Culture*. Abingdon: Routledge.

Honey, J. (1989), *Does Accent Matter?* London: Faber and Faber.

—(1997), *Language is Power. The Story of Standard English and its Enemies*. London: Faber and Faber.

House, J. (2007), 'Communicative styles in English and German'. *European Journal of English Studies* 10(3): 249–67.

Howard, M. (2008), *Spoken Dialogues in English Language Teaching Text Books: The Speech Genre of Asking for and Giving Directions*. MA Dissertation, London Metropolitan University.

Hua, Z. (ed.) (2011), *The Language and Intercultural Communication Reader*. Abingdon: Routledge.

Hymes, D. (1967), 'Models of the interaction of language and social setting'. *Journal of Social Issues* 23(2): 8–28.

—(1972), 'Models of the interaction of language and social life', in Gumperz, J. and D. Hymes (eds), *Directions in Sociolinguistics: The Ethnography of Communication*. New York: Holt, Rinehart & Winston, pp. 35–71.

—(1996), *Ethnography, Linguistics, Narrative Inequality: Toward an Understanding of Voice*. London: Taylor and Francis.

Inal, D. (2009), 'The early bird catches the worm: The Turkish case', in Enever, J. Moon, J. and U. Raman (eds), *Young Learner English Language Policy & Implementation: International Perspectives*. Reading: Garnet Education/IATEFL, pp. 71–8.

Ivanic, R. (1998), *Writing and Identity: The Discoursal Construction of Identity in Academic Writing*. Amsterdam: John Benjamins.

Ivanic, R., Edwards, R., Barton, D., Martin-Jones, M., Fowler, Z., Hughes, B., Mannion, G., Miller, K., Satchwell, C. and Smith, J. (2009), *Improving Learning in College: Rethinking Literacies Across the Curriculum*. Abingdon: Routledge.

Jackson, H. and Stockwell, P. (2010), *An Introduction to the Nature and Functions of Language,* 2nd edn. London: Continuum.

Janson, T. (2004), *A Natural History of Latin*. Oxford: Oxford University Press.

Jefferson, G. (2004), 'Glossary of transcript symbols with an introduction', in Lerner, G. H. (ed.), *Conversation Analysis: Studies from the first generation*. Amsterdam: John Benjamins, pp. 13–31.

Jenkins, J. (2013), *English as a Lingua Franca in the International University. The Politics of Academic English Language Policy*. London and New York: Routledge.

Jenkins, J., Cogo, A. and Dewey, M. (2011), 'Review of developments in research into English as a lingua franca'. *Language Teaching* 44(3): 281–315.

Jibril, M. (1982), 'Nigerian English: an introduction', in Pride, J. B. (ed.), *New Englishes*. Newbury House: Rowley, pp. 73–84.

Jikong, S. Y. (2000), 'Official bilingualism in Cameroon: a double-edged sword'. *Alizés* 19: 117–35.

Jørgensen, N. (2008), 'Polylingual languaging around and among children and adolescents'. *International Journal of Multilingualism* 5(3): 161–76.

Kachru, B. J. (1994), 'English in South Asia', in Burchfield, R. (ed.), *The Cambridge History of the English Language (Volume 5)*. Cambridge: Cambridge University Press, pp. 497–626.

—(1998), 'English as an Asian language'. *Links and Letters* 5: 89–108.

Kemper, S. (1994), '"Elderspeak": speech accommodation to older adults'. *Aging and Cognition* 1: 17–28.

Kerswill, P., Cheshire, J., Fox, S. and Torgersen, E. (2007), *Linguistic Innovators: The English of Adolescents in London: Full Research Report*. ESRC End of Award Report, RES-000-23-0680. Swindon: ESRC.

Khan, I. A. (2013), 'Sun and Crescent Most Sought-After Election Symbols', *Dawn News*, http://dawn.com/news/795743/sun-and-crescent-mot-sought-after-election-symbols [accessed 19 November 2013].

Khubchandani, L. M. (1997), *Revisualizing Boundaries: A Plurilingual Ethos*. New Delhi: Sage.

Kim, H. (2008), 'The semantic and pragmatic analysis of South Korean and Australian English apologetic speech acts'. *Journal of Pragmatics* 40(2): 257–78.

Kredens, K. and Morris, R. (2010), 'A shattered mirror? Interpreting in legal contexts outside the courtroom', in Coulthard, M. and A. Johnson (eds), *The Routledge Handbook of Forensic Linguistics*. Abingdon: Routledge, pp. 455–69.

Kress, G. (1994), *Learning to Write*, 2nd edn. London: Routledge.

—(2003), *Literacy in the New Media Age*. London: Routledge.

—(2010), *Multimodality: A Social Semiotic Approach to Contemporary Communication*. London: Routledge.

Kress, G. and Hodge, R. (1979), *Language as Ideology*. London: Routledge Kegan Paul.

Kress, G. and van Leeuwen, T. (1996), *Reading Images – The Grammar of Visual Design*. London: Routledge.

—(2001), *Multimodal Discourse*. London: Bloomsbury Academic.

Labov, W. (1972), *Sociolinguistic Patterns*. Philadelphia: University of Pennsylvania Press.

Lamb, M. (2004), 'Integrative motivation in a globalizing world'. *System* 32(1): 3–19.

Larsen-Freeman, D. and Cameron, L. (2008), *Complex Systems and Applied Linguistics*. Oxford: Oxford University Press.

Lave, J. and Wenger, E. (1991), *Situated Learning: Legitimate Peripheral Participation*. Cambridge: Cambridge University Press.

Lenhart, A., Arafeh, S., Smith, A. and Macgill, A. (2008), 'Writing Technology and Teens', Report for *The National Commission on Writing*, Washington DC: Pew Internet & American Life Project available at http://www.pewinternet.org/Reports/2008/Writing-Technology-and-Teens.aspx [accessed 20 November 2013].

Le Page, R. (1981), *Caribbean Connections in the Classroom*. London: The Mary Glasgow Language Trust.

Le Page, R. and Tabouret-Keller, A. (1985), *Acts of Identity: Creole-Based Approaches to Language and Ethnicity*. Cambridge: Cambridge University Press.

Lewis, G. (2002), *The Turkish Language Reform: A Catastrophic Success*. Oxford: Oxford University Press.

Lewis, G., Jones, B. and Baker, C. (2012), 'Translanguaging: origins and development from school to street and beyond'. *Educational Research and Evaluation* 18(7): 641–54.

Lewis, M. P., Simons, G. F. and Fennig, C. D. (eds) (2013), *Ethnologue: Languages of the World*, 17th edn. Dallas, TX: SIL International.

Li Wei (2011), 'Moment Analysis and translanguaging space: discursive construction of identities by multilingual Chinese youth in Britain'. *Journal of Pragmatics* 43: 1222–35.

Lillis, T. M. (2001), *Student Writing: Access, Regulation, Desire*. London: Routledge.

—(2013), *The Sociolinguistics of Writing*. Edinburgh: Edinburgh University Press.

Liu, Y. and O'Halloran, K. L. (2009), 'Intersemiotic Texture: analyzing cohesive devices between language and images'. *Social Semiotics* 19(4): 367–88.

Machin, D. and Mayr, A. (2012), *How to do Critical Discourse Analysis: A Multimodal Introduction*. London: Sage.

Mackenzie, I. (2013), *English as a Lingua Franca. Theorizing and Teaching English*. London and New York: Routledge.

Makoni, S. and Pennycook, A. (eds) (2007), *Disinventing and Reconstituting Languages*. Clevedon: Multilingual Matters.

Malinowsky, B. (1923), 'The problem of meaning in primitive languages', in Ogden, C. K. and I. A. Richards (eds), *The Meaning of Meaning*. London: Routledge, pp. 146–52.

Marinova-Todd, S., Marshall, D. and Snow, C. (2000), 'Three misconceptions about age and L2 Learning'. *TESOL Quarterly* 34(1): 9–31.

Marr, T. (2005), 'Language and the capital: a case study of English "Language Shock" among Chinese students in London'. *Language Awareness* 14(4): 239–53.

—(2011), '"Ya no podemos regresar al quechua": modernity, identity and language choice among migrants in urban Peru', in Heggarty, P. and A. J. Pearce (eds), *History and Language in the Andes*. New York: Palgrave Macmillan, pp. 215–38.

McArthur, T. (1999), 'On the origin and nature of Standard English'. *World Englishes* 18(2): 161–9.

McCallum, A. (2012), *Creativity and Learning in Secondary English*. Abingdon: Routledge.

MacRuairc, G. (2011), 'They're my words – I'll talk as I like! Examining social class and linguistic practice among primary school children'. *Language and Education* 25(6): 535–59.

Mesthrie, R., Swann, J., Deumert, A. and Leap, W. L. (2009), *Introducing Sociolinguistics*. Edinburgh: Edinburgh University Press.

Milroy, J. (1999), 'The consequences of standardisation in descriptive linguistics', in Bex, T. and R. Watts (eds), *Standard English: The Widening Debate*. London and New York: Routledge, pp. 16–39.

—(2001), 'Language ideologies and the consequences of standardization'. *Journal of Sociolinguistics* 5(4): 530–55.

Milroy, J. and Milroy, L. (1985), *Authority in Language. Investigating Standard English*. London: Routledge & Kegan Paul.

Milroy, L. and Muysken, P. (eds) (1995), *One Speaker, Two Languages: Cross-disciplinary Perspectives on Code-switching*. Cambridge: Cambridge University Press.

Mithun, M. (2010), Foreword to Berez, A. L., Mulder, J. and D. Rosenblum (eds), *Fieldwork and Linguistic Analysis in Indigenous Languages of the Americas*. Honolulu: University of Hawai'i Press.

Mooney, A. S., Peccei, J., LaBelle, S., Henriksen, B. E., Eppler, E., Irwin, A., Pichler, P., Soden, S. (eds) (2011), *Language, Society and Power Reader*. Abingdon: Routledge.

Montes-Alcalá, C. (2009), 'Hispanics in the United States: more than Spanglish'. *Camino Real* 1: 97–115.

Morales, E. (2002), *Living in Spanglish: The Search for Latino Identity in America*. New York: St Martin's Press.

Moriset, B. (2004), 'The rise of the call center industry: splintering and virtualization of the economic space', Centennial Meeting of the Association of American Geographers, Philadelphia, 14–19 March.

Nadeem, S. (2011), *Dead Ringers: How Outsourcing is Changing the Way Indians Understand Themselves*. Princeton: Princeton University Press.

Office for National Statistics (2011a), *It's Time to Complete your Census Questionnaire*.

Office for National Statistics (2011b), http://www.ons.gov.uk/ons/taxonomy/index.html?nscl=Language [accessed 20 April 2014].

Olawsky, K. (2006), *A Grammar of Urarina*. Berlin and New York: Mouton de Gruyter.

Ong, W. (1982), *Orality and Literacy*. London: Routledge.

Ostler, N. (2005), *Empires of the Word. A Language History of the World*. London: HarperCollins.

—(2007), Ad *Infinitum. A Biography of Latin and the World it Created*. London: Harper Press.

Otheguy, R. and Stern, N. (2011), 'On so-called Spanglish'. *International Journal of Bilingualism* 15(1): 85–100.

Otsuji, E. and Pennycook, A. (2010), 'Metrolingualism: fixity, fluidity and language in flux'. *International Journal of Multilingualism* 7(3): 240–54.

Paltridge, B. (2012), *Discourse Analysis: an Introduction*, 2nd edn. London: Bloomsbury.

Pavlenko, A. (2008), '"I'm very not about the law part": non-native speakers of English and the Miranda Warnings'. *TESOL Quarterly* 42: 1–30.

Pennycook, A. (2010), *Language as a Local Practice*. Abingdon: Routledge.

Phansalkar, S., Edworthy, J., Hellier, E., Seger, D., Schedlbauer, A., Avery, A. and Bates, D. (2010), 'A review of human factors principles for the design and implementation of medication safety alerts in clinical information systems'. *Journal of the American Medical Informatics Association* 17: 493–501.

Phillipson, R. (1992), *Linguistic Imperialism*. Oxford: Oxford University Press.

Picone, M. (1996), *Anglicisms, Neologisms and Dynamic French*. Amsterdam and Philadelphia: John Benjamins.

Quinion, M. (2005), *Port Out, Starboard Home and Other Language Myths*. London: Penguin.

Rahman, T. (2009), 'Language ideology, identity, and the commodification of language in the call centers of Pakistan'. *Language in Society* 38: 233–58.

Ramat, A. G. and Ramat, P. (eds) (1998), *The Indo-European Languages*. Abingdon: Routledge.

Rampton, B. (1995), *Crossing: Language and Ethnicity among Adolescents*. London: Longman.

—(2006), *Language in Late Modernity: Interaction in an Urban School*. Cambridge: Cambridge University Press.

—(2010), *From "Multi-ethnic Urban Heteroglossia" to "Contemporary Urban Vernaculars"*. Working Papers in Urban Language and Literacies No. 61.

Riley, P. (2007), *Language, Culture and Identity*. London: Continuum.

Roach, P. (1991), *English Phonetics and Phonology: A Practical Course*, 2nd edn. Cambridge: Cambridge University Press.

Rose, D. (2004), 'Don't Call Me Handicapped!' On *'Ouch'*, BBC website http://news.bbc.co.uk/1/hi/magazine/3708576.stm [accessed 26 September 2013].

Rosewarne, D. (1984), 'Estuary English', *Times Educational Supplement* [19 October 1984].

Ryan, E., Anas, A., Hummert, M. and Boich, L. (1995), 'Communication predicaments of aging: patronizing behavior toward older adults'. *Journal of Language and Social Psychology* 14(1–2): 144–66.

Sarno-Pedreira, K. (2004), *Speaking English, Behaving Brazilian*. Unpublished MA dissertation, London Metropolitan University.

Scollon, R. and Scollon, S. W. (2003), *Discourses in Place: Language in the Material World*. London and New York: Routledge.

Scovel, T. (2000), 'A critical review of the critical period research'. *Annual Review of Applied Linguistics* 20: 213–23.

—(2006), 'Age, acquisition, and accent. Linguistic insights'. *Studies in Language and Communication* 22: 31–48.

Seidlhofer, B. (2001), 'Closing a conceptual gap: the case for a description of English as a lingua franca'. *International Journal of Applied Linguistics* 11(2): 133–58.

Sindoni, M. G. (2013), *Spoken and Written Discourse in Online Interactions: A Multimodal Approach*. Abingdon: Routledge.

Singleton, D. and Ryan, L. (2004), *Language Acquisition: The Age Factor*. Clevedon: Multilingual Matters.

Skutnabb-Kangas, T. (1988), 'Multilingualism and the education of minority children', in Skutnabb-Kangas, T. and J. Cummins (eds), *Minority Education: From Shame to Struggle*. Clevedon: Multilingual Matters, pp. 9–44.

—(1996), 'Educational language choice – multilingual diversity or monolingual reductionism?', in Hellinger, M. and U. Ammon (eds), *Contrastive Sociolinguistics*. Berlin and New York: Mouton de Gruyter, pp. 175–204.

Snow, D. (2004), *Cantonese as Written Language: The Growth of a Written Chinese Vernacular*. Hong Kong: Hong Kong University Press.

Spencer-Oatey, H. (ed.) (2008), *Culturally Speaking: Culture, Communication and Politeness Theory*, 2nd edn. London: Continuum.

Street, B. (1984), *Literacy in Theory and Practice*. Cambridge: Cambridge University Press.

—(2001), 'Introduction', in Street, B. (ed.), *Literacy and Development*. London: Routledge.

Stubbs, M. and Hillier, H. (eds) (1983), *Readings on Language, Schools and Classrooms*. London: Methuen.

Svalberg, A. M.-L. (2007), 'Language awareness and language learning'. *Language Teaching* 40(4): 287–308.

Swan, M. and Smith, B. (eds) (2001), *Learner English, Second Edition: A Teacher's Guide to Interference and other Problems*. Cambridge: Cambridge University Press.

Turner, J. (2010), *Language in the Academy: Cultural Reflexivity and Intercultural Dynamics*. Bristol: Multilingual Matters.

United Kingdom Literacy Association (2012), *Phonics Screening Check Fails a Generation of Able Readers*, United Kingdom Literacy Association Report available at: http://www.ukla.org/news/story/phonics_screening_check_fails_a_generation_of_able_readers/ [accessed 20 January 2014].

Vertovec, S. (2006), *The Emergence of Super-diversity in Britain*. Centre on Migration, Policy and Society, Working Paper 25, Oxford University.

—(2007), 'Super-diversity and its implications'. *Ethnic and Racial Studies* 29(6): 1024–54.

Vigouroux, C. B. and Mufwene, S. S. (eds) (2008), *Globalization and Language Vitality: Perspectives from Africa*. London: Bloomsbury.

Volosinov, N. ([1929] 1986), *Marxism and the Philosphy of Language*, trans. L. Matejka and I. R. Titunik. Cambridge, MA: Harvard University Press.

Wang X., Spotti, M., Jufermans, K., Cornips, L., Kroon, S. and Blommaert, J. (2014), 'Globalization in the Margins: toward a re-evaluation of language and mobility'. *Applied Linguistics Review* 5(1): 23–44.

Wardhaugh, R. (1998), *An Introduction to Sociolinguistics*. Oxford: Blackwell.

—(2010), *An Introduction to Sociolinguistics*, 6th edn. Chichester: Wiley-Blackwell.

Wenger, E. (1998), *Communities of Practice*. Cambridge: Cambridge University Press.

Wigglesworth, G. and Yates, L. (2007), 'Mitigating difficult requests in the workplace: what learners and teachers need to know'. *TESOL Quarterly* 41(4): 791–803.

Williams, A. (2007), 'Non-standard English and education', in Britain, D. (ed.), *Language in the British Isles*, 2nd edn. Cambridge: Cambridge University Press, pp. 401–16.

Williams, D. (1998), *Romans and Barbarians.* London: Constable.
Williamson, J. and Hardman, F. (1997), 'Those terrible marks of the beast: non-standard dialect and children's writing'. *Language and Education* 11: 287–99.
Winkler, E. (2012), *Understanding Language: A Basic Course in Linguistics.* London: Bloomsbury.
Woolard, K. (2004), 'Codeswitching', in Duranti, A. (ed.), *Companion to Linguistic Anthropology.* Malden: Blackwell, pp. 73–94.
Yule, G. (2006), *The Study of Language*, 3rd edn. Cambridge: Cambridge University Press.

Index